# Christmas in Minnesota

MINNESOTA
HISTORICAL
SOCIETY PRESS

# Christmas
## IN MINNESOTA

EDITED BY

*Marilyn Ziebarth
and Brian Horrigan*

*Acknowledgments*

The authors thank Minnesota Historical Society Press editor Shannon Pennefeather for her assistance. The St. Paul Public Library's online book request system proved indispensable. Thank you to other Minnesota Historical Society staff, including Dana Heimark, and to volunteer Mary Kay Nutzmann.

www.mhspress.org

The Minnesota Historical Society Press is a member of the Association of American University Presses.

Manufactured in the United States of America

10 9 8 7 6 5 4 3 2 1

♾ The paper used in this publication meets the minimum requirements of the American National Standard for Information Sciences—Permanence for Printed Library Materials, ANSI Z39.48–1984.

International Standard Book Number

978–0–87351–542–0 (cloth)

978–1–68134–142–2 (paperback)

Library of Congress Cataloging-in-Publication Data

Christmas in Minnesota / edited by Marilyn Ziebarth and Brian Horrigan.
p. cm.

Includes bibliographical references.
ISBN 0-87351-542-0 (alk. paper)
1. American literature—Minnesota. 2. Christmas—Literary collections. 3. Minnesota—Literary collections. 4. Christmas—Minnesota. I. Ziebarth, Marilyn. II. Horrigan, Brian.
PS571.M6C48   2005
810.8'0334—dc22

2005164458

Title page photo: Genoa Mine, 1919, Minnesota Historical Society.
Jacket photo by Phoebe Dunn. Jacket design by Brian Donahue.
Book designed and composed in Adobe Jenson by Wendy Holdman and manufactured by Maple-Vail Book Manufacturing Group.

# Contents

———•◦•———

*Wanda Gág,* Christmas Eve *(1927)*

* * *

# Introduction

BRIAN HORRIGAN

In a memorable passage from F. Scott Fitzgerald's *The Great Gatsby*, narrator Nick Carraway remembers coming home to Minnesota from the East Coast for Christmas every year. As the train heads west, he watches out the window and reflects: "That's my Middle West—not the wheat or the prairies or the lost Swede towns but the thrilling, returning trains of my youth and the street lamps and sleigh bells in the frosty dark and the shadows of holly wreaths thrown by lighted windows on the snow. I am part of that...."

So many themes emerge from these simple, singing lines (excerpted below in Chapter 3): memory, youth, the passage of time, home. For Nick—as for most of us—the Christmas season evokes feelings of nostalgia and self-reflection. Fitzgerald helps us remember how important the sense of place is to our identity—"I am part of that"—and, incidentally, how closely our memories of Christmas are bound up with our memories of the places of our lives, both present and past.

This is a book of stories about Christmas with one place—Minnesota—in common. Most are passages from memoirs, letters, diaries, and reminiscences; a few are excerpts from fictional works. Real or imagined, however, all are "true"—or at least they have at their core the clear ring of believability. Christmas also has a unique ability to bridge time and cultures. And so our chapters are organized around familiar themes: "Finding Christmas," in places from Bohemian Flats to the Gunflint Trail; "Celebrating the Holidays," marking it with pageants and music; "Coming Home," with stories of homemade traditions, old and new; "The Giving Season," about the "stuff" of Christmas; "Eating and Making Merry," with tales of food and festivities; and "Family Matters," with stories that remind us where the word "familiar" comes from.

Christmas is our most literary of holidays. The book you hold in your hands is itself an artifact of the peculiarly "printed" character of Christmas. Books have long been popular as Christmas gifts, and not just because they are easy to wrap. A book is a symbol of permanence, something sturdy, uncomplicated by moving parts or batteries.

But the real reason for this book is the simple axiom that Christmas is a time for storytelling. In fact, many of the stories in *Christmas in Minnesota* are *about* storytelling. Christmas stories are the way we talk about our families, our rifts and losses, our beliefs and values, our histories.

There is a great story at the very heart of Christmas—the New Testament story of the Christ Child. Although celebrations of the birth of Jesus span Christian history and cultures, the "American Christmas" has become a thing apart—a singular combination of the secular and the religious, the civic and the private, the invented and the "traditional." But it was not always so. In 1850s Minnesota, for example, church observances were by no means universal; it was predominantly Catholic and Episcopal congregations that celebrated Christmas in any special way. This would change within just a few years, however, as other denominations adopted Christmas services, festivals, and tree lightings.

Still, in reading through accounts from territorial Minnesota, one never gets the sense of Christmas as the all-consuming event it became over the intervening century. One 1857 commentator in the *Daily Minnesotian* went so far as to rail against people who "call themselves Christians" but were using Christmas Day to do marketing or housecleaning or laundry.

But at least by the 1860s, Americans had transformed traditions from Scandinavia, Holland, Germany, and England to create a new cultural hybrid. This American Christmas emerged largely from places like New York, New England, and Pennsylvania—regions that many Minnesota settlers knew as home. Their celebrations would be entirely familiar to us today: midnight Mass and lengthy church services, Santa Claus and reindeer, shopping and gift-wrapped packages, decorated evergreen trees, cookies, caroling, cards, and crowded family gatherings on Christmas Eve.

Unlike most holidays, Christmas is firmly rooted in place—a number of places, some authentic, some legendary: Bethlehem (for starters), the North Pole, the early Victorian streetscape of Dickens's *A Christmas Carol*; "Santa's Villages" popping up year-round in tourist destinations. We even recreate some of those places in our own homes, with elaborate miniature Christmas villages and scenes marketed by collectible companies such as Minnesota-based Department 56. No other holiday in our annual calendar can be so literally or figuratively "visited."

Minnesota can lay fair claim to being among the most "Christmassy" of places. Of course, others are in the running: the New England village square, or the archetypal small town in *It's a Wonderful Life*. Although many Americans live in places where the landscape has a hard time mustering an appropriately seasonal look, in our hearts Christmas is a quaint and snowy place with evergreens abounding. In other words, it looks a lot like the Minnesota of myth and memory.

The state's vast stretches of northern forest, filled with spruce and pine and the fragrant balsam fir, were once a major source of the nation's Christmas trees, especially for the treeless towns of the prairies and plains. Today, Christmas trees are grown and tended in neat farms, and Minnesota supplies nearly 500,000 trees a year. In Chapter 1 we have a story by Robert Treuer from the "supply side" of this industry. Many of us have memories of cutting "just the right tree" with our families, as Barton Sutter tells us in Chapter 3.

Cold and snow are other essential ingredients for the "perfect" Christmas. I say this as someone who grew up in Houston, Texas, barefoot in shorts and tee shirts throughout December. Although that outfit felt normal most of the year, at Christmas it didn't seem quite right. How could I avoid feeling somehow second-rate without a white Christmas? The Bobbsey Twins celebrated Christmas with sleigh rides; snow fell on Charlie Brown's Christmas tree; the radio played songs about snowmen, reindeer, jingle bells, and winter wonderlands. And so we draped sparkly white cotton "snow" around the base of our tree and sprayed fake snow on our windows.

No such problem affects "cold-enough-for-you?" Minnesota, although climatology statistics tell us the Twin Cities has only had white Christmases (at least an inch of snow cover) in seventy of the past hundred years. Despite the statistics, our memories of the really cold ones trump all those brown, dry Decembers, and Minnesota Christmas stories abound in details about wintry weather. Childhood reminiscences— like those of Melvin Frank (Chapter 1), or Charles Schulz (Chapter 2), or Jerry Fearing (Chapter 3)—typically center around wintertime play, maybe with a pair of skates or a sled left under the tree by Santa. Adult memories of snow and cold usually fall into two categories: The Romantic, such as Swedish traveler Hugo Nisbeth's account (Chapter 1) of his visit in 1872 to a sod house on the prairie ("Outside the snow fell slowly and spread its white Christmas mantle over the endless prairie . . ."); or The Grim, such as Emily Carter's story (Chapter 3) about a quixotic trek through south Minneapolis ("He was just about to kick a clump of black, hardened snow."). It doesn't matter how often we are reminded that late December in Bethlehem is rarely cold and never snowy; we know that *our* Christmas is supposed to look like the picture on the cover of this book.

In celebrating the holiday, we confront a kind of divide—on the one hand, we commemorate the Biblical story of Christmas, and, on the other, we have adopted many secular and even pagan traditions, such as lighted trees, feasting, and gift giving. The Janus-headed nature of Christmas is noticeable even in frontier Minnesota. The 1849 *Minnesota Chronicle and Register* reported that the "grave and devout" in St. Paul planned to go to church, while "those that love worldly pleasure" would go to balls, sleigh rides, or "eating and drinking parties."

Sounds familiar enough, although this chasm between churchgoers and partygoers may not be as wide as it once was. Many of us manage to reconcile our allegiances to both God and Mammon. Samuel Hynes' memories (Chapter 4) may come closest to capturing the neatly divided scenario so often played out at Christmas: first, the public and religious, then the private and secular. An awed reverence at church, holding candles, "the light of the Christmas spirit;" then to home, and family, to the "feasting and present-giving part."

As devout as we may be (or like to think we are), we cannot escape the fact that the American Christmas is, and always has been, a highly commercialized affair. Certainly, Minnesota takes a back seat to none in providing a sufficient number of places to part with one's money. Although the state's current claim to the highest square footage of retail space per capita in the United States may be largely attributable to the eruption of the Mall of America, before that the metro area had all of those "Dales," and even before those we had not one but two bustling downtown shopping districts. It's remarkable to read, in "What a Christmas Shopper Saw" (Chapter 4), of the stunning variety of Christmas shopping opportunities in St. Paul in 1915, or Harrison Salisbury's memories (Chapter 4) of the dazzling wonders of turn-of-the-century department and toy stores in Minneapolis.

Forget fishing: Shopping is Minnesota's favorite way to pass time outside the home. (Inside the home there is the television, urging you to get out and shop.) Surrounded as it is by relatively undermalled places, Minnesota and its malls have an almost electromagnetic power. Shopping and Christmas intertwine in a state of mutual dependency, with some businesses making more than half their annual sales during the season. Thanksgiving Day parades, Santa's villages, elaborately animated store windows, and brilliant displays of lighting and decorations have been deployed for decades to entice shoppers into stores. More recently, downtown interests in Minneapolis came up with another "instant tradition"—the Holidazzle parade, which began in 1992. This was the year the Mall of America opened 10 miles away, and retailers wanted an attraction to keep customers coming into the city to shop at Christmas, something besides the famous Dayton's (later Marshall Field's) windows and indoor displays.

It's not just our imaginations that the Christmas "season" gets longer every year. It has always been a holiday with elastic boundaries, stretching out and folding in other year-end traditions and mythologies—giving thanks at the end of harvest, marking the solstice, celebrating a new year. Even Hanukkah, the Jewish "feast of lights," has come to share features of Christmas—gift giving and lighting candles and telling stories. Some immigrant groups, such as those who lived on Bohemian Flats in Minneapolis (Chapter 1), brought Old World traditions that carried the Christmas season into the new year to the Feast of Epiphany, which marks the Wise Men's adoration of the Christ Child. Thanksgiving, too, was once much more closely tied with Christmas. In fact, before it was a permanent national holiday, Thanksgiving Day was a moveable feast, declared yearly in individual states or territories, sometimes set for the day after Christmas, as it was in 1850 by Minnesota's territorial governor, Alexander Ramsey.

The "fullness of the season" can be a two-edged sword; we can become "afflicted by Christmas," as Garrison Keillor felt as a boy (Chapter 2). Coming in the "dead" of winter, the last two weeks of the year can sometimes feel just too crowded with a whole year's worth of anxieties, unaccomplished tasks, and unfulfilled expectations. The holiday makes us feel compelled to perform, to keep up appearances, to construct perfect Martha Stewart events that our families will cherish forever. The result can be exhaustion, stress, or just plain unhappiness. Some of the stories in Chapter 1 make it clear that Christmas stress is not a recent phenomenon. Look at the letter a miserably lonely Anna Ramsey writes to her husband on Christmas Day 1849: St. Paul is "a horrid place" and "intolerable" and it's giving her huge headaches. Or Ann North, "sad and discouraged," writing a Christmas Day letter to her parents in 1853. Or yet another Christmas Day and another woman writing (Mary Dodge Woodward, on a farm in the Red River Valley in 1885): The "wind howls dismally" and she feels "so lonely" knowing she can't get away.

In her essay (Chapter 2), Jonis Agee comes to the conclusion that "maybe this holiday thing is a kind of journey," an odyssey fraught with danger: "We get stranded from home, we're among strangers, we must invent, invent, invent. Our very identity is at stake. But we suffer and pine and salvage something anyway." Let's be honest: Aren't all Christmas "traditions" invented? Bill Holm is helpful here (Chapter 3). Although he writes that at Christmas the "gavel of tradition bangs on the table to call the house to order," he notes that tradition in the Midwest is "a strangely jackleg affair, hardly old enough to qualify as tradition at all, rather only invented procedure." Christmas is filled with yearning, a longing for simpler times, for reconnecting with family and childhood, with whatever we have defined as "tradition."

If Christmas is always about the past, nothing feeds the fires of nostalgia more surely than food, and this book is stuffed with the aromas and memories of food. The smells wafting from an 1850s Minnesota kitchen at Christmas would be mostly familiar to us today, except perhaps for the frequently mentioned buffalo tongue. Cranberries and lots of pies and cakes were usually on the menu, along with roast turkey with oyster stuffing. Amazingly, fresh oysters, densely packed with seaweed in wooden barrels, were shipped all over the country in the nineteenth century, even to cold and frozen Minnesota. During the Civil War, Union soldiers from Minnesota, yearning for a home-like Christmas dinner, managed to find—and write home about—oysters. Christmas dinner treats in turn-of-the-century logging camps included pumpkin pie and cookies with raisins.

In our more recent Christmas food stories (Chapter 5), such as those by Nick Fauchald and Susan Hauser, cookies play starring roles, which isn't surprising. Just thinking about cookies—let alone eating one!—can bring back a flood of memories. And we include accounts of two meals that could hardly be farther apart—Helen Hoover's story about a turkey dinner in a Boundary Waters cabin and Colleen Kruse's memory of Christmas Eve at an all-night downtown eatery.

Eating is only one of a myriad of otherwise mundane details of life thrown into high relief by Christmas. Acts of charity and acts of crime both skyrocket during the holidays. Everything is magnified, including gender roles and expectations. In these stories, women are forever setting forth abundant meals, wrapping presents, remembering relatives' names, soothing over rough edges and anxieties, keeping the engines of Christmas running. Sociologists call this "kin work," and there is a *lot* of it to do as December rolls around. Look for the larger-than-life character of Anni in the excerpt from Shirley Schoonover's novel about Iron Range Finns (Chapter 5); or Justine Kerfoot's mother, inviting all of her Ojibwe neighbors to the family cabin for Christmas dinner (Chapter 1); or the Presbyterian church ladies who raise money for charity at Christmas in 1851 St. Paul (Chapter 1); or Ulrika Jackson, from Vilhelm Moberg's "Emigrant" novels, whose generous feast transports her homesick Swedish neighbors back across time and distance (Chapter 5).

Meanwhile, where is Dad? He can be counted on, perhaps, to carve the bird at the table, stoke the fire, and bring home the bacon and the Christmas tree, like Louie

Anderson's dad (Chapter 3). In some of these stories, though, we find men happily taking on "women's work": Sam Cook (Chapter 4) actually makes a pair of slippers for his wife; Bill Holm deals manfully with a vast Christmas card list, the "December duty," that rattles after him "like Jacob Marley's chains" (Chapter 3); in Jon Hassler's story (Chapter 6), a divorced dad drives hours to spend Christmas with his grown-up son and even brings dinner, sort of.

If it's true that throughout the year we all have our roles to play, then at Christmas the stage lights seem to shine a little stronger. The theme of performance frequently edges into these stories: an 1857 Christmas puppet show (Chapter 1); Florence Jaques's party for her Ojibwe neighbors, where everyone dresses up in funny hats (Chapter 1); an affable drunk channeling Elvis in Kevin Kling's story (Chapter 4).

But we don't have to stray too far from home to find Christmas "performances." Our living rooms are decked out like stage sets, perfect backdrops for reenacting holiday rituals. Outside, the house is an electric extravaganza, the front yard full of cutout characters and the roof outlined with lights, all for an audience encased in warm automobiles slowly cruising the neighborhood, as Cathy Mauk remembers in her story (Chapter 2). Our Christmas dinners are carefully orchestrated dramas (comedies, if we get lucky), with family members reprising accustomed roles, recorded year after year by someone with a camera, as in Michael Fedo's family (Chapter 6). We dress up as Santa—or better yet, we get somebody else to put on that beard and stuffed costume, as Roger MacDonald recalls (Chapter 2).

Our devotion to Christmas-as-performance requires at some point that we troop off together to watch *other* people perform: the inevitable Scrooges and Tiny Tims, the Messiahs, the perennial Nutcrackers. More than other performances, however, it's the children's pageant that touches an irresistible emotional chord, becoming a kind of collective memory and a stand-in for other kinds of performances in our lives. Wendell Anderson remembers learning about public speaking at a childhood pageant (Chapter 1). In Faith Sullivan's story (Chapter 2), fourth-grader Sally Wheeler learns why people come to a pageant in the first place: "They want somebody to tell them a story, help them understand what's going on." And Noah Adams ends our collection (Epilogue) with a visit to an elementary school pageant, where the "light is really coming from the stage to the audience, shining from the energy and pride of the young faces."

And so we invite you to this substantial pageant, this *Christmas in Minnesota*. The packages are wrapped, the candles lit, the cookies decorated, the table is set. It's time to indulge—even over-indulge—in a feast of memories. Enjoy the celebration.

*A snowy Christmas Day in Minneapolis, 1932 (Norton & Peel)*

• • •

# Christmas in Minnesota

## · 1 ·

# Finding Christmas

—◆·◆·◆—

## Christmas Chronicles

*Settlers in pioneer-era Minnesota adapted Christmas traditions to their new frontier circumstances as soon as they arrived, as the following excerpts from letters and newspaper accounts suggest.*

*Not surprisingly, it was the cold weather around Christmas that held the attention of many unprepared new settlers, including Anna Ramsey, wife of Alexander Ramsey, the first territorial governor. Spending her first holiday season in Minnesota, Anna wrote on Christmas Day, 1849, to her husband, who was—heartlessly—back east on political business.*

My dear but very negligent Husband, Oh, Alex, could thee be here and know how we suffer with cold, thee would never want to winter again in St. Paul. I know I will not, I nearly froze to death in bed as well as out. Today is Christmas and such a one making a shirt for thee and nothing in the house to eat but strong butter and coffee without cream. Every potato and vegetable is frozen up. . . . My health is not very good I suffer so much with headaches. I do hope thee will hasten home, it is such forlorn living alone in such a horrid place as this. I think it is intolerable. . . . The thermometer stands at 22 degrees below zero and if it gets much colder I shall have to close the house as the four windows and five doors besides innumerable cracks give more air than we really require. . . . I tell thee now thee shall never leave me again so long. I will not stay.

· · ·

*Wild game was on many a Christmas menu in the frontier era. Here Catherine Goddard, who ran Winona's first boarding house, writes to her sister and describes a holiday feast in 1852.*

This Christmas, dinner was given in the upper story of the Winona House on Water Street, in which Edwin Hamilton was keeping what was called Bachelors' Hall. The young men set up stoves and Mrs. "Elder" Hamilton and myself looked after the culinary part of the dinner. In the absence of the bird that usually graces the Christmas dinner, we were obliged to use coon, or rather several coons, with entrees of venison and wild goose. At the request of the young men, who said it would not be a Christmas feast without them, we fried enough [dough]nuts in coon's fat, and they were much relished.

By 11 o'clock, every resident of Winona, old and young, big and little . . . some thirty in all, were present. In addition to these were several from Minnesota City, besides some St. Paul men who were hauling goods on the ice from LaCrosse to St. Paul and who shortly before noon broke through the ice on the river opposite the business part of the town. These men were assisted in rescuing their teams and goods by our townsmen and invited to share the hospitalities of our Christmas dinner.

◆ ◆ ◆

*An 1851 St. Paul newspaper report—written by someone simply identified as "A Bachelor"—described a "Ladies' Fair," which had inaugurated the Christmas season in a genteel fashion almost out of place in a frontier village.*

The ladies of Rev. Mr. Neill's society—the 1st Presbyterian Society—held a Fair on Tuesday evening last. A stock of articles, of the various descriptions usually got up for sale on such occasions, was disposed of at a fair profit; and the tickets for supper were sold probably to some 150 persons at a living rate. The amount of the proceeds was about $350.00.

The supper was excellent. It was made up of nearly every good eatable that the various tastes and abilities of the contributors may have laid in store—there were at least seven baskets full left. Ninety plates were set on linen covered tables at one time. The ware was all white, as the fashion is. Let us consider some of the viands which one would scarce expect to see so far northwest, in the early times of St. Paul. There were oysters, and sardines, and turkey, and lobster, and ice cream, made without freezing—pastries, and the more staple meats, including buffalo tongue.

It seemed to have a salutary effect upon the feelings of everyone present. . . . Indeed, one great good of churches to the community is the civilizing and refining effect upon the social feelings. . . . Here applies the principle that man without the society of woman, is a barbarian.

◆ ◆ ◆

*The Minnesota Daughters of the American Revolution preserved interviews with old settlers in* Old Rail Fence Corners *(1914), a compilation of "authentic incidents." Between the sweet, nostalgic lines of most of these memories are glimmers of the hardscrabble life "in those hard times."*

Nothing could be cozier than our cabin Christmas eve. We had brought solid silver knives, forks and spoons. These hung from racks. Quantities of copper and brass utensils burnished until they were like mirrors hung in rows. In Sweden mother had woven curtains and bed coverings of red, white and blue linen and these were always used on holidays. How glad we were they were the national colors here! We covered a hoop with gay colored paper and set little wooden candleholders that my father had made all around it. This was suspended from the ceiling, all aglow with dips. Then, as a last touch to the decorations, we filled our brass candlesticks with real candles and set them in the windows as a greeting to those living across the lake. A sheaf for the birds and all was done.

◆ ◆ ◆

Christmas in those hard times did not mean to us little pioneer children what it does now. There was no spare money with which to buy presents. We always hung up our stockings, but got nothing in them but a little cheap candy, and perhaps a few raisins. But one year, father determined to give us and the other children of the village a little better Christmas than usual. So he went out to his woods and cut enough firewood to exchange in St. Cloud for a barrel of apples. Then he divided off one end of our sitting room with a sheet and arranged a puppet show behind it. And with the village children in one end of the room eating apples, and father in the other managing the puppets, we celebrated the day in a very happy way.

◆ ◆ ◆

*John Wesley North, an abolitionist lawyer and land speculator, moved with his bride, Ann—who was just seventeen at the time—to a log cabin on Nicollet Island at the Falls of St. Anthony in 1849. For several years Ann pined for the comfort and companionship she had enjoyed among her extended family in New York. Her sadness and discouragement were magnified, of course, at Christmastime.*

December 28, 1849

My dear Brothers, Christmas has passed—but it seemed not like a holy day to me, for I was here with Mr. North alone. None of my dear home friends could come and make it merry with us, and, of course, we were very quiet. . . . The sleighing is now fine, especially on the river. And we have the brightest, sunniest days I almost ever saw in winter.

December 26, 1852

My dear Parents, This is bright beautiful weather, but anything but a "merry Christmas" did I have yesterday. Mr. North went to Stillwater the day before and did not return till last night. . . . I was alone with Elisabeth Eichard, who stays with me during Clara's absence, and Charlie was at home at his meals. Of course we made no particular account of the day, none of us receiving any presents but Charlie and Emma.

December 25, 1853

My dear Parents, This is a bright, beautiful Christmas morning. How I wish all within me was as bright—but I have not felt so sad and discouraged for many a day—I seem to work hard every day—at all events, I keep tired all the time—and yet nothing seems accomplished by my hands. . . . My children are neither trained nor clothed as they ought to be.

◆ ◆ ◆

*In 1925 Britania J. Livingston of Fairmont recorded her reminiscence of a simple rural Christmas, probably in the 1860s. She recalls a time when "having a Christmas tree" meant staging a community event, usually at a church or school, during which a decorated tree would be "unveiled" and the gifts hanging from it distributed to the children in attendance.*

Most of the children had never seen a real Christmas tree. The idea started between the teachers and two or three ladies—perhaps it was evolved by a sort of mental spontaneous combustion. It was spoken of only a week before Christmas. The weather was so bad—snowy and blustering—that no committees could get their heads together for consultation; but during that week after school house, the fine floury snow of Minnesota was melted off the trim overcoat of our teacher beside nearly every hot stove in his school district. . . .

Then every mother laid her plans to help Santa Claus. Mrs. H. counted up the little children that were sure to be there, and found that they numbered twenty. So that every child should certainly have something, she cut twenty stockings out of blue mosquito netting, made them neatly and wrote each child's name and fastened it to the stocking, and then made a few extra ones for any extra children that might happen to come.

Mrs. S., with the same thoughtful purpose, counted also, and made twenty little stockings and a few extra ones, and pinned on the names with only this difference—the mosquito netting was pink. Mrs. P., not knowing the counting and planning going on at the snow-bound neighborhood, counted also and made neat little white bags with fancy strings for twenty. Mrs. L. did the same thing. So you can see for yourself that the thing was a success from the start. But wait: the teacher had not done all of his part yet. Fearing that some might be slighted or overlooked by the saint in a crowded house, he went to town counting, as he rode along, up to twenty, and he invested in twenty toys.

Christmas evening was clear and beautiful. All day long the teacher and his aids were at the school house arranging the tree, the evergreen decorations, and receiving those who came on business. . . . At early candlelight the sleigh bells began to ring up their merry loads. The schoolhouse was crowded to an overflow. A brighter, prettier tree we never saw, although we have looked on those of ten times the value. It was a graceful red cedar well lighted with candles and well loaded with presents, as was also a table nearby and the floor at its roots. . . .

The "twenty" soon had received their pairs of pink and blue stockings which Santa Claus had filled with candies, nuts, maple sugar, etc., and the children that were unexpected had their names called and were served just as well as the others. But the tree was still loaded, such sights of pretty mittens, suspenders, leggings, neckties, slippers, dolls, drums, dolls' clothing, books, pictures, and several pairs of small boots and hoods. O, I cannot begin to mention the things. Nothing costly, nearly everything useful, but so bright and handsome.

# Christmas Eve in a Sod House

## Hugo Nisbeth

*In 1872 Swedish traveler Hugo Nisbeth visited Minnesota and spent a few days before Christmas in St. Paul before heading out onto the prairie in search of some homesteading countrymen. Nisbeth remarks—twice, in fact—that Swedes in America somehow manage to get through Christmas dinner without lutefisk.*

Much activity prevailed in St. Paul when I got there. . . . It is not only the Scandinavians who celebrate Christmas here in America in a true ancient northern fashion, but even the Americans themselves have in late years begun to give more and more attention to this festival of the children and have as nearly as possible taken our method of celebration as a pattern. For example, most of them use fir trees with candles, confections, and other decorations, and so far as the number and costliness of the presents are concerned they often display a liberality that would amaze us Swedes. These Christmas presents are given in various ways. In the public schools, especially for younger children, the school officials usually arrange a huge fir, which stands for about eight days. On this tree the children's parents and friends hang small presents, which are distributed by the school-teacher. In the home the presents are sent with a message if the giver is someone outside the family, or they are distributed by a dressed-up Christmas mummer, who here goes under the name of "Santa Claus." Still another custom exists, although it is not used so commonly perhaps as the first two. If there is reason to expect presents, a stocking is hung up at bedtime in some convenient and well-known place and in it in the morning will be found the expected presents. Not a trace of our traditional *lutfisk* and rice porridge is found. There is no special menu for Christmas Eve. On the other hand there are few American homes in which the customary turkey is not served on the following, or Christmas, day.

As I had planned to spend my Christmas Eve with some of my countrymen out on the prairie, I left St. Paul a few days before Christmas and went by the St. Paul and Pacific one hundred English miles northwest to the Litchfield station. Here, after some trouble, I was fortunate enough to secure a sled in which I set out over the prairie to the west. There was no road, of course. The way was not particularly difficult to traverse, for on the flat prairie the snow distributes itself comparatively evenly. Toward nightfall on the day before Christmas Eve I perceived far off the smoke from a human habitation, which, from what I could make out at a distance, should be a sod house. I had not steered wrong, for I had reached the house of the man I sought, Jan Erikson from Wermland, who had been in America for three years and for the last two years had been living on his large eighty-acre homestead. I was received by him and his friendly wife with that cordiality which I have been accustomed to find among my countrymen on the prairie. Nor did I need to put forth any request that I might stay over Christmas Eve, for I was anticipated in this by my friendly hosts, who simply but heartily bade me remain and help myself to whatever they had to offer. To the two children, a girl of seven named Anna and a boy of three, Eric, the visit of a strange gentleman seemed particularly surprising, but the sight of some packages I had brought along, which the dwelling's smallness made it impossible for me to hide, soon made us the best of friends.

Early in the morning of the day before Christmas my hosts were at work, and when I arose I found a huge ham already sputtering over the fire, while outside I heard my host's great ax blows, for he was busy getting the necessary Christmas wood ready. I hurried out and was met with a picture that was for me entirely new and particularly striking. The sun was about twenty degrees above the wavy horizon of snow and from the snow-clad tops of countless hillocks the sun beams were thrown in a dazzling bewilderment all around. Yet, except for this tiny world in which I now found myself, I could not discern another sign of human presence other than two columns of smoke, which arose, nearly perpendicularly, from the horizon, one in the northwest and one in the southwest. After the wood was chopped and carried in, a task in which the two children took part with a will, the cattle were fed and watered, and a small sheaf of unthreshed wheat was set out for the few birds that at times circled around the house, in accordance with the lovely old Swedish custom.

With these and other chores the morning passed, and right after twelve o'clock we were invited in by the housewife for the midday meal. The bread that we dipped in the kettle was freshly baked and tasty, and the fat chicken that was later served in a sort of stewed pie form, which awakened especially the children's delight, had clearly not fared ill during the short time allotted him to live. And so came the afternoon with its small arrangements for the evening meal and the Christmas table, for this could not be omitted. There was no Christmas tree, for fir trees are not yet planted in this part of Minnesota, but two candles stood on the white covered table and round these were placed a multitude of Christmas cakes in various shapes made by the housewife and such small presents as these pioneers were able to afford, to which I added those I had brought. Nor were *lutfisk* and rice porridge to be found on the table, but the ham which took the place of honor in their stead banished all doubt that the settler's labor and sacrifice had received its reward.

The meal was eaten in the happiest of moods and afterward the few presents were distributed to the children. The gifts were neither costly nor tasteful, but they were *gifts* and that was all that was necessary. On the wooden horse I had brought, the little three-year-old galloped over the hard-packed dirt floor of the sod house with as much joy and happiness undoubtedly as the pampered child upon one polished and upholstered. All was joy and thankfulness, and when later the head of the family read a chapter from the Bible about the Christ Child I am certain that from the hearts of these poor people there rose many warm thanksgivings to Him who smoothed their path and gave them courage and strength to conquer the hardships of the New World.

Outside the snow fell slowly and spread its white Christmas mantle over the endless prairie. Now and then a snowflake fastened itself on the single window of the sod house, its curtains faded by the summer suns, and quickly dissolved and disappeared as if its icy heart had melted with joy at sight of the peace that reigned within. And later, from the corner of the room where the housewife's kind hands had made my bed, I heard the small voice of the youngest child, still clutching his wooden horse, repeating after his mother, "Good night, kind Jesus."

*Icy branches at St. Anthony Falls, about 1870 (Benjamin F. Upton)*

· · ·

# "No sound of joyous Christmas bells"

## MARY DODGE WOODWARD

*In 1882, the recently widowed Mary Dodge Woodward moved with her two grown sons and daughter to a "bonanza farm" in the Red River Valley. As evident in these diary entries from the 1880s, Mary became reflective, wistful, and more than a little sad around Christmastime—feelings that are probably familiar to many of us. Contrary to one of her bleakest reflections, however, she did indeed get away from the howling prairie, and returned in 1889 to her Wisconsin home.*

December 24, 1884

The mercury goes into the ball at forty, and it is now out of sight, so we shall not know how cold the weather is. Katie is thawing the frost from the front windows with a warm flatiron so as to let in the light. A fine snow has been drifting by all day. Tonight the sun is setting with three large dogs, the like of which I never saw before. I suppose it is always so in the north. I do not believe apples or any other fruit will ever grow here.

This is Christmas Eve. The wind howls dismally around the house. We will not be likely to hear Santa Claus' bells way out on the cold prairie where we dwell, but I have no little stockings for him to fill. The children are grown to manhood and womanhood, and scattered far apart, and their father has gone to return no more. Tomorrow I shall wish the family a Merry Christmas and give them a good dinner on this, the third Christmas I have passed in Dakota Territory.

December 24, 1885

The ground was studded with diamonds of frost this morning, the whole yard of twenty acres gleaming and taking on lovely colors in the sunlight. The snow falls gently, great flakes sailing by as they used to in Vermont. But the winter cannot be long now. This is Christmas Eve. Walter, Katie, and I are alone.

December 25, 1885

The mercury fell thirty degrees last night. . . . Nellie's package contained presents for all of us: a photo album and beautiful nightgown for me; slippers and an embroidered

## Burning Coals to the Altar

*In early winter 1878, missionaries journeyed from St. John's Abbey and St. Benedict's Convent to the White Earth Ojibwe reservation in northern Minnesota. Expecting to find the mission provisioned, they found no tools and log buildings with leaking roofs and wide cracks that let in snow. Father Hermanutz remembered:*

Never in my life did I suffer so much for the cold as I did that winter and then more in the house and church than outside. . . . I had sent the [church] bell away to be recast. To give the signal for the midnight Mass on Christmas, I had procured three mortars, which some Indians were to fire off at the proper time. Wrapped in my buffalo coat, I had been sitting in the confessional from 6 o'clock in the evening. It was 40 degrees below zero. When the mortars were discharged at the specified time, the violence of the explosion shattered every windowpane on the north side of the church. We covered the openings with blankets. . . . During Mass the cold in the church became so intense that burning coals had to be brought to the altar to keep my hands and the contents of the chalice from freezing. The Indians did not complain and said they had a glorious Christmas.

Quoted in Sister M. Grace McDonald, *With Lamps Burning* (Saint Benedict's Press, 1957)

handkerchief for Katie; for Walter, two hemstitched linen handkerchiefs; and for Fred, a pair of mittens and a scarlet silk handkerchief with his initials embroidered in yellow silk. Katie and I each received a very elegant fringed Christmas card.

The day has been cold and windy and not a very merry Christmas at the Dodge farm. No sound of joyous Christmas bells on the lone prairie where we dwell. Tonight the wind howls dismally and we sit close to the fire, we three, where we will be found for many nights to come. It is not the being here on a night like this that makes one feel so lonely, but the knowing that, in any case, one could not get away.

December 24, 1888

It is Christmas Eve and I am thinking of the merry times we used to have, all of us at home on this night, many years ago. The happiest part was when the children hung their stockings in a long row on the mantelpiece. Their father always saw that they were filled with good things such as candy and nuts, whatever else they received.

December 25, 1888

A bright, peaceful Christmas morning with a beautiful mirage. I have been wishing that Christmas bells could ring out on the prairies on this clear, shining day. But they can be heard only in imagination. The boys brought Katie a pair of fine silk stockings and a Wirt fountain pen. Fred gave Walter Dante's *Inferno* for a Christmas present. The book is beautifully bound in morocco, but oh, the illustrations are horrible! They make me shudder. Katie presented me with a candlestick and Elsie Lessing brought us a cup and saucer.

December 31, 1888

> Another year is dying fast,
> A checkered year of joy and woe,
> And dark and light alike are past,
> the rose and thorn at once laid low.

This is the last entry in this diary. Very soon the year 1888 will have passed into history. But if it were not for the end of the year, where would we find time to make new resolutions, to swear off from old vices, and to commence on a new plan? It is a sort of fetching up place. The shadows lengthen as the night draws near, and with the advent of another day a new year will be born.

———•◦•———

# "In the American fashion"

## Works Progress Administration

*Bohemian Flats was a "shantytown" of Eastern European and other immigrants that grew up in the nineteenth century along the Mississippi River in Minneapolis, near what is now the university's West Bank. In the 1930s, writers from the New Deal's Works Progress Administration produced a detailed account of life in the Flats, which included a consideration of how the immigrants reconciled old-world Christmas traditions with new American expectations.*

In the Bohemian Flats as in the old country, holidays were closely associated with the church. The Santa Claus myth was not fostered; mothers told their children at Christmas that the Christ Child brought the presents. Christmas began on the evening of December 24 and dinner was not served until the stars came out. In many homes a place was set for the family dead because it was felt that they were present on special occasions. Before the dinner was eaten, families partook of holy bread, brought from the church, which they dipped in honey. Some of this bread was also fed to the cows to insure a plentiful supply of milk during the coming year.

Just as the sun was setting and before the church bells rang for the evening service, young girls who wanted to be married began to sweep the kitchen floor. When the first chime of the bell was heard, they would run outside with the sweepings and look about for a man. The name of the first man a girl saw would be the name of the man she would marry. The boys knew the girls would be coming out, so they waited around their doors. "They not only got a kick out of it but often a kiss," laughs a Slovak father. "The best part of the custom was that it really worked!"

After dinner everyone went to the candlelight service at the church. The first Christmas tree on the Flats was set up there and was decorated with tiny candles of twisted wax. An old resident remembers that "we were so afraid the Christmas tree would burn the little church down that we had two men sitting by it all through the service." Carols were sung and the church windows opened wide, so that the light shone on the snow and the songs could be heard far down the street.

Christmas Day was strictly observed. For many years the villagers forbade all work on this day. They could not even sweep the floors. Visiting was postponed until the following day. The only chores permitted were milking and feeding the cows.

Morning services were held at the church. The girls and women did not take seats but stood in front of the altar during the entire service, which frequently lasted two and a half hours. Sometimes a woman fainted before the service was finished, but it was considered disgraceful to sit down. For this occasion older women wore shawls and young married women wore gaily decorated hats, which were later put away until the next Christmas.

The dinner was prepared on the preceding day and typically consisted of mushroom or beef soup, roast pork or fowl, fish and potatoes, sauerkraut, koláče, and dried berries or fruits. Sausages were prepared weeks in advance. Heaps of wild nuts, gathered in the fall, were a traditional part of the holiday feast. Christmas bread was made from dried dough cut into small rounds, which were baked and rolled in honey and poppy seed. The old grandmothers told the girls that if they wanted the boys to like them they must put one of the little biscuits under their pillows at night.

The year following the first appearance of the Christmas tree at the church, many homes adopted the custom. In the old country only people of considerable means had had Christmas trees, and some of the villagers had never heard of them until they came to America. The first home Christmas trees in the Flats were decorated by the children with small homemade cookies, nutshells painted in bright colors, bits of rags or paper, and small candles of twisted wax. Long strings of popcorn and cranberries were also used, in the American fashion.

The custom of exchanging gifts during the Christmas season was not general in old Bohemia, but it was universally adopted in the Flats. The women crocheted square shawls, or fascinators, and made bright sweaters and socks. Boys carved wall plaques from blocks of wood salvaged from the Mississippi. Girls fashioned dolls from straw and rags and finished them off with eyes of bright beads. Families exchanged complete dinners, packing them in split-willow baskets and sending them up the road with the children, who stopped at each house along the way to sing Christmas carols and gather cookies or pennies in return. The church choir also made the rounds of the village, singing carols in front of each home.

New Year's Eve, called St. Sylvester's by some of the Flats dwellers, was celebrated in the streets or in the beer house. They played music and danced all night, and welcomed the new year just like their fellow Americans "on the hill." In the early days the lads gathered on the streets, formed circles, and fired guns into the air three times. This custom, known as "shooting the witches," apparently had no significance when practiced here; its original intent, however, was to frighten away any witches that might be lurking in the neighborhood. The holiday season ended with Epiphany, January 6, which was marked by a church service and was said to be in commemoration of the journey of the three Wise Men to Bethlehem.

# "Screaming their excited delight"

## MELVIN L. FRANK

*Every year, Minnesota kids keep their collective fingers crossed for a really wintry Christmas— not for any Bing Crosby-nostalgia reasons, but because the snow and the cold mean that the new Santa-provided sleds and skates can get a workout. Such was the case for the energetic young Melvin Frank, who grew up on Minneapolis's north side—"Sawmill City"—in the 1910s.*

*Sleighs and sleds crowd Minneapolis's Park Avenue, about 1885*

· · ·

Now and then when conditions were right, the city would ice up Twenty-sixth Avenue from Lyndale to Washington, a distance of four blocks, for a bobsled run. When this happened the bobsled owners would break out their equipment and head for the hill. Some of the sleds were long jobs with room for a dozen riders or more. The old-time bobsled is pretty obsolete now, but it was a fun thing in those years. It rode on two sleds with steel runners, one front and one back, with ropes for steering attached to the front sled and handled like reins by the front rider. Passengers sat on long planks that stretched from front to back. When all the riders were on board, a couple of older fellows at the rear would push off and give the thing a running start and then climb on.

The bobsled gathered speed, and we would go whizzing down the grade, with the girls in particular screaming their excited delight. It was great for us little kids when the bobsled owners invited us to ride. So it was that, when the word was out that the big sleds were running, we would hurry to Twenty-sixth in eager hope of snagging a ride.

Experimenting with homemade equipment was also a part of winter fun. My favorite homemade sliding toy was the "Johnny jumper," as we called it. Where the name came from I do not know. I took one wide barrel stave and mounted it on a one-foot length of four-by-four, and then capped it with a piece of one-by-six about ten inches long for a seat. We got our odd pieces of wood for free from the scrap lumber pile at the sawmill. This made the "Johnny jumper" a one-runner ski-sled that a boy sat on and balanced as he rode it downhill. The ride was exciting and usually ended in a spill. I also made two-stave models of the jumper. They were not so tough to balance but were not as much fun either.

Most of us were lucky to have a sled. To own a Flexible Flyer or another model of a steel runner put us on the hills with a first-class outfit. Many boys had wooden sleds their fathers built in their home shops. These were substantial jobs but lacked the advantage of flexible runners that simplified steering. Only rich kids had toboggans. The rest of us made "cheese box" toboggans from the round boxes in which cheddar wheels were shipped.

Farview Park offered another winter attraction besides hills for sliding—skating. When freezing weather arrived, usually between Thanksgiving and Christmas vacation, the Park Board each year flooded the baseball diamond to make ice for skating, and the shelter would be converted into a warming house, with fires started in the big oil-drum wood burners.

My first skates were steel clamp-ons that attached to everyday shoes. Web straps helped hold the skates on and at the same time lent support to the skater's ankles. . . .

Next I tried screw clamp skates. These were a hockey model, unlike the rocker runners of the old clamp style. They were handsome and well designed, but the trouble was they called for heavy shoe soles and mine were not up to requirements. Dad resoled my shoes, using leather from old sawmill belts. It was good leather but tended to be limber, flexible, and not hard enough so the screw-on clamps gripped solidly. The result was a repeat of the problems of the clamp-ons they replaced.

Shoe skates came in about 1916, but who could afford them? Knowing how I loved to skate, Dad undertook to make me a happy skater. So for Christmas I got a pair of shoe skates. Dad had bought a set of runners and attached them to a pair of my best shoes. But the shoes fastened with buttons! Dad had not anticipated that the buttons would pop or come undone under the pressure of skating. Dear man, he tried. Having never skated with anything but clamp-ons himself, he figured that shoes were shoes even with skates on, but he was wrong. Button shoes with skates just did not work. They were one of the biggest disappointments of my boyhood. Shoe skates had to wait until I earned a pair of Nestor Johnsons myself.

If Dad's effort to furnish me with skates did not work out, he did succeed in making me a pair of skis that were sheer joy. They came as a gift another Christmas. He made them at the powerhouse workbench, and they were beautiful to behold. Crafted in the best Norwegian style, they were long enough so I could just reach the tips. Dad had steamed the fine-grained birchwood and gradually achieved the bend at the front and the curve in the long blades. He had attached buckled straps to fit my shoes. No boy on Sixth Street had finer skis. It was a great day when I first took the skis, newly waxed and polished, for a ride; and then, day after day as long as the snow lasted, it was ski, ski, ski.

*Composer F. Melius Christiansen, long-time director of St. Olaf College's Christmas choir concerts, described carols as "innocence and purity . . . the constant, quiet falling snow of a mild winter day." (1951 photo, Wally Kammann)*

*Simple holiday decorations (and a stop sign) on Minneapolis's Seventh Street, 1927*

. . .

## Minneapolis claims brightest Christmas

Mayor George E. Leach has sent telegraphic challenges to ten American cities defying them to dispute this city's claim to the title of brightest Christmas city in the United States. Boston, Pittsburgh, Detroit, Buffalo, Kansas City, Davenport, Denver, Fargo, Duluth and La Crosse were invited to compete for the honor. The challenge read:

Minneapolis is the brightest Christmas city in America. A downtown district with streets under a canopy of evergreen festoons and thousands of tiny lights twinkling from the streamers. Every downtown lamppost a Christmas tree against a lighted background of red. A towering municipal Christmas tree in the loop gateway, its branches glittering with the light of thousands of tiny color lights and its top holding a flashing star of Bethlehem seventy-five feet in the air.

Ten thousand lighted outdoor Christmas trees in the residential sections. . . . Christmas carols broadcast by radio and carried through every street and alley of the city by hundreds of loud-speakers set in windows of Minneapolis homes.

Minneapolis challenges the world to dispute its claim to the brightest Christmas city in America.

*New York Times*, December 25, 1927

# Christmas on the Gunflint

## JUSTINE KERFOOT

*Christmas comes to all parts of Minnesota, even the most remote. The near-legendary Boundary Waters guide and lodge-owner Justine Kerfoot wrote in her memoir about a Christmas feast in the 1930s and about her family's newfound friends among the area's Ojibwe (Chippewa) people.*

At Christmas Mother invited all the Indian neighbors for a big feast. Word spread among them but there was no indication of how many would appear. On the appointed day, we watched for signs of movement across the lake, a mile away. The snow-draped timbered hills made a backdrop to the white ice of the lake, and we could see one moving tiny speck appear on the far shore and then another. The figures of Abie Cook, Bessie and their youngsters were strung out in a long line and became ever larger. In another 10 minutes Netowance Plummer and Mary Cook would appear, snowshoeing with ease, one behind the other. Their layered skirts swayed with each step as they slowly came closer. Although they spoke no English, when they came in, their broad smiles and twinkling eyes revealed their pleasure. Eddie Burnside and his wife arrived next, carrying their youngster in a tick-a-noggin. Charlie Cook joined the Plummers—Walter, Butchie and George—who came, one following the other.

Parkas, caps and mitts were piled in a corner of the dining room. The Indians carefully swept the snow from their moosehide mukluks to keep them dry. The dining room tables were arranged in a long line so we were all seated as one big family. Our friends sat on chairs along the wall waiting and watching quietly while the feast was brought from the kitchen.

One Christmas Mother prepared a large roast. When it was passed to the two older ladies, they looked at it but took none. When we asked, we were informed, "They no eat cow." It was evident that they had eaten contaminated beef once and become ill. Mother quickly found slices of cold turkey, which was agreeable to them.

Following Christmas dinner we cleared the table and all joined in a game of poker, the one game everyone knew. We played plain stud poker for several hours, shifting the piles of chips back and forth. The Indians laughed and joked. I enjoyed hearing them speak. The Chippewa language flows quietly and smoothly like water gliding over a smooth submerged rock. As they tired, they left one by one as quietly as they arrived.

# "A Christmas tree for birds"

## FLORENCE PAGE JAQUES

*Naturalist Florence Page Jaques spent Christmas 1942 in "Snowshoe Country" on Gunflint Lake with artist-naturalist husband Francis Lee Jaques. They shared their holidays with their neighbors, including Justine, Bill, Bruce, and Patty Kerfoot, the operators of the Gunflint Lodge, and several friends from the Ojibwe (Chippewa) communities in the area.*

December 23d

We decided to get ready for Christmas today; the Chippewa families are coming over for dinner. We brought the turkey in to thaw, and made cakes, and Bruce and I strung cranberries and popcorn for the tree. I haven't done that since I was very small.

At sunset Bruce and Lee and I started up the cliff trail to get a Christmas tree. It was a delight to have such thousands to select from, but almost impossible to choose among them. On a ridge we found a beauty, and I begged a tiny one besides. I've always wanted to have a Christmas tree for birds. Coming down, the spicy air and the great snowy landscape were so inspiriting that Lee and I surprised Bruce by bursting into carols. The lake was a giant mosaic in pastel colors as the sunset reflected on various surfaces. It was as if a rainbow had been shattered there.

Since everyone will be in for their Christmas mail tomorrow, we decorated the tree tonight. All of us, that is, except Justine, who chose this evening to skin Bill's mink and weasel.

December 24th

A delicious day, crisp but not cold, and I always love the day before Christmas better than Christmas itself. I put our birds' Christmas tree outside the west windows on a tall stump and decorated it with jackpine cones dipped in melted suet, strings of popcorn and cranberries, small bright apples, and birch-bark cornucopias filled with fat and sunflower seeds. A scarlet Christmas ornament shone on the tip. It looked very festive.

Everyone for miles around came for the mail. Ahbutch came across the ice with her dogs, pulling a rowboat she had borrowed in the summer. We decorated Ferdinand [the calf] with a mammoth bow of scarlet oilcloth and dog-sled bells, which he wore with a quiet perplexity.

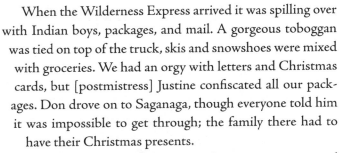

When the Wilderness Express arrived it was spilling over with Indian boys, packages, and mail. A gorgeous toboggan was tied on top of the truck, skis and snowshoes were mixed with groceries. We had an orgy with letters and Christmas cards, but [postmistress] Justine confiscated all our packages. Don drove on to Saganaga, though everyone told him it was impossible to get through; the family there had to have their Christmas presents.

After everyone left we ate a hasty supper, arranged the packages around the tree, and had Christmas eggnogs, while carols from radio archangels rang around us. It was a lovely Christmas Eve.

Christmas Day

It is thirty *above!* Scandalous! This isn't the Christmas weather we are supposed to endure!

After breakfast Bruce distributed the presents, glittering like the Christmas tree in his excitement. Later, the Indians arrived by dog team and Charlie Olsen came along. My family had sent Christmas crackers in our box of gifts, and everyone wore the gay paper caps. The Indians love any sort of fun and frolic. I wish I had a picture of old Charlie and Butchie's mother in their carnival hats.

Nettahwense is a wonderful old woman, with much character in her face. She is shy, but she has great poise. Justine says nobody else can make one feel as awkward as an Indian can. She told me, as we were getting dinner, of going over to ask Nettahwense what moss to use to chink this cabin. . . .

I liked listening to the Indians talking together. Chippewa holds the same place in Indian languages as French has held in European; it is the language of courtesy and grace.

While we ate the turkey dinner, Charlie Olsen told us about his boyhood in Norway, herding cattle above the timberline. Patty, busy with the boxes of chocolates, paid no attention to the dinner or the toys. In the middle of the festivity Ferdinand stuck his head in the door, like a goblin spirit of Christmas.

December 27th

We have been lucky in escaping the flu which has swept the North Shore, but now Justine and I have both caught colds. . . .

I've spent most of the day in bed, watching the birds at their Christmas tree. The whiskeyjacks and one blue jay came first, and gobbled like mad. They have an exasperating charm! Then the hairy woodpeckers, in white plush and gleaming black. They are supposed to be solitary through the winter, but here the male and female came together. A timid downy came hesitantly now and then. Last of all the chickadees flew in daintily.

December 29th

I can never forget the utter clarity of these winter dawns. The complete *stainlessness* in the coloring of early morning is what affects me most deeply. What did I say, when the snow first fell, about the monotony of white landscapes?

These subtle colors have no richness, but a strange and deliberate power. The infinite gradations of faint rose, clear blue, or pale gold over the vast stretches of snow come from no frailty, but from a hidden strength such as a pearl has. The purity of line, too—however fragile it may be, it is distinct and sure. These simplicities of curve and shadow make me feel that they are preliminary sketches of a fresh earth made just before I came upon them.

---

# "Once again it is Christmas"

## WENDELL R. ANDERSON

*For its Christmas issue in 1976 (perhaps in a surge of Bicentennial fervor),* Redbook *magazine invited U.S. elected officials to reflect on the Christmas season. Then-governor Wendell R. Anderson, at the time something of a national celebrity because of his "Good Life in Minnesota"* Time *magazine cover, recalled his early Christmases on St. Paul's East Side.*

The words "Christmas in Minnesota" evoke a rural picture—deep snow, people bundled up against the cold temperatures while they run last-minute Christmas errands, travel from farmhouse to church for special programs and services or to make their way across the countryside to the homes of their relatives for Christmas Eve and Christmas Day.

*The warming house
at Minneapolis's
Franklin Steele
Square, 1949*

  · · ·

For many Minnesotans, Christmas is like that. But the world of my childhood Christmases was much smaller and my own memories are different.

My brothers, Orv and Rod, and I grew up on the East Side of St. Paul. In those days people tended to think of the East Side as almost a separate community, so closely knit were the Polish, Italian, Irish, and Scandinavian families who then inhabited the area. And so we shared our school time and playtime with boys and girls who on Sundays went to churches with names like St. Casimir's, St. Patrick's, St. Ambrose, and Gustavus Adolphus.

For us the best part of the week before Christmas—besides the fact that school was out—was ice hockey. We played it in the morning, we played it in the afternoon, and we played it in the evening when we could. We shoveled and flooded the outdoor rink constantly at Phalen Park, across the street from our house. This was a required job in our part of Minnesota if we wanted to keep the ice smooth.

As we grew older we had to give up part of our skating and hockey time to earn money shoveling snow or bagging groceries or helping to deliver Christmas mail. But some of the best times we had, even then, were spent in front of the red-hot, potbellied stove in the Phalen Park warming house, thawing out amid the fumes of steaming wet clothing and swapping dreams about our brilliant hockey futures.

Of course, there was more to Christmas than hockey. Our family Christmas customs were rooted largely in Swedish traditions that my grandparents brought with them to Minnesota in the 1890s. Our Swedish history goes back hundreds of years, and we share this heritage with many Minnesotans; the customs of the Swedes and their Scandinavian brethren are a part of the Christmas celebrations of most of us.

Christmas week was a time of intense activity in our home, most of it related to baking Christmas goodies and taking care of last-minute shopping. There was the annual trip to Olson's Swedish meat market for *lutefisk*, an ocean fish preserved in lye. It was chosen with care from large barrels in the store and brought home to be prepared for dinner on Christmas Eve. There was the trip to Jacobson's bakery for cinnamon toast, Swedish rye bread, and their special Christmas cake, *julekage*. And there was the trip to the YMCA lot for the selection of a Christmas tree—an annual ordeal for my dad. Mother was particular about the shape and the condition of the tree but she never went along to help pick it out. So it was necessary to worry all the way home, where she reluctantly gave her approval to our selection.

Then there was the church Christmas program. If you were unlucky, you had to stand up and recite a piece you had struggled to memorize. If you were a little more fortunate, you were chosen instead to be a shepherd—and silent—in the pageant. I still remember the first phrase of a Christmas piece that I was required to memorize and deliver over 30 years ago. I was the first person to speak, and I began: "Once again it is Christmas."

———◆•◆———

# "Where are the trees?"

## ROBERT TREUER

*Christmas memoirs are full of nostalgic scenes of trudging through snowy woods and cutting that special tree. But rare is the memoir by someone who has actually grown those trees. Austrian-born Robert Treuer, who began tree farming outside Bemidji in 1958, here recalls a tree-selling season when he enlisted the help of his son Derek. Things do not go well.*

Cutting trees that one has planted is a little like death: an irrevocable action. I've taken my own Christmas trees from the natural woods and from the wild, unwilling to cut one we'd planted ourselves. But necessity and prudent ecological management have brought harvest close. Cutting the trees is a form of death, but it is also a form of death to let the trees grow. Yesteryear's seedlings are now twenty-five to thirty feet high, a foot thick at the butt; and some are much too close to each other. Soon they will crowd each other to the point of mutual damage and exhaustion—two stags with horns locked in competition and unable to free themselves.

They grew so slowly the first few years—a few inches a year at the most. Then they set roots more deeply, grew faster, a foot a year, then two, and sometimes three. Now the time of harvest is coming like first-morning tints; first wisps of breeze after wind-still night are brushing my cheek.

I'd given Derek 300 trees for a Christmas present. "If you cut and haul them, you should be able to sell them in the Cities and make out quite nicely. Do you want them?"

"Oh, yes. That's great! Of course I have exams at the university and don't have much time. But I think we can manage. Yes!"

"Take them from the east plantation, from the far northeast corner. Every other tree; they're too thick there."

"Okay."

"I won't be around; I've got to be away. . . ."

"We'll manage. Thanks."

I wanted to caution Derek that the enterprise would work only if he did the cutting and hauling himself, that otherwise the profit margin would be very small. But the telephone connection was broken, and I solaced myself that we had talked about the economics of the tree business often enough that he would know this.

Work obligations kept me away, and it was after Christmas that Derek, looking haggard and unhappy, told me about it. His examination schedule had been more demanding than he had anticipated, and on his only trip to the farm he had enlisted the help of erstwhile high school friends who lived and worked nearby. They had agreed to do the cutting and hauling for a fee; meanwhile, Derek and his wife, Elissa, would secure a lot in Minneapolis. The trees would arrive about the time the exams ended, and he could be at the lot to sell them. But the plan went awry.

"Where are the trees?" Derek pleaded with his friend over the phone. First the truck wasn't working, then the saw broke down. The help didn't show and his friend had domestic problems.

Derek—tied by exams, his frustrations fed by the passing days and his inability to do anything about the delay—became more vociferous in his demands; his friend became more dilatory. Finally the old friendship ruptured, and friends of friends were found to do the work—and had to be paid.

"I couldn't believe it when the truck pulled up," Derek later told me. "The trees were so huge, so bushy, they couldn't possibly fit into anybody's living room."

I had been recalcitrant about "shaping" the trees over the years—a pruning process whereby new growth is cut off with a machete to remove extra-long branches and to give the Norway pines a more traditional Christmas tree shape. So although I knew these trees would have their natural, uneven shapes, I did not expect them to be too large and too bushy; neither did Derek.

He and Elissa did what cutting and trimming they could on their loaned neighborhood-center lot, obtained lights, made signs, and distributed handbills. They opened for business, but few people came. The neighborhood residents were too poor; there was not enough passerby traffic composed of more affluent buyers.

"People came at night and ripped us off," Derek said. "I took my sleeping bag to the lot and slept there. That stopped most of it."

Then they decided to flock the trees, to spray them in garish pink, blue, white, to each customer's order. A few more trees were sold. When it was over—after several sleepless nights, the end of a long and close friendship, and much distress—he had lost money.

"A nightmare," he said, and Elissa concurred. "Never again."

I did not have the heart to tell him that the trees had been cut from the sparser west plantation, not the overcrowded east planting. No wonder they were too large, too bushy: these west-plantation trees had been properly spaced and distanced already, and were on their way to becoming posts and poles. The crowded ones were more suitable in size, had a better shape, and now still needed thinning. I smart at the sight of the open gaps in the west, and feel anew dismay at the waste. Most of all I regret that my well-intentioned gift was ill-timed and that it misfired, bringing grief and a broken friendship for my son.

But it's not concern with the past that triggered nostalgia the other night, it is that I must face up to harvest preparations of my own. It's an adjustment that I have to make, and that everyone in the family will have to prepare for. The east planting has to be gone over; trees have to be selected for posts, others marked for poles. Many should be trimmed and sheared accordingly, because in a year or two the first ones must come out. They are growing too close in spots. Here and there on the west side we will have to do the same. Timing of the harvest is still indeterminate: one, two, three years from now. Maybe four. But the preparatory work and planning must start now.

I fret about how the older boys will feel about it, but I think I'm really coping with my own feelings. Tree farming has a particular effect on my sense of time—on how I perceive its passage. I measure it in days and hours like everyone else, and in the seasons of the year, as do farmers and gardeners and others aware of their external surroundings. But growing trees makes me perceive of time in decades and longer spans as well. I look forward and backward in terms of generations, and this gives me an added sense of personal place in the scheme of things. We each assert our thrust, our will to live, in different ways. This happens to be mine. Not my only way of course; being able to give and receive love is another. So is creativity and constructiveness in many forms.

Coming to grips with the harvest makes me philosophical.

*At the nightly Holidazzle parade on Minneapolis's Nicollet Mall, lighted floats, singers, storybook characters, and marchers bring merriment to cold December nights.*

• • •

# ⋄ 2 ⋄

# Celebrating the Holidays

———◆————

## "They want to hear a story"

### Faith Sullivan

*A Christmas celebration would hardly be complete without a school pageant. Here novelist Faith Sullivan places fourth-grader Sally Wheeler in front of an audience that includes her depressed mother, Stella, and an ample representation of her extended family. Wise beyond her years, Sally learns that a good story well told can be a wonderful gift at Christmas.*

"I won't cry I won't cry I won't cry," Sally chanted in her head as she stood, eyes closed, leaning against the cool, smooth plaster wall of the grimly lit hallway. It was Friday evening, December 22, 1939, night of the dreaded Christmas Program.

Beyond this thick wall and beyond the athletic equipment rooms that lay behind it, the auditorium/gymnasium was alive with the running-water sound of murmuring townspeople edging down rows of folding chairs. Rubbers and galoshes squidged on the highly varnished floor.

High up, on either side of the gymnasium, the balconies were filling, according to Miss Borgen the fourth-grade teacher who had sneaked out on the stage; peeped through the curtain; and returned to the long, linoleumed hallway where kindergarten through sixth grade huddled in shapeless little individual masses. Chewing fingernails and pigtail ends, scratching scabs, and picking noses, they waited. A couple of kindergarteners had begun to cry and wanted to go home.

The teachers, in their Sunday best, smiled and whispered encouragement or

*Children hold a long pose for a turn-of-the-century photographer at a
Lutheran Christmas program in Hawley. (Flaten/Wage)*

· · ·

frowned gimlet-eyed and shook their heads. Except for Miss Bailey (who was in every
circumstance the same imperturbable enthusiast), the elementary schoolteachers were
prancy on their best high heels, like skitterish horses at the starting post. They wore
cologne and a bit of makeup, brooches, and, one or two, a bracelet.

The children thrilled to see their teachers dolled up and feverish, to glimpse the woman
that teacher might be when she wasn't teacher, when she took the train to the Black Hills
on vacation or had her female chums over to her little apartment above Lundeen's Dry
Goods for an evening of bridge.

It was incredible, heady, and slightly disturbing to pupils to think that teacher had a life she enjoyed beyond the classroom. Oughtn't *they* to be enough?

Sally, wearing her rose velveteen dress, long white stockings, and Mary Janes, did not chew the ends of her braids, which Grandma Elway had tied with thick, luxurious rose satin ribbons brought from Mankato. Rather, she stood cold and still as a funerary angel, wishing that she could fly away to heaven.

The kindergarten was led away, through the door at the end of the hall and up the short flight of steps leading to the stage. Sally's eyes sprang open. Only the first grade remained to perform before she would be led down the same path to the brilliantly lighted stage where humiliation waited.

Her lips stuck to her teeth. Her fingers, holding the script, were icy and paralyzed, and she doubted she'd be able to open them when the time came to lay the pages on the music stand.

Her mother was in the audience. Grandma Elway, who'd arrived by train from Mankato that day, had insisted. "Our Sally is a narrator!" she'd exclaimed.

Donald had dropped Sally at school soon after dinner, so she had not heard all the cajoling, scolding, inveigling, and begging that had resulted in Stella's presence at the program, clean, made-up, and wearing a burgundy wool dress with a soft flounce collar.

Stella could prevail with Donald but not with her mother who, although she loved Stella with a daunting passion, did not believe that giving in to Stella's megrims was the way to see her through the Change.

Edna did believe that if one forced oneself to get out of bed in the morning, as she occasionally had to force herself; if one bathed and dressed in clean clothing from the inside out; then ate a proper breakfast and picked up the house before sitting down with a second cup of coffee to draw up a grocery list, well, one soon cleared the vapors from one's head. Work, organization, proper nutrition, and cleanliness. Marching down that path, you'd soon be right again.

Edna Elway occupied a center aisle seat about midway back in the rows of folding chairs. To her left sat Stella, fastening and unfastening the clasp of her handbag, and beyond Stella, in the third seat, Donald.

Edna held her head up and studied the motley assemblage with satisfaction. Her tiny tribe compared well, and soon Sally, her Christmas angel, would appear, a child sweeter and lovelier than any other in this school. A true beauty.

Sally, like Stella, had inherited the tall, pale-skinned, dark-haired beauty of Herb's side of the family, Edna was quick to admit. Her own people were attractive, but they were squat. Well, what did one expect? Until emigrating, they'd been Alsatian miners for as far back as anyone knew.

But they'd been the sort who took hold, took advantage, and made something of themselves. Backbone and wits. That was what she'd come from. Was there something wrong with that? Ambition it was called. God knew, its importance had been borne in upon her. Hard work, respectability, ambition.

Edna had always had a tender and unquestioning regard for her parents. They had been strict but generous. She had tried never to disappoint them, and their assurances that this filial regard and obedience would bring her happiness had not been wrong.

She had married the "catch" of her girlhood, Herbert Elway, whom she adored. And she had raised a pretty, sweet-natured daughter. A good and loving daughter.

Edna poked daintily at her coiffure. A hairpin was stabbing someplace just there where she seemed unable to reach it. She closed her eyelids until the tears behind them were dispelled.

Across the aisle and near the last row of chairs, Harry and Irmgard Wheeler settled themselves, Harry with his hat on his knee. The Wheelers had almost been late. Something had come up at the last moment down at the registrar of deeds office, and it was nearly six by the time Harry had got home from work. A quick bowl of tomato soup, the twenty-five mile drive, and here they were, slightly out of breath, but none the worse for wear.

Irmgard Wheeler observed Edna Elway poking at her beauty parlor hairdo, but immediately reminded herself that her hair, too, had been styled by a beauty operator, Vera Swenson, at Clarice's Beauty Parlor in Worthington.

Poor Bub, Irmgard thought, craning a bit to catch sight of her son. He looks almost as old as his dad. Stella's Change was going to put him into an early grave. Out on the road all week, then back to look after things at home on the weekends. It was too much.

Irmgard eased her right foot out of the plain, squared-off black pump. Her bunion was tender. More snow, no doubt about it.

Was Sally someplace back there behind the blue curtain, waiting to perform her turn? Tied up in knots, she probably was, poor little thing. If only there'd been time beforehand to tell her that everything would be just fine.

Behind the blue velvet curtain, back in the grim hallway leading to the stage, Sally breathed shallow flutters of air, little bird breaths, her knees rigid as clothesline posts.

Miss Bailey placed a firm hand on each shoulder and delved into Sally's eyes, way back where she knew the fear monster sat. "Take a deep breath."

Sally tried. Her expelled breath came out in a shudder.

"Again. Fill your lungs all the way down."

Sally sucked in air with a ragged gasp.

"Now, out. Get rid of it all."

Thus they stood for two or three minutes, Miss Bailey coaching Sally's breathing.

"Now, I want to tell you something about your job as narrator," Miss Bailey said. "Three hundred or more people are in the auditorium."

Sally's eyes widened, her lips compressed in a thin grimace.

"They want to hear a story. People love stories. Don't *you?* Didn't you say that your daddy was reading you *The Wind in the Willows?*"

Sally nodded, unsure where this was heading.

"And you really get caught up, don't you, when you hear about those nasty stoats moving into Toad Hall?"

Again Sally nodded. Miss Bailey straightened, glaring at Ronald Oster, who kept untying Sue Ann Meyer's sash. Ronald thrust his hands into his pockets and stared at his shoes.

"Well," Miss Bailey resumed, "when people come to a play, that's what they want . . . somebody to tell them a story, help them understand what's going on, and make it exciting." Her large hands on Sally's shoulders gave them an affectionate squeeze. "Our play isn't about how scared Sally Wheeler is or how bad a reader she thinks she is."

She smiled and Sally smiled back. "Tell yourself 'I'm giving everybody a Christmas present tonight. For fifteen minutes, I'm going to make them forget that the car wouldn't start this morning, and the dog died last Saturday, and all we had to eat this week was beans and bread.'" She held Sally's chin in one of her big hands and said, "I chose you for narrator because I knew that you could do that."

*Young actors in an annual municipal pageant in St. Paul, 1956 (Ted Strasser)*

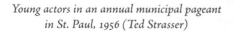

They heard the first grade concluding "Up on the Housetop." "All right, class," Miss Bailey said softly, "it's time."

Just before the blue curtain parted, she reminded Sally, "Don't rush. You are the hostess."

And when the audience was revealed to her, programs rattling as they looked down to mind who this little girl in the rose velveteen dress might be, unhurriedly she carried the music stand to the apron of the stage, placed it beside the microphone, then calmly lay the text before her.

Smiling, she said, "Hello." This "hello" was not part of the script. Sally wasn't even aware that she'd said it, but Miss Bailey's words had filled her with a tender generosity and sense of responsibility toward the audience.

And when she greeted them, they responded, smiling back, some mouthing the word *hello*. She saw that they had indeed come to hear a story, and she began slowly and clearly to tell them one, coloring the words, when appropriate, with disdain, sadness, or delight so that the dead battery and the dead dog and the memory of beans all week would slip away, under the folding chairs, for fifteen minutes.

---

# "Like the haunting croon of Goodman's clarinet"

## ROGER MACDONALD

*Roger MacDonald describes being guest of honor at an Ojibwe children's Christmas pageant in Cass Lake in northern Minnesota. Santa struggles to keep his beard attached, and to find enough presents to go around.*

Children's Christmas pageants always seemed to me barely a notch above a session at your friendly dentist's office. One year Barbara and I were invited to stay after clinic and attend one put on by the Chippewa Lake Elementary School. We sat in honored seats near the front of the basement cafeteria in the schoolhouse, the only space large enough for such an extravaganza. The place was already steamy hot. I sighed, pondering my impending martyrdom.

A pair of bed sheets had been stitched together to serve as a curtain, hiding the kitchen and area designated "stage." It fluttered suddenly: show time, magic time. Someone hidden from sight pulled on the rope that was supposed to draw it aside. It merely wiggled. A voice that sounded remarkably like that of Foxy Bronson when coping with a behavior problem in class commented on its putative heritage. The curtain fell in a heap; Foxy made his escape into the kitchen, under cover.

An angel choir led off: first- and second-graders. I wasn't sure what song was intended, but it sounded Christmassy. Precarious halos and gauzy wings created authenticity.

Adeline Dubois and Cissy Portier marched front and center to recite *The Night Before Christmas*. Eight-year-old Adeline started things off. She was a waif: fatherless, her mother shackled to beer; pinched of face; her limbs skin, bone, and wisps of muscle. No childhood plumpness. Her dress, with its uneven hem, was twice handed down. She lisped through the gap in her front teeth, shared wistful yearnings for stockings filled with wonders. Cissy took over the recitation at the point when reindeer landed on the roof. Her enthusiasm and eloquence were so persuasive that more than one of us glanced up at the ceiling.

The manger scene came next. Mary was played by sixth-grader Margo Little Frog. Joseph strode down the aisle, his worn tennis shoes squeaking like a troop of mice, and resolutely arraigned himself next to the shepherds. "Get over here" Mary snapped, the gleam in her Madonna eyes boding ill for Joe, on- or off-stage.

One of the wise men knocked over a pasteboard cow. (Paper towels shined defiantly through its black-and-white hide.) The youngster wrestled it upright, then fled down the aisle to his mother.

Irene Basswood sang "Silent Night," once in English, again in Ojibwe. The girl's voice was like the haunting croon of Goodman's clarinet when he was at his most introspective.

Lex Bullhead ended the production by reciting the Lord's Prayer in Ojibwe.

It happened that kindly ladies from three of the churches in Northpine had adopted the children at Chippewa Lake, to the extent of buying and wrapping gifts for the party. Barbara and I had brought them with us: Claus Enterprises, Transportation Division. As our personal contribution, she and I had brought two large containers of ice cream.

It was time for Santa!

Tossing off "Ho-ho-hos!" along with pieces of hard candy, St. Nick staggered down the aisle under the weight of a sack—very similar to a pillowcase—bulging with packages. To my skeptical ear, Santa sounded for all the world like James Squint-eye. (The man's title was school custodian. In truth, he was an innovative magician whose genius kept the place functioning. Every institution needs someone like him.) White chin whiskers kept slipping up over his mouth. Since Indians have the good fortune not to bear genes for facial hair, he had no practical experience in coping with shrubbery.

To the children, there was no doubt as to Santa's authenticity. Arriving at the front of the room, he delved into his bag of mystery. Beaming and strutting or shy and hesitant before such a marvel, children filed past James. Santa. The pillowcase—sack—shrank upon itself until. . . .

Three children waited while Santa dived headfirst into the bag. When he popped back out his eyes were as round as those of the children, they wondering aloud what they were about to receive.

Barbara beckoned to Jim. She took three precious packages from her purse, red and green and silver. Thankful for her foresight, Santa crossed himself and accepted them.

The ledger balanced.

*A small sampling of the Christmas music recorded in the Twin Cities in the 1970s and 1980s, including the Dale Warland Singers, St. Ambrose Catholic Church choir, 3M Music Makers, Federal Reserve Club Choir, and Minnesota Mutual Life Insurance handbell chorus (Eric Mortenson)*

• • •

# "This is my favorite part"

## LORNA LANDVIK

*What if instead of Bethlehem, Jesus had been born in Minneapolis? This is just one of many thoughts that a pregnant Patty Jane and her mother-in-law, Ione, ponder as they celebrate the Christmas miracle together while Patty Jane's husband, Thor, sleeps off dinner on the couch. The characters belong to Lorna Landvik's first novel,* Patty Jane's House of Curl.

On Christmas Eve, the first time she could see for certain that Patty Jane was indeed carrying, they gathered at Ione's small house near Lake Hiawatha. Flickering light from candles in their wall holders reflected onto the floors Ione had waxed twice. Straw angels and crocheted snowflakes hung from the Christmas tree and the smell of evergreen competed with the aromas of cider mulling in a blue speckled pot on the burner and the turkey roasting inside the oven.

To Patty Jane, it seemed a Christmas she had only read about. . . .

After dinner, as the two women did dishes, Ione reached out her sudsy hands and patted Patty Jane's stomach.

"Uff-da mayda, I'm sorry," she said quickly, plunging her hands back into the dishwater.

"Please," said Patty Jane and she stood facing her mother-in-law, arching her back and thrusting her new belly outwards.

Ione dried her hands on the embroidered dishtowel and laid her hands on Patty Jane's stomach and held them there, as if she were warming them over a fire.

"I can't think of anything more wonderful to touch," she said, her eyes shut.

Patty Jane held Ione's hands under hers, feeling Ione's hard sharp knuckles against her palms.

"Thor doesn't like touching my stomach," whispered Patty Jane. "I guess he thinks he'll hurt the baby."

In the silence that followed, Patty Jane wondered if Ione believed her. She herself desperately wanted to find some excuse for Thor's coldness. Ione gave a final pat to Patty Jane's roundness and then began attacking the turkey roaster with a shiny pad of steel wool.

Dishes done, the two women discovered Thor asleep on the davenport in front of the fire, his stockinged feet crossed and one big toe, pink and hale, poking out of a hole.

"Seems I never get to my darning basket," said Patty Jane. She didn't admit that she didn't have one to get to.

Ione was about to offer Patty Jane a glass of gooseberry wine, but reading the time on the small filigreed clock on the mantel, she said impulsively, "Patty Jane, Christmas Eve services are so lovely at my church—will you go with me?"

Patty Jane pulled the afghan up under Thor's chin. Normally nothing could tear her away from the privilege of watching her husband sleep. She could study each of his fine features, could watch the firelight play against his butter-colored hair. But these weren't normal times.

"I'd love to," said Patty Jane.

"You see, I usually go to the midnight service—there's such a sense of adventure getting out and about at that hour—but the eight o'clock has good singing—mostly the Chancel Choir—and if Thor's asleep . . ."

"Sure," said Patty Jane when Ione paused for breath.

A small shiver of pleasure zipped up Ione's spine. She was too shy to meddle, but the nonchurchgoing habits of Thor and Patty Jane nagged at her. She knew they weren't destined to hell because they didn't have a regular pew in the church, but still, she was certain God enjoyed the attention and shone His grace upon those who regularly added to the collection plate and knew the Nicene Creed by heart.

They drove the half-mile to Kind Savior's Lutheran Church in Ione's well-tended green Plymouth. Ione was an overly careful driver, leaning into the steering wheel as if she were trying to chin it; so close that occasionally her chest bumped the horn, startling her every time.

The church vestibule smelled of hot radiators and wet wool, and puddles of slush formed an irregular path to the double doors leading into the sanctuary. An usher greeted Ione and seated them. Ahead of them bobbed rows of haberdashery: special-occasion hats with velvet flowers and iridescent feathers, Russian hats of curly wool, long stocking caps, striped and tasseled.

"My Naomi Circle made the banner," whispered Ione. It read, "He is Born" in red and green letters and was draped behind the altar.

A long chord signaled the beginning of the service and the entire congregation rose to sing "Joy to the World." Ione and Patty Jane stood close, sharing a hymnal, and Ione remembered how as a young woman she had loved sharing the book with her husband, his thumb solid and square-nailed on the left page, her small painted one on the right. . . .

She cocked her head slightly to better hear Patty Jane's voice. It didn't soar like her

## Company Christmas party, 1919-style

*The Washburn-Crosby Company's employee newsletter described a Christmas party that brought employees and owners together in an unusual display of solidarity.*

The biggest Christmas party ever given in Minneapolis—that was the consensus of opinion concerning Washburn-Crosby Company's mill employees party which was given in the Armory Saturday afternoon and evening.

Approximately 4,500 officials of the company, mill employees, their families, and friends enjoyed the entertainment which lasted from one o'clock in the afternoon until the last of the hundreds of dancing couples left the floor at midnight.

Not one hitch marred the festivities, and everyone voted it the biggest social event of their lives and the best thing ever attempted by Washburn-Crosby Company.

It was a genuine family party and, as Mr. John Crosby stated in his address of welcome, the family is bigger than anyone had even imagined. Many of this family, strangers when they came to the party, went home fast friends. Directors hobnobbed with office boys; head millers told of the days when they were learning the great game of milling: position, salaries and greed was forgotten as all mingled, laughed and joked in the regular old time love feast.

The big Armory was brilliantly decorated with evergreen, flags, tinsel, and Christmas colors until it seemed to fairly radiate Christmas cheer. When the kiddies, big, little and intermediate, arrived in the afternoon, things started with a bang. First came the vaudeville with the Washburn-Crosby Company band and orchestra. Early in the evening the adults began to flock toward the Armory in a solid stream. . . . The Minneapolis Quartet, led by George Hodgkins, offered various songs and the yodels always so popular. After a group sing, Mr. John Crosby welcomed the guests.

*The Eventually Yours,* December 31, 1919

---

sister Harriet's, but it was serviceable and Ione summoned her thin alto to join her: "Let earth receive her king. . . ."

Pastor Nelson's sermon was lively with humor and Ione was happy to see Patty Jane chuckling with the rest of the congregation. The deep-voiced minister imagined the holy birth happening in the city of Minneapolis—would the Dyckman or the Francis Drake Hotels turn Mary and Joseph away?

"Would you," he asked, and everyone felt certain he was speaking directly to them, "would you give up your sofa in the den to a poor couple, to a woman about to deliver? Or would you make feeble excuses about a lack of space? Would you eat your

Christmas ham and linger over coffee and cookies, making jokes about the brazen, unkempt couple who wanted to spread fleas in your guest room?"

Patty Jane hugged her belly, imagining Mary's terror at laboring on a donkey, not knowing if she was going to give birth under a roof or a cold winter's moon. Considering the unusual circumstances of conception, surely Mary must have known everything was going to be fine? She probably wasn't even bothered by the contractions ("pains like a hatchet working its way out of your insides" was how her mother Anna put it); if God had chosen her to bear Jesus, she was probably the serene type who smiled while others screamed.

Pastor Nelson eased his grip on the pulpit and smiled.

"Friends," he said, and there was a collective relaxation of shoulders as everyone heard the shift in tone; they were off the hook and could stop feeling guilty. "Friends," the minister continued, "let us see in the faces of our loved ones, in the faces of strangers, the face of Jesus, for he truly does live in us all. Amen."

Patty Jane was startled when the congregation murmured "Amen." It was too abrupt an end to a sermon she wanted to go on and on; she wanted to think of Jesus in Thor's face (an easy task), to hear the resonant assurance in Pastor Nelson's voice.

Near the end of the service, after the gospel reading and the collection, the lights were dimmed and ushers standing at the end of the pews began to pass out small candles. Parishioners lit their candles from their neighbors' until all the rows were lit.

"This is my favorite part," said Ione, her head bent to her daughter-in-law's, watching the flame from Patty Jane's candle ignite the wick of hers.

---

# Celebrating Christmas in Lake Wobegon

## GARRISON KEILLOR

*The Sidetrack Tap, the Statue of the Unknown Norwegian, tubs of lutefisk at Ralph's, a familiar sermon in a Lutheran church: where else could this be but Lake Wobegon? Garrison Keillor takes us on a familiar Yuletide tour of the town "out there on the edge of the prairie."*

Now an older guy, I've gotten more moist and when the decorations go up over Main Street from Ralph's north to the mercantile, I walk down alone to look at them, they are so beautiful—even old guys stand in wonder and are transported back to childhood, though of course these are the same decorations as when we were kids so it doesn't take much imagination. The six-foot plywood star with one hundred Christmas bulbs, twenty on each point, was built by Mr. Scheffelmacher's shop class in 1956; I flunked the quiz on electricity and didn't get to work on it. I sanded the edges a little, though I had flunked wood too. Later, I flunked the ballpeen hammer and was kicked out of shop and into speech class—Mr. Scheffelmacher said, "All you do is talk, talk, talk, so you might as well learn how." I begged him to let me stay in shop, which was getting into sheet metal and about to make flour scoops, but he said, "You couldn't even pass wood. You couldn't even make a decent birdhouse!" and he was right. My birdhouse leaked, and the birds were so mad about it, when I tried to caulk the roof, they attacked me, Mr. and Mrs. Bluebird. So I dragged myself into speech and had to make up the work I had missed: five speeches in one week: humorous, persuasive, extemporaneous, impromptu, and reflective, and suddenly, talking, which had been easy for me at the shop bench, became impossible. I dragged my feet to the front of the room, afraid my loafers would flap (they had been my brother's), and stood there, a ridiculous person six-feet-three and a hundred fifty pounds, trying to keep my jaw slack as I had practiced in a mirror to make up for a small chin, and mumbled and got hot across the eyes and had to say, "Anyway, as I started to say. . . ." which Miss Perkovich marked you down for three points for because "Anyway" showed disorganization, so I failed speech, too, but speech was the end of the line—if you couldn't speak, where could you go? To reading? I sat in speech and drew stick men hanging on the gallows, listening to Chip Ingqvist's reflective, entitled "A Christmas Memory," which was about his dear old aunt whom he visited every Christmas, bringing sugar cookies, and was so good he did it twice in class and again for school assembly two weeks after Christmas and then in the district speech tournament, the regional, and the state, and finished first runner-up in the reflective division, and yet it always sounded so sincere as if he had just thought of it—for example, when he said, "And oh! the light in her eyes was worth far more to me than anything money could buy," a tear came to his voice, his eyes lit up like vacuum tubes, and his right hand made a nice clutching gesture over his heart on his terrific brown V-neck sweater, which I mention because I felt that good clothes gave him self-confidence, just as the clothing ads said, and that I might be sincere like him if instead of an annual Christmas sweater I got a regular supply. Anyway, Christmas decorations sure bring back a lot of memories for me.

Depending on your angle, the stars seem to lead the traveler toward the Sidetrack Tap, where the old guys sit and lose some memory capacity with a glass of peppermint schnapps, which Wally knows how to keep adding to so they can tell the old lady they only had one. After one of those continuous drinks, they try not to look at the bubble lights on the little aluminum tree on the back bar. Bud is there, who gets a twinge in his thighs around Christmas, remembering the year the ladder went out from under him as he was hanging decorations, and he slid down the telephone pole, which was somewhat smoother after he slid down than before. In addition to the large star, you see smaller ones that look like starfish, and stubby candles, and three wise men who in their wonder and adoration appear a little stupid, all made by shop classes on a jigsaw, and angels that, if you look at them a certain way, look like clouds. The manager stands in front of Our Lady church, the figures (imported from Chicago) so lifelike, it gives you the chills to see them outdoors—it's so cold, they should take their flight to Egypt! The municipal Christmas tree stands in front of the Statue of the Unknown Norwegian who seems to be reaching out to straighten it. It leans slightly toward the south, away from the wind.

One bitter cold night, a certain person stepped out of the Sidetrack Tap and crossed the street under the clear starry sky toward the gay lights of the municipal tree and noticed that he needed to take a leak. It was three blocks to home, and the cold had suddenly shrunk his bladder, so he danced over toward the Unknown and picked out a spot in the snow in the dark behind the tree where nobody would see him.

It was an enormous relief at first, of course, like coming up for air after a long submersion, but it also made him leery to be so exposed right out on Main Street. So many dark windows where someone could be watching, and what if a car came along? They'd know what was up. Him, profaning a monument to the Norwegian people. "I should stop—right now!" he thought. His capacity, though: it was amazing! Like a horse. Gallons, already, and it didn't feel like he could put the cork back in. Then he saw the headlights. Only for a moment, then the car turned the other way, but in that moment he hopped six feet to one side and stood in shock until the taillights disappeared, and only then did he hear the hiss of liquid on the hot bulb and look and see what he was doing. He was peeing on the tree! Pissing on Christmas! Then the bulb burst. Pop!

"Oh God, what a pig I am!" he thought. He expected the big spruce to fall on him and crush him. Pinned under the tree, found the next morning, frozen to death with his thing in his hand. The shame to his family. The degradation of it. Finally he was done (*you pig!*). There was a stain in the snow as big as a bathtub, and another one where he had stood before. He dumped handfuls of clean snow on them, but it turned yellow. Then he walked home, got a snow shovel, came back, and carried his mess, shovel by shovel, across the street to the side of the Sidetrack Tap, and brought back shovels of clean snow to fill in. He smoothed it over and went home to bed.

It was not such a happy holiday for him for the recollection of what he had done (*pig*), which if any of his children had done it he would have given them holy hell. He bought them wonderful presents that year and a gold watch for his wife, and burned when they said what a great guy he was, and it wasn't until January after the tree came down that he started to feel like he could drop in at the Sidetrack and relax with a couple of beers.

We get a little snow, then a few inches, then another inch or two, and sometimes we get a ton. The official snow gauge is a Sherwin-Williams paint can stuck to the table behind the town garage, with the famous Sherwin-Williams globe and red paint spilling over the Arctic icecap. When snow is up to the top of the world, then there is a ton of snow. Bud doesn't keep track of the amount beyond that point because once there is that much snow, more doesn't matter a lot. After the ton falls, we build a sled run on Adams Hill, behind the school, with high snow embankments on the turns to keep our sleds on the track at the thrilling high speeds we reach once the track is sprayed with water and freezes. Everyone goes at least once, even Muriel. Up at the Pee Tree, you flop on your belly on the sled and push off, down an almost straight drop of twenty feet and *fast* into a right-hand turn, then hard left, then you see the tree. It is in the middle of the track and will bash your brains out unless you do something. Before you can, you're in the third turn, centrifugal force having carried you safely around the tree, and then you come to the jump where some cookies are lost, and the long swooping curve under the swings, and you coast to a stop. You stand up and look down and see that you've almost worn the toes of your boots. You had the brakes on and you didn't notice.

At the swimming beach, the volunteer firemen have flooded the ice to make a glass sheet and hung colored lights in a V from the warming house to the pole on the diving dock. The warming house is open, the ancient former chickenhouse towed across the ice in 1937 from Jensens' when he gave up poultry after some exploded from a rich diet that made their eggs too big. When Bud fires up the cast-iron Providence wood stove, a faint recollection of chickens emanates from the floor. The stove stands in the middle, the floor chopped up around it where decades of skaters stepped up and down to get feeling back in their feet, and the benches run around the walls, which are inscribed with old thoughts of romance, some of them shocking to a child: news that Mother or Dad, instead of getting down to business and having you, was skylarking around, planting big wet smackers (*XXXXX*) on a stranger who if he or she had hooked up with her or him you would not be yourself but some other kid. This dismal prospect from the past makes a child stop and think, but then—what can you do?—you lace up and teeter down the plywood ramp and take your first glide of the season. It's a clear night, the sky is full of stars and the brilliant V points you out toward the dark, the very place your parents went, eventually, holding hands, arms crossed, skating to the

Latin rhythms of Cully Culbertson and His Happy Wurlitzer from the *Rexall Fun Time* album played through a mighty Zenith console put out on the ice, where some of the oldsters still cut a nice figure. Clarence and Arlene Bunsen, for two: to see him on the street, you'd know he has a sore back, but on the ice, some of his old form returns and when they take a turn around the rink in tandem, you might see why she was attracted to him, the old smoothie. Once two people have mastered skating the samba together, it isn't that much harder to just get married, says Clarence. She has bought a new pair of glasses, bifocals, that, when she looks at him, bring his ankles into sharp focus, slightly magnified.

In some homes, decorations don't appear until Christmas Eve afternoon, except for the Advent wreath on the supper table, its candles lit every night during supper. Catholics believe in abstaining before a feast—it sharpens the appetite—so Father Emil gives up his 9 P.M. finger of brandy for weeks so that his Christmas Eve brandy will taste more wonderful, even when Clarence brought him a bottle of Napoleon brandy far more wonderful than the Dominican DeLuxe Father buys for himself. "None for me," he said. "Oh, come on," Clarence said, "you only live once." Clarence is Lutheran but he sometimes drops in at the rectory for a second opinion. It is Father's opinion, however, that a person does not only live once, so he put the Napoleon on his bookshelf behind *War and Peace* where he would remember it. Even on Christmas Eve, one finger is the correct portion, by him, and it's a miserable mistake to think that two would be twice as good, and three even better, or putting both hands around the bottle and climbing into it. That's no Christmas. The true Christmas bathes every little thing in light and makes one cookie a token, one candle, one simple pageant more wonderful than anything seen on stage or screen.

The Kruegers ask him over to watch the Perry Como Christmas special and out of respect for their tremendous contributions over the years, he goes, and sits in glum silence watching tanned, relaxed people sing "O Little Town of Bethlehem" on a small-town street like none he's ever seen. A man appears on the screen to talk about Triumph television sets as the perfect Christmas gift, as behind him a viewing couple turn and beam at each other as if TV had saved their marriage. The Kruegers enjoy martinis, a vicious drink that makes them sad and exhausted, and the Mister gets up during commercials to adjust the picture, making it more lurid—greenish faces like corpses of the drowned, then orange, the victims of fire—and then the Krueger boy says, "Oh, *Dad*," and fixes it to normal, but even that looks lurid, like a cheap postcard. They sit, enraptured by it, but what dull rapture: not fifteen words spoken between them in the whole hour until, in the middle of "Chestnuts," the phone rings—it's Milly's sister in Dallas—and though it's only a commercial, Milly doesn't take her eyes off the screen, doesn't make a complete sentence, just says "uh-huh" and "oh" and "all right, I guess" as if the lady demonstrating the dish soap is her sister and her sister is a telephone salesman. A dismal scene compared to church, people leaning forward to catch the words coming from their children's mouths, their own flesh and blood, once babes in arms, now speaking the Gospel. What would the Kruegers do if during Perry's solo the doorbell rang and they heard children singing a carol on the porch?—would they curse them?

The German club from high school goes caroling, most of them Catholic kids but it's Luther they sing: *Vom Himmel hoch da komm ich her, Ich bring euch gute neue mar.* Luther League goes out, Catholic youth, Lutheran choir, Miss Falconer's high school choir, the Thanatopsians troop around and warble in their courageous ruined voices, Spanish Club, G.A.A., 4-H, even Boy Scouts sidle up to a few doors and whisper a carol or two. *O Christmas tree, O Christmas tree / How brightly shine thy candles.* The Scouts carry candles, which drip onto their jackets. Jimmy Buehler, Second Class, whose mother confiscated his phonograph because AC/DC's song "Highway to Hell" made her nervous, is their best singer; his sweet tenor leads the others. *And from each bough, a tiny light / Adds to the splendor of the sight.*

The carols that Miss Falconer's choir sings along Elm Street are a relief from the *Hodie* they practiced so hard for the Christmas assembly. Day after day, they sat and looked at the floor, which reeked of disinfectant, and breathed quietly through their mouths as she stood over them, still as a statue, and said, "Well, maybe we should cancel the whole concert. I'm not getting one bit of cooperation from you." She sighs at the shame of it and folds her arms. In a school this small, you don't get to specialize: one day Coach Magendanz is trying to bring out the animal in you, and then you are Ernest in *The Importance of Being*, and then you are defending the negative in the question of capital punishment, and the next day you're attempting sixteenth-century polyphony. "Tenors, open your mouth, you can't sing with your mouths shut. Basses, read the notes. They're right in front of you."

So great is the town's demand for Christmas music, some of them are going straight from this practice to Mrs. Hoglund's at the Lutheran church or to Our Lady choir practice and a different *Hodie* under Sister Edicta, a rehearsal in parkas in the cold choir loft, Father Emil having blanched at the latest fuel bill and turned the thermostat down to fifty-five. A cold Advent for Catholics, thanks to Emile Bebeau, the itinerant architect who designed this pile in 1878, no doubt intending the soaring vaulted ceiling to draw the hearts of the faithful upward; it also draws heat upward, and the parish is in hock to a Lutheran fuel-oil supplier. Father is dreaming of a letter from Publishers' Sweepstakes: "Dear Mr. Emil: It's our great pleasure to inform you—" or an emergency check from Bishop Kluecker, though Our Lady is not a diocesan parish but a mission of the Benedictines and Father reports to an abbot in Pennsylvania who observes the rule of silence, at least in financial matters.

The Sons of Knute don't carol in person, God having given them voices less suitable for carols than for wallies and elmers, but they do sponsor a choir of fourth-graders who learn two Norwegian carols well enough to sing them in dim light and make the rounds in the snow after supper, alternating carols house to house. One is usually enough to make any Knute wipe his eyes and blow his nose—*Jeg er så glad hver julekveld, Da synger vi hans pris; Da åpner han for alle små, Sitt søte paradis.* ("I am so glad on Christmas Eve, His praises then I sing; He opens then for every child The palace of the King")—and two might finish him off for good. Even Hjalmar, who sat like a fencepost through little Tommy's rare blood disease on "The Parkers" while Virginia put her head down and bawled, even Hjalmar hears *Jeg er så glad hver julekveld*; his pale eyes glisten, and he turns away, hearing his mother's voice and smelling her *julekake,* the Christmas pudding, Mother sitting in a chair and working on her *broderi,* a pillowcase with two *engler* hovering over the *krybbe* where Jesus lies, the bright *stjerne* in the sky. "*Glade Jul!*" the fourth-graders cry, and back come Hjalmar's own boyhood chums in fragrant memory to greet him. "Hjally! Hjally!" they call, standing in the frame of bright windowlight on the brilliant snow of 1934.

Custom dictates that carolers be asked in and offered a cookie, a piece of cake, something to nibble, and so must every person who comes to your door, otherwise the spirit of Christmas will leave your house, and even if you be rich as Midas, your holiday will be sad and mean. That is half of the custom; the other half is that you must yourself go visiting. Everyone must get at least one unexpected visitor, otherwise they'll have no chance to invite one in and Christmas will be poorer for them. So, even if when they open the door, their thin smile tells you that you have arrived at the height of an argument, and even if, as you sit and visit, sulfurous looks are exchanged and innuendos drop like size-12 shoes, you are still performing a service, allowing them to try to be pleasant, even if they don't do it well.

Baking begins in earnest weeks ahead. Waves of cookies, enough to feed an army, enough to render an army defenseless, including powerful rumballs and fruitcakes soaked with spirits (if the alcohol burns off in the baking, as they say, then why does Arlene hide them from her mother?). And tubs of *lutefisk* appear at Ralph's meat counter, the dried cod soaked in lye solution for weeks to make a pale gelatinous substance beloved by all Norwegians, who nonetheless eat it only once a year. The soaking is done in a shed behind the store, and Ralph has a separate set of *lutefisk* clothes he keeps in the trunk of his Ford Galaxie. No dogs chase his car, and if he forgets to change his *lutefisk* socks, his wife barks at him. Ralph feels that the dish is a great delicacy and he doesn't find *lutefisk* jokes funny. "Don't knock it if you haven't tried it," he says. Nevertheless, he doesn't offer it to carolers who come by his house because he knows it could kill them. You have to be ready for *lutefisk*.

Father Emil doesn't knock *lutefisk*; he thinks it may be the Lutherans' penance, a form of self-denial. His homily the Sunday before: we believe that we really don't know what's best for us, so we give up some things we like in the faith that something better might come, a good we were not aware of, a part of ourselves we didn't know was there. We really don't know ourselves, our own life is hidden from us. God knows us. We obey His teaching, even though painful, entrusting our life to Him who knows best.

The faithful squirm when he says it. What comes next? they wonder. No Christmas this year? Just soup and crackers? Catholic children see Lutheran children eating candy that the nuns tell them they should give up until Christmas and think, "Ha! Easy for nuns to talk about giving up things. That's what nuns do for a living. But I'm twelve— things are just starting to go right for me!"

Lutherans also get a sermon about sacrifice, which the late Pastor Tommerdahl did so well every year, entitling it "The True Meaning of Christmas," and if you went to church with visions of sugarplums dancing in your head, he stopped the music. Santa Claus was not prominent in his theology. He had a gift of making you feel you'd better go home and give all the presents to the poor and spend Christmas with a bowl of soup, and not too many noodles in it either. He preached the straight gospel, and as he said, the gospel is meant to comfort the afflicted and afflict the comfortable. He certainly afflicted the Lutherans.

I only heard his sermon one year, and I liked it, being afflicted by Christmas, knowing how much I was about to receive and how little I had to give. I was ten, my assets came to eight bucks, I had twelve people on my list and had already spent three dollars on one of them: my father, who would receive a Swank toiletries kit with Swank shaving lotion, Swank deodorant, Swank cologne, Swank bath soap on a rope, and Swank hair tonic, an inspired gift. I walked into Detwiler's Drugstore and there it was, the exotic Swank aroma that would complete his life and bring out the Charles Boyer in him, so I said, "Wrap it up," and was happy to be bringing romance into his life until the cash register rang and I realized I had five bucks left and eleven people to go, which came to forty-five cents apiece. Even back then forty-five cents was small change.

I imagined a man walking up and giving me fifty dollars. He was fat and old and had a kind face. "Here," he said, and made me promise I wouldn't tell anyone. I promised. He gave me two crisp new twenty-five-dollar bills, a rarity in themselves and probably worth thousands. A Brink's truck raced through town, hit a bump, and a bag fell out at my feet. I called the Brink's office, and they said, "Nope. No money missing here. Guess it's your lucky day, son." Crystal Sugar called and said that the "Name the Lake Home" contest winner was me, and would I like the lake home (named Mallowmarsh) or the cash equivalent, fifteen grand?

But there's nothing like a sermon against materialism to make a person feel better about having less. God watches over us and loves us no less for knowing what we can't afford. I took the five dollars and bought small bottles of Swank lotion for the others, which smelled as wonderful as his. If you splashed a few drops on your face, you left a trail through the house, and when you came to a room, they knew you were coming. It announced you, like Milton Cross announced the opera.

Dad was so moved by his gift, he put it away for safekeeping, and thanks to careful rationing over the years, still has most of his Swank left.

Father Emil still has the bottle of Napoleon brandy.

I still have wax drippings on the front of my blue peacoat.

The *Herald-Star* still prints the photo of Main Street at night, snowy, the decorations lit, and underneath, the caption "O little town of Wobegon, how still we see thee lie"—the same photo I saw in the paper when I was a boy.

*Junior choir members rehearsing for a concert at a St. Paul church, 1958*

· · ·

# "Christmas . . . is really a terrible day"

## Charles Flandrau

*The excesses of Christmas celebrations inevitably attract the irritated comments of curmudgeons and naysayers, and it has always been so. Here Charles Flandrau, writing in 1909, calls for observing Christmas "by not observing it at all."*

Christmas—As I grow older, its original significance, its reason for being a holiday at all, becomes more full of meaning, more touching, more beautiful. It is not in the least obligatory to be religiously inclined in order to be profoundly moved by the symbolism of its pathos and poetry. The incident stands out, sums up, crystallizes for us, all that in our gentlest and best moods we believe about the great fact of birth, of motherhood, of infancy, or the family relation. . . . The birth of the Infant Jesus, the attendant circumstances, the general scene and the significance of it all is, I happen to know, one of the few things that can cause a hard-faced, avaricious old billionaire to sink his head on his library table and burst into uncontrollable sobs.

But Christmas itself! I mean the day we have made of it. It is really a terrible day unless, perhaps, you are pretending to relive it with the children which some of us don't possess. Just as I can recall delirious Fourths of July, I can recall Christmas days that were a scream of delight from energetic dawn until tired and sleepy midnight. The delicious, exciting smell of the pine tree, the feel of the "excelsior" in which the fragile ornaments were packed, the taste of those red and yellow animals made out of transparent candy, the taste of the little candles (for some strange, youthful reason we always purloined several of the candles and chewed them, even green ones, in secret. I can't imagine now why they didn't poison us), the thrilling effect of cotton-batting spread on the floor at the tree's base (there were always, of course, acres of real snow just outside the front door but it quite lacked the power to entrance possessed by a few square feet of cotton-batting)—for years I haven't smelled or tasted or seen any of these things. But how wonderful they used to be. Even the Christmas we spent in Gibraltar, and where our tree consisted of a small orange tree propped up in a slop-jar, was the real thing. Every moment of it returns palpitating with the old Christmas sensation.

But now the day, aside from its real significance, to which apparently no great attention is paid, has, as far as I am concerned, lost all its old magic and charm. Of late years, when I have been sufficiently foolish to attempt to "make merry" on Christmas,

I have found the twenty-fifth of December merely a memory that one can revive, but to which one may not give life or even a very successful, galvanic semblance of life. If, nowadays, I permitted Christmas to make any particular impression on me, which I don't, it would, I fear, be chiefly an annoying impression that I ought to be spending more money than I can afford in order to give, to persons I take but little interest in, presents they don't need. At any rate, that is the principal impression I seem to derive from the ante-Christmas conversation of most of my acquaintances who still conventionally observe the day. . . .

This sort of thing, unless one happily possesses a temperament unusually innocent and robust, has but one result: holidays become mere dates on a calendar. They are welcome intruders if one happens to be tied down day after day, as most of us are, to any one exacting and monotonous occupation, but the way to enjoy them, to extract the best from them is, I have found, to ignore them. It is an immeasurable satisfaction when you at last haul down the flag and tell yourself that you don't in the least care what other people are doing on a certain day; when you finally cast out the disturbing belief that you ought to engage in some irritating or melancholy activity, generally supposed to be in keeping with the occasion. To observe Christmas by not observing it at all but by doing what you really feel like doing on a day of leisure, to dine on bread and butter and a cup of tea on Thanksgiving Day because they are what you most want, to seek on the Fourth of July a locality in which there is absolute quiet, all require some courage and, I regret to say, a certain age, but it is worth it.

---

# "Off the hook"

## CHARLES M. SCHULZ

*For schoolchildren, celebrating Christmas means enjoying a glorious winter reprieve from the daily grind. Blissfully long, too, as vacations go—but never long enough. As Peanuts cartoonist Charles M. Schulz remembered, the days fly by, and the day of reckoning, in that awful, dark, freezing month of January, is too soon upon you.*

It is probably impossible to discuss holidays and children without talking about school. No matter how much meaning we try to put into holiday ceremonies, children will always look to these times primarily as a reprieve from schoolwork.

When I recall my childhood in St. Paul, Minnesota, the memories invariably are memories of school. I was not overfond of the class routines, but I must admit there was always one project that I enjoyed. Just as English class meant the inevitable theme "What I Did on My Summer Vacation," art class always included a project requiring us to draw our friends engaged in some form of winter activity. Now, in Minnesota this meant that we drew a group of children skating on a pond. This did *not* mean that any of us had actually experienced such an activity; we were city kids, and very few of us had ever seen a pond that had frozen hard enough to be skated on. But we always tried to depict these scenes, and it was a certainty that every child included a hole in the ice out of which projected a sign that read "Danger." Most likely we had seen these in comic strips.

I noticed that all the kids had trouble drawing those holes in the ice. Somehow they just looked like black spots. My own interest in cartooning led me to discover that by drawing a double line in the ice, one could depict the thickness of that ice. I was very proud when the teacher came around and complimented me on my discovery.

This was one of my very few moments of triumph in school. Unfortunately, the memory of a Minnesota Christmas that always came back to me has to do with another, less-successful project.

At the beginning of each December I looked forward to the holidays as happily as any child. I loved the decorations in the downtown shopping areas and I eagerly anticipated the gifts I might receive. But the best part of the holiday was the knowledge that we would have a two-week vacation from school—and how I looked forward to that! Inevitably, however, there always seemed to be one teacher who could not resist darkening the vacation days with a homework assignment, and one particular vacation was spoiled by our having to read *Silas Marner*. Why couldn't this be read during the regular school term? Why couldn't we be allowed to relax for 14 days and read our comic books and our magazines about football and hockey heroes? *Silas Marner* was pure drudgery.

Now, of course, we all know that 14 days, even to a teenager, is close to an eternity. There would be no reason at all to begin reading a novel during the first few days of vacation, for wouldn't the vacation stretch on forever? And then, of course, as the first week disappeared, why would you want to begin reading the novel during the first part of the second week? After all, you still had seven full days. And then as those days disappeared, one by one, and you drew near the end of the second week, there was still no reason to panic—you had the whole weekend, and anyone who read reasonably fast could surely read *Silas Marner* over the weekend. So, of course, there was nothing to worry about.

But weekends go very fast, and before you know it, Sunday night has arrived. The book has not been opened and there is no possible way to finish it in one evening. The only thing left is to dread Monday morning.

Snoopy co-stars in Charles Schulz's popular television holiday program, A Charlie Brown Christmas (1965). (PEANUTS © United Feature Syndicate, Inc.)

· · ·

Why do teachers have to give such assignments? Why can't we read books that are more interesting? Why are teachers so unreasonable? Why do we have to go to school anyway? Why do Christmas vacations go by so fast? Why are Monday mornings the worst kind of morning ever created?

Oh, how I hated to return to school that day! When was I ever going to learn? The next time we got an assignment like this, I would know better, but it was too late now. I was on my way to school and I was on my way to certain doom.

When I walked into English class that Monday morning there was a strange excitement in the room. Our teacher had not shown up yet and no one knew why. Then we were given the news. During Christmas vacation she had slipped and fallen on the ice and had broken her arm. Off the hook! We were off the hook! Our assignment was canceled and we would not have to finish *Silas Marner* until our teacher returned to school.

This may not be the kind of memory adults like to think children have about Christmas holidays, but I am afraid this is the kind they have.

Merry Christmas. If you have any homework, do it early, and be careful walking on ice.

—◆—

# "It's the light"

## Cathy Mauk

*A reindeer-drawn sleigh may be the archetypal Christmas conveyance, but most of us experience the glittering delights of the holiday looking out from the inside of our cars. Cathy Mauk remembers a childhood cruising the Christmas lights in the Red River Valley's twin cities of Fargo and Moorhead.*

Long ago, when fast food was the lunch counter at Woolworth's, when the mall was a cornfield and Herbst Department Store seemed destined for eternal merchant reign, our family launched a tradition. We'd go out to eat, a rare treat, and then we'd pile in the car and spend the evening driving up and down the streets of these two towns looking at Christmas lights.

As little children, my brother and I were most impressed by the houses that wore the most lights, believing, as do most children, that more is better. The houses with the most lights, or the most garish display of lights, always won our award. And if a house had both thousands of lights, preferably blinking lights, and a plywood Santa atop the roof—with loudspeakers blaring "Up on the Housetop"—the others didn't stand a chance.

As adolescents, we fancied ourselves arbiters of cool. We most liked those lighting displays with a touch of whimsy, or silliness, or impressive, avant-garde design.

Too, it was in our adolescence that, with some encouragement from a parent whose sense of humor runs toward the absurd, we began selecting the winner of our very own award for tacky. This tradition became firmly entrenched in family history when we noticed that those displays that made us snicker often were named winners in the very real contest sponsored then by the Chambers of Commerce.

Because of our family lights-viewing tradition, I consider myself something of a fan, if not an expert, of Christmas lighting displays. Even in adulthood, even in a hurry as I drive down a Fargo street late for an appointment, I consider which of those houses would have been a contender when we were kids.

As I grew older, my travels exposed me to exquisite Christmas lighting displays. I have seen the president of the United States light the national Christmas tree and the White House a-drip with Christmas splendor. I have seen 300-year-old tidewater

Virginia mansions festooned with greenery, beeswax candles and tree ornaments of spun gold. I have seen an estate in Maryland with a room constructed for the display of the owner's village of miniature Victorian houses, each lit from within, each surrounded by sparkling artificial snow and the whole town circled by a gold-plated limited edition Lionel train.

There was a time when they impressed me.

Now I far prefer humbler displays. I like the displays of small towns, their one or two strands of lights swathed in faded green plastic garland, swaying in the wind over the near-empty streets. I like thinking that someone—maybe the local cop, maybe one of the few remaining merchants—hauled out the ladder and put up the lights that the city council bought in 1967. I like to think that when he hung the lights, he felt he was doing an important thing in making ready for Christmas.

I liked places like the Cash Town cafe and bus station in Ortonville, Minnesota, before it was recently remodeled. Then, it had cracked linoleum and tables that always rocked and the rips in the brittle gold plastic of the booths were sutured with duct tape. I like that they decorated for Christmas. On a wall behind a counter was a cardboard banner of cut-out letters spelling "Happy Holidays." The green and red had faded to lime green and pink and the second "P" hung out of kilter, but you got the message. On the serve-yourself coffee table, near the two-burner Bunn coffee maker and the plastic wrapped slices of pie and the glass canister of doughnuts was a two-foot Christmas tree made of pipe cleaners and graced with little pink balls so old that half their paint had rubbed off to expose swatches of silver. It was the warmest sight I saw that cold day.

Now, I prefer the single electric candles hung in the windows of dilapidated houses, or the lights of an artificial tree twinkling from an attic apartment.

For it's the dingy little house that dares celebrate Christmas that reveals the holiday's message. It's the grubby little cafe and bus station that most needs to greet travelers with the Christmas promise of hope and grace. It's the empty streets of small valley towns that, lit by the single string of old Christmas lights, most need something in which to rejoice.

It's the light amid the commonplace and the ordinary that can make even an adult think perhaps there's a Christmas after all.

*House lights brightening the winter night in St. Paul, 1960*

· · ·

# The Christmas Question

## JONIS AGEE

*Novelist and short-story writer Jonis Agee remembers when she asked a number of friends to share one of their memories of celebrating Christmas, good or bad. The stories she heard—each of them "something simple and alive"—led her to reflect on her family and one sweet invented holiday ritual.*

Riddle me this: Why do even bleak holidays so often provide good memories?

Let's get one thing straight: I'm not gaga over the whole holiday thing. Don't get me wrong. I'm not against it—I try to do my part. Some years I string those hopeless little lights up in the euonymus tree outside the front door so my yard looks like a used-car lot. I give dollars to the old guy who plays the quavery off-key violin for the Salvation Army at Har Mar Mall. I even try going to midnight church every few years. The last time at the St. Paul Cathedral went about as expected. The TV cameras and bigwigs got the best view. Next to me, the old nun's garlic snores were strong enough to cut the incense. Instead of magnificent raiments, the bishop and his buddies wore those harvest-gold dealies that looked like the cotton throws my mother used to buy when the furniture got too dirty. I expected more. We were on TV, for heaven's sake.

When I told my friends I was going to write about Christmas, they laughed.

"Why would you do that?" one asked suspiciously.

"Can't you get a better holiday? Halloween, that's your holiday."

"I don't hate Christmas," I said, a little hurt that my ambivalence had been so misunderstood.

I didn't dare mention the holiday business again until I was safely out of town in late August. Having breakfast in Valentine, Neb., with friends I'd made while researching my new book, I decided to try once more. When the Christmas question came up, they didn't even laugh.

"What's your worst or best Christmas memory?" I asked Dave to my left.

"We had all the usual—get in the old pickup, drive to Shlagel Creek, chop down the tallest pine we could find, top it and cut all the boughs, load 'em in the truck, then drive back. Now, we don't bother." Dave gestured with his nearly empty coffee cup and the obliging waitress strode over to fill it.

I told Ed it was his turn. I'd just met him, a printmaker hiding in Crookston, working nights at the halfway house in Valentine with Chris, who was from Baltimore. "Well, the one that stands out, I mean that I do remember, was the one we didn't celebrate at all. I was in California with some friends and none of us were near family, so we just took the day off and went to the woods. Horsed around and threw those slimy banana slugs at each other. It was the best day because we weren't trying to make anything." He was wearing a seed cap that framed his graying hair. His eyes were wary and sad. It wasn't hard to imagine that his holidays haven't been wonderful.

"Notice we're telling our best—not our worst times. You said tell either one." Dave's always making a point, as if somehow everyone in the world is wrong, including him.

"Well, I remember a bad one, my last one in Baltimore," Chris said, flipping his long hair behind one ear. "I was in a basement apartment with these friends. It was the night before Christmas, and there was a bad storm and cold. I mean, colder than it gets out here even. We were sitting around, miserable and unhappy. We didn't even have a tree. Then someone suggested we photograph each other naked—we were all photographers—and things cheered up a lot after that. We got all these neat effects with a flashlight. Afterwards we called all over the city and finally found a Shop and Go that was open 14 blocks away. So we bundled up and walked the 14 blocks, each bought a candy bar and a cup of coffee and walked back. We had a great time."

"There was guy here in Valentine named Cash," Dave began, pushing his plate away. "He decorated his car and drove around in this old fedora pulled down like this, and his elbow stuck out the window. No matter what the weather. The car—everybody called it Cash's Christmas Car. It had these little red lights and everything."

"In Baltimore everyone put wreaths on their cars," Chris announced. "I might put a wreath on this year."

"Cash is dead," Dave said. "Died in his Christmas car. Hit a patch of ice, spun around and flipped over, and he flew out. Broken neck. Everyone still remembers that car, though."

Ed watched us tiredly.

"Some years I have the town come out with their big crane and string lights on the giant pine in my front yard," Dave said. "You know, those tiny white blinking lights? Mary Bonnard came up to me one year and said, 'You cost me $50 in gas I didn't have this year. My little girl, every night, begged me to drive her over to see your tree.'" He smiled at the memory.

We sat silently, each sunk in a holiday mind.

That morning in Valentine, asking the Christmas question, I was reminded of the one ritual that remains in our little family. It began after my divorce when my 4-year-old daughter and I moved to upstate New York in the late '60's so I could attend graduate school. It was our first Christmas alone. There was little money and no ornaments. My daughter and I went to the local discount store to buy a few things, provided they were cheap enough. She chose a green plastic stocking and some reasonable little birds made out of feathers and paper. I found a large white dove, which seemed important in the Vietnam days.

I was in the check-out line, carefully adding things up, when my daughter handed me the ugliest thing I'd ever seen. A concoction of leftover bird parts—with an orange toucan's beak that sprang from the thick turquoise head, yellow and black wings that clamped its sides. Ragged red feathers that sprayed from the butt and stumpy legs that looked like they were wearing black support hose. The stiff yellow plastic feet might have been liberated from a chicken. We already had more stuff than we could afford, but of course we bought it. And every year until she was a teen-ager, my daughter dragged that thing out and put it in a prominent place, despite my grimaces.

I felt better after I remembered the Christmas ritual and realized that maybe this holiday thing is a kind of journey—personal, intimate and public all at once. And like every odyssey, it's fraught with danger: We get stranded from home, we're among strangers, we must invent, invent, invent. Our very identity is at stake. But we suffer and pine and salvage something anyway. The first thing that came to mind whenever I asked people the Christmas question over a period of weeks was something simple and alive and maybe even fine, regardless of religion or politics.

After my daughter entered high school, the clumsy bird ornament began to embarrass her. It looks even worse now. The white of the cardboard body shows through where the felt cover has dried and split. The few feathers are clumpy and disgruntled looking. One black plastic eye has popped off, leaving a discouraged white patch, not even a circle, something more like a skin disease. As soon as she went to college, she began to leave it in the bottom of the ornament box. She even tried to hide it a couple of times.

But every year I find it, and discreetly I wrap the wires protruding from its big chicken feet to a branch and let it perch drunkenly through the whole season, peering at us, head cocked, with its one good eye from the very back of the tree, resigned apparently to the inevitable fate of its demise. Now, despite the new ornaments we buy to commemorate each year—the bear on skis when Paul and I got married, the engraved silver bell for his mother's visit—it's that stupid bird I like best.

———— • ✦ • ————

*Young girls follow an older dancer during a rehearsal of the popular Nutcracker ballet, Stillwater, 1998.*
*(Keri Pickett)*

• • •

# CHRISTMAS
## IN THE CITY

"Once upon a time"
Being the Sequel to
CHRISTMAS IN THE COUNTRY

That was the year when Uncle Erik and Aunt Stella got the Thorkelsons to care for the farm while they went "up to the city" to spend the Holidays with John and Clara.

Scat!

"fresh fruit, chewin' gum, magazines"

They took the 6:17 A.M. "accommodation train"

Illustrations by LEE MERO

(It "accommodated" freight, livestock and people)

**E**rik and Stella arrived at the Union Depot, which was even BIGGER than they had imagined!

"A Hack", says Mr Webster, "is a carriage for hire."

An almost endless line of hacks waited to drive folks to their destinations

**T**hey got a real thrill, though, when John said they would ride out home in one of the new E-LEC-TRIC CARS--complete with trailer!

"Faster and more comfortable", he said, as they found seats next to the stove for the two mile ride--

Erik's telescope grip

"Yes sir!" said John, "these are going to put horse-cars right out of business!"

Next morning, after the grocer had called for his daily order, everybody left home for a trip downtown, "to go through the stores".

"Just like fairy-land!" exclaimed Stella.

She didn't forget to buy a souvenir coffee spoon for Mrs. Thorkelson

On the way home the Turkey was bought,

Next day, the wood-box was filled to overflowing

Good things fairly popped from the oven!

The Turkey was plucked,

The children had a final rehearsal for the Sunday school program

Uncle Erik "slicked up" his celluloid collar

And a nice goose was sent over to the parsonage

That evening they went over to the Exposition Building to hear the "Messiah"

And Stella got a chance to observe what the ladies up in the city were wearing

Ice-boats made a pretty picture

The day after Christmas, being a very nice one for this time of year, John rented a team and a two-seated sleigh and took the family on his favorite ride around the parkways.

The Park was thronged with skaters

Stella thought "the Falls" were "just like fairy-land!"

John "saved up" the most exciting entertainment for the last evening! Then, they went to the neighborhood fire-barn, where, promptly at eight, the fire drill took place. The gong rang, the horses pranced to their places, a fireman slid down the pole and "a pleasant time was had by all!"

the Captain

MASCOT OF COMPANY EIGHT

Erik thought "the dappled grays were just wonderful!"

They didn't want to appear too much like "country cousins" while they were with John and Clara, but on the way home, they talked about:

"The man who lit the gas light with a newfangled device on the end of a stick",

How "Clara didn't have to pump water"

And how he thawed it out with a long iron rod when it froze up!

"Those good, hot chestnuts at five cents a bag"

"The steaming kettle sign for a tea and coffee store"

"How much they enjoyed the Christmas music"

"All those pieces of Grandma's china that Erik could mend with that new cement the man sold him!"

But, after all, it was good to be "HOME AGAIN" when the Thorkelsons met them at the station with the bob-sled!

*Loading freshly cut trees atop a car, about 1926 (Kenneth Wright)*

• • •

# Coming Home

—•◦•—

## "My Middle West"

### F. Scott Fitzgerald

*F. Scott Fitzgerald's* The Great Gatsby *contains this memorable passage in which the narrator, Nick Carraway, realizes that his story has been "a story of the West." The scene brings together trains and transitions and moving through distances and time—and Christmas.*

One of my most vivid memories is of coming back West from prep school and later from college at Christmas time. Those who went farther than Chicago would gather in the old dim Union Station at six o'clock of a December evening, with a few Chicago friends, already caught up into their own holiday gayeties, to bid them a hasty good-by. I remember the fur coats of the girls returning from Miss This-or-That's and the chatter of frozen breath and the hands waving overhead as we caught sight of old acquaintances, and the matchings of invitations: "Are you going to the Ordways'? the Herseys'? the Schultzes'?" and the long green tickets clasped tight in our gloved hands. And last the murky yellow cars of the Chicago, Milwaukee & St. Paul railroad looking cheerful as Christmas itself on the tracks beside the gate.

When we pulled out into the winter night and the real snow, our snow, began to stretch out beside us and twinkle against the windows, and the dim lights of small Wisconsin stations moved by, a sharp wild brace came suddenly into the air. We drew in deep breaths of it as we walked back from dinner through the cold vestibules, unutterably aware of our identity with this country for one strange hour, before we melted indistinguishably into it again.

That's my Middle West—not the wheat or the prairies or the lost Swede towns but the thrilling returning trains of my youth, and the street lamps and sleigh bells in the frosty dark and the shadows of holly wreaths thrown by lighted windows on the snow. I am part of that, a little solemn with the feel of those long winters, a little complacent from growing up in the Carraway house in a city where dwellings are still called through decades by a family's name.

◆◆◆

# "You could hear sleigh bells"

## Walter O'Meara

*When someone writes a memoir, it is a kind of "coming home." Walter O'Meara remembered growing up in the lumber-milling town of Cloquet, a place where people were happy every year just to make it through the winter. Christmas, with its feelings of peace and joy mingled with bustling celebration and sheer loveliness, came as a welcome interlude in the bitter winters on the edge of the north woods.*

In our town, as everywhere else in those days, Christmas was celebrated in a quiet, almost sedate way. The early 1900s were not lacking in business enterprise, but the observance of Christ's birth, at least, had not yet turned into a commercial promotion. Christmas, as I happily remember it, was a time of profound peace and quiet in a small town silenced by a heavy blanket of snow. On Christmas Eve you could hear sleigh bells at an extraordinary distance. To children wide awake in bed there was always the wild surmise that maybe they were Santa's.

For a small boy, however, Christmas did have a certain commercial aspect: it presented him with the problem of how to earn enough money to buy presents for everyone. Billy Horan and I usually went into the Christmas tree business. On Saturdays and after school we trudged through the drifts to Tamarack Swamp with an ax and length of rope. To find a good tree, we usually had to force our way for some distance

*Santa and the company tree, topped with a fluttering flag, at northern Minnesota's Genoa Mine, 1919*

• • •

into the muskeg. After finally selecting and felling one, we attached the rope to it and dragged it back to town. Often it would be dark when we arrived starved and half-frozen. The next day we would canvass the neighborhood, hoping that a customer of previous years would again buy a tree from us. If we were lucky and made a sale, we usually received twenty cents to divide between us.

Even in those days you couldn't buy much for many people at that rate. One year I made only enough from the sale of our trees to buy my mother a pair of scissors for her sewing basket. I had seen them weeks before in the window of Mr. Freeman's jewelry store, and had persuaded him to put them aside for me. They were in the form of a gilded stork, with the stork's beak functioning as blades.

Each family in Cloquet had its own way of celebrating Christmas, and its own idea of how to decorate a Christmas tree. Ours was set up in the parlor, always in exactly the same spot near the piano, with the same battered Santa Claus at the very top. It was hung with a few German-looking ornaments, carefully preserved in cotton from Christmas to Christmas, and with garlands of popcorn and cranberries we had gathered in a swamp across the river. Besides paper chains, the decorations also included pink popcorn balls, oranges, and apples. It was at Christmas that the oranges made their sole appearance in our house. The apples on the tree looked oddly special and unfamiliar, although they were really no different from those we ate every winter evening.

Our tree was lighted with little candles of different colors clipped to the branches in tin basins to catch the drippings. They gave a soft, wavering light to the dim parlor on Christmas morning, and a smell of balsam boughs warmed by their tiny flames. On Christmas Eve candles were also placed in the parlor windows of houses all over Cloquet—to light the way of the Christ Child, it was said. The effect of so many candles gleaming between the lace curtains of dark windows was very pretty on a snowy night.

Christmases in our town may not have been so different from those in other homes and other towns around the turn of the century. But in a few minor ways they may have been unique; I could not think of our own holiday season without recalling us children trooping to the Company Store on Christmas morning to receive a shiny little dinner pail—just like our fathers'—filled with candies as a gift from the lumber company; the highly polished apple left under the tree for Santa and how we marveled, when we were younger, at the big bite taken out of it; the excitement of going to the Railway Express office with my sled to haul home the box of presents from our aunts in the Twin Cities; the freezing walk to church with my mother for midnight Mass on Christmas Eve; and the feeling of incompleteness and sadness with my father "up in the woods" and his place at the table empty for Christmas dinner.

# "Closer to the ground"

## Jerry Fearing

*Home for cartoonist Jerry Fearing was the working-class neighborhood near West Seventh Street in St. Paul. His Depression-era childhood was a time when snow seemed a lot deeper, when December afternoons were spent dreamily paging through the "wish books" of big mail-order catalogues, and when a kid could jump on a sled and take a ride that would live in memory forever.*

Then, as now, the religious significance of Christ's birthday was the last thing on a kid's mind. It was the colorful trappings, the Santa legend, and *gifts* that captured and held our attention. Preparations for the big day started soon after Thanksgiving. Wreaths went up on doors, electric candles appeared in the windows, and soon through those windows could be seen Christmas trees glittering in living rooms. In my memory, the scene seems to glow like a Terry Redlin painting.

Maybe it's because I stood closer to the ground then, but the snow in our yard and on the streets seemed a lot deeper in those days. There wasn't much snow removal at that time so the snow cleared from streets, sidewalks, and driveways ended up as huge mounds along the curbs. Playing on these was as close as we kids ever got to mountain climbing.

There were none of the glitzy-blinking lights in yards or along roofs that we see today. Nor did I see Santa's sleigh on rooftops or hear loud speakers blaring Christmas music at the neighbors.' It was more subdued, less commercial. For me a sure sign that Christmas wasn't far off was being asked to draw pictures on the school blackboards. The teacher knew I spent most of my time drawing pictures anyway, so she put me to work going from room to room drawing Christmas scenes in colored chalk. Because I attended a parochial school, I usually chose as my subject the three wise men on their camels, Bethlehem with a big star shining above it, or the manger scene with animals. I enjoyed the assignment because it kept me out of class where I was supposed to be learning something about long division and spelling.

Then there were the lists of things we wanted for Christmas or what we hoped to buy as gifts for members of the family.

We didn't have the newspaper supplements from shopping centers with stores like Toys "R" Us. But we did have catalogs from Wards and Sears. My four-year-old brother,

six-year-old sister, and I would spend hours on the front-room floor paging through them, oh-ing and ah-ing over the array of products pictured there.

Unfortunately we were Depression babies who grew up being told "we can't afford that!" So we knew most of the items pictured in the catalog were out of reach. Our lists were made up of inexpensive items, like books, fingernail polish, slippers, hair combs and brushes, and bubble bath or simple items of clothing like ties or handkerchiefs.

Mom helped the younger kids buy the items they wanted to give each other, but when you got to be as old as I, you were expected to save up your nickels and dimes and buy them yourself. Those nickels and dimes were hard to come by. There was no such thing as an allowance at our house. You did your chores without pay. Nor did babysitting pay anything. I was expected to take and watch my little sister and brother when I went to the playground or to pull them along on the sled when I went sliding at Irvine Park. Running a special errand could earn you something. Shoveling snow for elderly neighbors was a good source of income during the winter months. You could earn a quarter if you did a good job, or even fifty cents if it was a corner lot. Another lucrative source of revenue was the front-room furniture. On the morning after our folks had entertained friends at the house, we'd rush to the livingroom couch and chair, remove the cushions, and search the furniture's lining for change that had slipped from the guests' pockets. It often paid very well.

To us kids Irvine Park was known as "Erving Park." It held the remnants of a stylish old area that once even had a fountain in the center. A high hill swept down from the west through the trees. Huge houses that were once home to the elite of St. Paul circled the park. But at the time we used the hill for sliding, the area had become just a deteriorating lower-middle-class neighborhood. Years later it was discovered by a new generation. The old houses were renovated, and today Irvine Park again reflects some of the glory of those early years. We kids knew nothing of the park's past. For us it was just one of the few good hills in the area for sliding.

We used runner sleds and toboggans, but the best ride was had with a large piece of cardboard curled back over the knees of the kids in front. As it started down the hill kids would come running and jump on. By the time it came to a stop at the bottom, the giggling mass was at least three-kids high.

I must tell you of the greatest sled ride in the history of "Erving Park." One night a freezing rain had left everything coated with a half inch of ice! A handful of us kids showed up at the park the next morning before the city got around to treating the streets. From the top of the hill, we belly flopped down through the park, over the curb, and down the block to Chestnut Street. There we made a sharp right turn and sped down Chestnut Hill, across the railroad tracks, all the way down to the Mississippi River. It must have been at least an eight-block run. I think of that ride every time I see the bobsleds in the Olympics on TV. We hurriedly made the long slippery walk back to the park for another go at it. By the time we got back the trucks had arrived, spreading cinders in the street and putting an end to our glorious sled ride.

I usually had to bring my sister and brother along sliding. I hated that. It was pretty cold on that windy hill, but when you're busy climbing back up and running around, it didn't bother you much. My sister was old enough to handle it. But my little brother, who was too young and over-dressed to be very active, was a problem. I would slide and fool around with my friends, ignoring his complaints as best I could. Finally his crying would start drawing attention. So I'd put him back on the sled and pull him home. By the time I got him there and upstairs, his feet and hands were painfully cold. While Mom held his feet and massaged warmth back into him, she'd scold me for not taking better care of him. My answer, of course, was not to send him along in the first place. As I look back now, I realize what a painfully miserable experience it must have been to be my little brother.

# "My December duty"

## Bill Holm

*A town with a name like "Minneota, Minnesota" might easily be mistaken as a place of pure
fiction or nursery rhyme. But it's not. Minneota was—and is—essayist and poet Bill Holm's
hometown, a place where the "gavel of tradition" bangs loudly on the Christmas table.*

My interior Christmas begins early, sometimes the first snow in October, sometimes
the last scorcher in August. The Christmas letter rears up in the mind's eye like a sudden thunderhead in a bright sky. I imagine the rummaging through drawers for last
year's pile of Christmas cards and the attempt at rationalizing my way into an escape:
"Why bother? No one reads them. I don't have time for this. I haven't seen some of
these people in years. Others don't bother. (I make a list.) It's a silly habit; habits can be
tamed and broken." The whine goes on. The excuses don't work.

　　During the first blizzard, I rummage, find not only last years' Christmas cards (a
sizable lump), but the last ten years', maybe twenty. Some senders are now dead from
inevitable age or bad luck. Some are divorced, some re-married, some not; some simply moved or disappeared. At Christmas, we want steadiness, a still point in a chaotic
world, but we get mutability, a mirror with the face of chaos staring back at us.

　　In the second blizzard, I brood and examine my own character, my passing life. I
cross-examine it, send it to the interior jury, convict it, sentence it—if not to death, at
least to exile. But either mercy or lethargy or both reprieve it. Of what am I guilty? Of
being silly and weak, a procrastinator, a carrier-out of orders from the dead, a skeptical
practitioner of ritual, of having arrived at middle age without entirely finishing youth.
Thus I am guilty of being human, more normal than I imagine in my more grandiose
moments.

　　By the third blizzard, I am steeled to the job, lashed to the grim wheel of duty. Since
recent Minnesota blizzards have been the three- or four-day variety with howling hur-
ricane winds—the world invisible inside a maelstrom of snow and wind-chills lethal
enough to finish you off in two or three minutes—there's not much else to do except
your duty. I write the Christmas essay, a half whimsical, half melancholy sermon on the
progress of another year, set out the sheets of stamps and boxes of envelopes, arrange
the pens next to the pile of cards, stare wistfully out the kitchen window at the icy
white scrim over the universe, and begin. Merry Christmas. . . .

What, you might ask, am I doing with ten or twenty years of old Christmas cards? For all I know, fifty-year-old cards may lurk in unopened boxes. At thirty-two, I found myself heir to my mother's and father's lifetime accumulations of stuff too valued to be thrown: old tools, photographs, boxes of crocheting, knitting, wood painting, every toy I ever played with, and every scribble of paper in my handwriting—childish poems, school essays, letters. I was an adored only child, but this—this was ridiculous! At the back of a closet sat a shoebox full of baby congratulations cards—from 1943.

Jona and Big Bill were both devoted pack rats. Raised without money in Icelandic immigrant farm families, they married in 1932 to slog through the whole Depression trying to buy back my grandfather's farm from a loan company. They narrowly escaped foreclosure, hanging tenaciously onto the old Holm farm at the edge of the Dust Bowl until World War II, Minnesota Governor Floyd B. Olson, and FDR saved them. One consequence of that chronology was the inability to get rid of anything that they actually owned. Neither of them was thrifty with money; rather they practiced mad generosity to friends, strangers, and of course to me, the beloved child. But a broken hayrake or iron tractor wheel, or a bag of holey nylon stockings, patched underwear, paper-thin overalls, and moth-eaten sweaters was different. They could be recycled, made useful, given new life, like half-gone leftovers disappearing into a hot dish. I once wrote a poem about my mother's habit with these lines:

> *You never know, she said,*
> *when it might come in handy,*
> *and you can always put it in the soup*
> *where it'll taste good.*

After more than twenty years of overseeing the Holm ancestral junk, I look around appalled to find that not only have I thrown out almost nothing, I have instead doubled the holdings. I am a genetic pack rat with a weakness for paper, not iron or craft supplies. Books, magazines, letters, musical scores, manuscripts, and old Christmas cards have eaten wall space, corners, window ledges, the floor up to the bed springs.

The ritual of the Christmas card list is a visible emblem of spiritual packrattery. Going through my mother's boxes after she died in 1975, I found her collection of old cards. What to do? I added my mother's list to my already sizable accumulation: more cousins, uncles, aunts, old neighbors, her stamp pals, schoolmates. After twenty years, the old family list shrunk though the attrition of death, but new cousins surfaced, new connections from strange parts of the world where I've lived and worked, old friends with grown children who have themselves become friends. My December duty now resembles Jacob Marley's chains. They rattle after me wherever I go.

But the Christmas letter is only half a burden. It is also a necessity, even a pleasure. No matter the awkwardness of tone or expression—Christmas letters are often comically guilty of two great human failings: bragging and complaining—its real message lives under the language. I am alive, it says, still on the planet. I have not forgotten you. The thread, whether of blood, nostalgia, or friendship, that sews us together has not been cut. In a culture Balkanized by technology and group-think, the Christmas letter is a human message in an envelope bottle, a small ritual where we name each other one at a time, even if only in a scribbled sentence at the bottom of a Xerox.

The old cliché to the contrary, a picture is probably not worth a thousand words. Language, like music, takes time; a picture slaps us in the face in an instant. It hardens and makes plain what language can sometimes soften and make subtle. Some find escape from an annual Christmas essay by sending the Christmas card snapshot with a cheery but brief printed greeting. I have never sunk to it. I take my photographs with sentences. But at the bottom of a dusty box of family memorabilia, I found evidence that my mother and father swallowed the whole bait—for years sending out "cute" photographs of their long-awaited single son. The sequence begins in the mid-forties, continuing until the mid-fifties. By then, teenage acne and surliness robbed the photographs of their "cuteness," so Jona and Bill retreated to Hallmark and hand-written notes.

I don't remember ever seeing those photos as a child. When I first found them, at about forty, I chuckled at the grotesque little boy who certainly didn't seem to have much connection to me as a grown man. But now, past fifty and barely recognizable as this dimpled young fellow, I realize with a kind of ironic dismay that I still contain the little cowboy of 1949. He's duded up with his Hopalong Cassidy outfit: chaps, six-gun in holster, bandanna, and Suzuki-size ten gallon hat, ready to fast draw on the photographer, proclaiming in his soprano grumble, "Stick 'em up!" My hand already clutches the gun. In 1950 the seven-year-old goose hunter sends "Seasons Greetings": Big Bill's twelve-gauge 1897 Remington pump in one hand and the neck of a dead Canadian honker in the other. The next year features the solemn boy in a floral shirt standing in front of the family's new brown Dodge, asphyxiating Andrew, the white barn cat. The cat, with terrified eyes and flat ears, looks ready to claw the boy and leap for freedom. In 1952 same boy, same shirt, but now he's squeezing an alarmed rabbit. Thick black spectacles adorn his pink nose. He's on his way to junior high nerd king!

No printed letter accompanies these cards depicting the progress of Little Billy. In time, the gun slinger and goose hunter grew up to be a devout pacifist who spent his twenties "clean for Gene" marching against Lyndon Johnson's war. The pet choker grew up to think that animals deserve to stay wild and outdoors. These Christmas photos announce to me (and to you, since your face probably appeared on similar cards) that I most certainly am not eternal, but that some stubborn core of character born early will last until my own death, whether I want it or not.

At Christmas, the gavel of tradition bangs on the table to call the house to order. We have always done it this way, so do it now. We have always eaten—oysters, lutefisk, ham balls, fill in the blank—so we shall eat them again. In towns like Minneota, the solid front of Christmas habit brought even the atheists to church on Christmas Eve. The Jewish doctor's children acted in the Sunday school Christmas pageant. A Hindu could not have escaped appearing in the manger scene, toasting the holiday afterwards with garishly decorated butter cookies dunked in thin coffee.

Yet tradition, anywhere in America (and certainly in the Midwest), is a strangely jackleg affair, hardly old enough to qualify as tradition at all, rather only invented procedure. A tradition must be so old that its true origin, while lost to us consciously, remains quick inside the cells of the body. Tradition grows from the texture of the grass, the shape of the hills, the color of rivers when the snow melts, the swampy pasture where our great-grandfather's horse stumbled and broke his leg. We haven't been long enough in Minnesota to earn that kind of tradition.

But what about the old country, you ask? Didn't tradition travel over on the boat from Ireland, Norway, Iceland, Belgium? A majority of Minnesotans descend from those stocks, hardly over a century ago. But traditions seem not to travel well over water; most sickened in mid-Atlantic and expired shortly after they stepped off the horse cart onto the tall grass prairie. This is a country of interrupted traditions, just entering a difficult puberty to start growing real ones. The physician poet, William Carlos Williams, described us well, if a little harshly, as "tricked out . . . / with gauds/ from imaginations which have no/ peasant traditions to give them/ character."

But at Christmas, my mother, Jona, "tricked out" her house with gauds that would have astonished even Dr. Williams, and as she would have briskly assured him, she had plenty of character. She might have defined tradition as anything you did once that looked good to you, so you practiced it forty or fifty times more—and behold you have invented "tradition."

Jonina Sigurborg Josephson Holm, my mother, was a woman of extraordinary energy and vitality. In her, the life force was not an idea but an eruption. Born in 1910 on a farm to parents who spoke little or no English, she longed for education, travel, adventure, the Big World. She escaped all of seven miles south to Minneota to graduate from high school, worked in Leland's Drug Store illegally filling prescriptions, and in 1932, after years of his courting and cajoling, married Bill Holm, her childhood sweetheart, to return seven miles north to yet another immigrant farm only a few miles from her parents. No college, no career, no New York—not even Minneapolis, half a lifetime away on mud roads. Just an unpaid-for farm, a drafty shack of a house, kerosene lamps, a pump over the sink, and a two-holer outhouse. These bare details of her life are not peculiar; her story is the story of a million women of her generation in the rural United States—and probably in the big cities too, though school was easier there.

*Women assembling holiday crafts, St. Paul, 1951*

• • •

*Department 56 (originally a unit of Bachman's, a Minneapolis floral company) produced its Original Snow Village—six hand-painted, lighted, miniature ceramic buildings— in 1976 after old friends gathering for a holiday meal shared a view over the twinkling lights of Stillwater.*

· · ·

Like most of that million, she didn't whine. If luck and circumstance thwarted her longing for beauty, elegance, an exciting life, she would act out her longing by inventing her own version of them wherever she was. Without having any idea what "art" or "taste" were, she possessed, probably from birth, the equipment of an artist; a skilled hand, a sharp eye, a willingness to make mistakes, and mammoth reserves of energy.

She crocheted, she knitted, she embroidered, she painted figurines and wooden plates and breadboards, she made ceramic ashtrays, lamps, bowls, casserole dishes, she glued beads and gewgaws on any recyclable object, however unlikely, she canned and baked and pickled, she collected stamps, hand ruling the pages with a Parker fountain pen after checking her perforation gauge, she sewed dresses, shirts, coats, and when they wore thin, she adorned them with decorative patches, and then patches on top of the patches. Whatever interested her at any given moment, she surrendered to in excess. Without ever having heard of William Blake, she practiced his maxim by instinct: *The road of excess leads to the palace of wisdom.* When wooden plates captured her attention she painted fifty for relatives, fifty for neighbors and friends, fifty to sell (though mostly she gave them away), and another fifty for storage under the bed, just in case. Not only was her enthusiasm contagious, she owned no resistance to the enthusiasms of others. If a neighbor learned from the radio or a crafts magazine how to make pink swan soap dishes out of plastic dish soap bottles, Jona swung into action and tried a few hundred herself. None of her projects, however, intruded into the time she spent on her real passion: human beings—creatures capable of language and conversation, the telling of stories. She entered a room talking, eyed the company to see who might need cheering up, finishing the sentence when she closed the door behind her. When she died, one of her friends, amazed that death had been tough or fast enough to do Jona in, sighed and said, "She had only two speeds, high and off."

Her house became the gallery for her projects, and at Christmas, her favorite season, the show doubled or tripled in size to overwhelm the cramped little farmstead. Out came the boxes of handmade tree ornaments, the painted figurines of Santa and his whole retinue—reindeer, elves, sleighs, a set of wise men and camels and an electrified manger scene with blinking lights, angels of various color and design, dishes and bowls decorated with poinsettias and mistletoe, the embroidered Christmas tablecloth and napkins, the rosemaled napkin rings, wooden plates painted with Christmas motifs and Yuletide greetings in four or five languages, Christmas bric-a-brac on every flat surface, handmade candle holders of maybe fifteen designs with scented candles burned nightly for a month, their smells of lavender sachet, pine forest, and spicy cinnamon oozing together in the drafty rooms, and finally, my favorites, the Christmas angels made from folded magazines shellacked and spray painted to a board-like stiffness, and the *piece-de-resistance*: the Christmas toilet seat cover with a gay red winking Santa Claus waiting for your hind end (this came after acquiring a flush toilet in 1950).

And it was a house of "gauds"; no subtle earth tones or delicate pastels for Jona—

she loved bright, intense, gypsy color: red, hot pink, purple, orange, gold, lime green. These wise men had *style*; these angels played tambourines, not ethereal harps. In a bleak old farmhouse on the bleak north crest of a bleak hill on a bleak prairie with the bleakest climate on the continent, this house, inhabited by Scandinavian Lutherans, looked like a Hungarian restaurant decorated for a Chinese wedding.

My mother cared little for the theology of Christmas. She was, at best, a nominal Lutheran, faithful to Ladies' Aid and do-good projects but casual in her piety. Her Christmas music consisted of breathy performances of *Heim Sem Bol* (*Silent Night* in Icelandic) and *Jingle Bells* on a Hohner harmonica—and this only after a well laced Tom-and-Jerry or two. She loved the festivity of Christmas, the chance to create some light and noise and gaiety at the bottom of the year's darkness, cold, and silence. If you had to live in this godforsaken place at least show some evidence of being actually alive. Maybe that's the real kernel of psychological wisdom underlying the Christmas rites anyway. Jona's extroverted nature guided her to stumble into that wisdom unconsciously.

What she made was not "kitsch"; kitsch implies a consciousness of fashionable taste satirically undermined. Jona invented beauty—as she understood it. Her creations connected not so much to her ego as to her affectionate desire to please others. If you admired a piece of her handiwork, you went home with it. As a boy, sometimes overwhelmed by the crowded gypsy camp atmosphere inside the house at Christmas, I kept wishing for more traffic, more guests to do a little thinning and pruning on the collection. It would have done no good; she would simply have swung into action and invented more. The Icelandic Christmas tradition inside her family and immigrant culture evaporated in the new world, except for a few Christmas recipes that were adaptations of food that had already begun to disappear from real old country tables. One ritual function of a tradition is to create connection inside a community. So, lacking Iceland, Jona made do, announcing: "This is now tradition; help yourself."

## A century of Minnesota cards

Minnesotans began sending Christmas cards to family and friends beginning in the 1860s. Included in this sampling are a small carte-de-visite fringed card from about 1870, a larger hinged and fringed chromolithograph card from the 1880s, an embossed and die-cut card of pansies from 1900, a block-print rooftops scene from the 1920s, a hand-crafted doorway image by Frances Dodge from 1936, patriotic message cards from the world wars, a Shipstads and Johnson Ice Follies card from 1951, and a pop Santa Claus greeting from the 1970s.

# "How much for this tree without limbs?"

## LOUIE ANDERSON

*The exasperations of family life, like so many other things, seem to enlarge at Christmastime. Here actor and entertainer Louie Anderson—one of eleven children of a long-suffering mom and an alcoholic dad—focuses his standup-comic beam on a familiar scene.*

During the holidays, there are all these rituals we go through with our families. One tradition I'll never forget is going to the Christmas tree lot with my dad who was always looking to outsmart the guy selling the trees.

"I know how to work these guys, Louie. They buy them for a quarter a piece, by the billions."

My mom would pick the tree out. "I'll take this one," she'd say, "but that one looks like it could use a good home . . . or maybe this one that smells so good. . . ."

Once she'd decided, Dad went to work negotiating.

"Hey, buddy, how much for this tree without any limbs?"

"Thirty-five dollars."

"What?! Are you going to come over and decorate it for us? I'll give you three bucks for it."

I'd be mortified. "Oh my God. He's not our legal father!"

Then my dad wouldn't pay fifty cents for the rope.

"I got the rope in the car."

We'd carry the tree over to the station wagon; he'd open the trunk and find nothing.

"You kids been taking that rope again?"

"Oh yeah, Dad. We wait until you and Mom fall asleep, we get those car keys, we open that trunk, we get that rope—we've got enough in our room to hang the whole neighborhood!"

Then we'd end up holding the tree on to the car, our hands freezing in the cold. Once we got the tree home, my dad would make us get the stand from the basement—the stand that came over on the Mayflower.

"That's a good stand!" he'd bellow. "When I was a kid, we didn't have stands! We had to take turns holding that tree!"

He'd get the saw and work on that stand for hours. Finally, we'd put the tree in the stand and inevitably the tree would lean over, crooked. My dad would frown and yell at the tree: "For thirty-five bucks, that thing should dance!"

You ever get your dad something that he already had for Christmas? Something he already owned? Something that was his?

My dad would open up his present and find one of his tools.

"Hey, I was looking all over for this."

I'd turn to my brother.

"Wait till he looks in that other box and finds all that rope."

---

# Afterthoughts on Christmas Trees

## BARTON SUTTER

*Transforming an ordinary living room into a "home for Christmas" comes down to one simple fact: a Christmas tree. Or maybe a tree is not such a simple thing. In this essay poet Barton Sutter looks at this symbol of renewal, and considers both its distant, ancient origins as well as its personal meanings and memories.*

Normally, a week or two into the new year, we plant our Christmas tree in a snowdrift with some suet for the birds dangling from the branches. This year, though, we took our tree to a recycle site where city workers ran it through a chipper. I like to think our tree, which served so well as a symbol of renewal, might have a practical afterlife. In Duluth, I'm told, the chipped-up trees are used as mulch on hiking trails. I hope that's true, because we sure go through a passel of trees. If this is a city of a hundred thousand, and you figure we average four people per household, that means we sacrifice twenty-five thousand trees every Christmas. . . .

I'm not opposed to this peculiar custom. Just the opposite, in fact. I'm growing more devoted to it as I go along. There were winters in my twenties when I did without a tree, for sure, but that was less from principle than laziness. Besides, I could always count on older friends and relatives to carry on the tradition. I'll bet if everyone had gone without a tree in those days, I would have been seriously upset. At any rate, here in middle age, the darkness of the winter months seems awfully deep to me, suggesting, I suppose, that final, utter darkness that comes closer every day. So I appreciate those old symbols of renewal—lights and greenery—a little more each year. The straight white spruce that stood in our back room this season, laden with tinsel and silly decorations, looked strangely brave to me. And I'm grateful, here in January, to see the odd wreath hanging on a neighbor's door and colored lights still twinkling on the trees and snow-caked houses. Did I once think that such displays were vulgar, dumb, and wasteful? I'm afraid I did. Now they seem cheerful and tragic. It's a cold planet, baby, and we come to a cold end. Trees and lights both help along the way.

But the idea of bringing a tree inside the house! You know, it's damn near as weird as if you'd suddenly decided to keep a cow in the living room. "There, now, Bessie. Stay." You give the tree a drink of water, too, now and then, don't you? This can't be a

Christian idea. Of course it's not. The Christians would like you to think so . . . stick a pretty angel on the treetop and pretend. But the habit of putting up a tree at Christmas time has much deeper roots. We know, for example, that the Romans traded greenery on the first of January. Celtic druids, the priests of ancient Ireland, believed that oak trees and mistletoe were sacred. My encyclopedia, speculating about the origin of Christmas trees, says straight out: "People in Scandinavia once worshiped trees." The primal truth is this: When we cut a living tree on one of the darkest days of the year, stand it up inside the home, and dress it with decorations, we are performing a pagan sacrifice to make the sun come back. When we sink a saw blade into the slender trunk of a young fir tree, we draw sap instead of blood, but in that moment we are one with the ancient people—pictured in the Bible, Homer's epic poems, and many other places—who cut the throats of oxen, sheep, and goats to offer up on altars.

Of course if you just buy your tree precut from a commercial lot, you're not apt to be reminded of blood sacrifice. But up here in northern Minnesota, there's plenty of opportunity to cut your own, and when I saw my dad during the holidays this year, I thought once more of the very first Christmas I can recall and the first Christmas tree I ever saw cut. I was four or five then, and those were the days when my father had black, wavy hair and strong arms. Today he is frail and unsteady, with dry, wispy hair, and glasses that slide down his nose. These days, my father forgets. More and more often he seems to be lost in some sort of internal blizzard, and as his memories gradually fade, I feel compelled to remember aloud for us both. That particular Christmas, I remember, the Nordvalls had invited us to take a tree from their woods. So my dad drove out to their place on Minnesota Hill and hauled me along. The Nordvall place was a subsistence dairy farm, located on the only high ground in that flat country, backed up against the Canadian border—a wild, hardscrabble, pioneer farm at the end of the road. The snow lay so deep that I had to ride my father's shoulders as he plowed across the pasture to the forest. The woods were full of shadows, and I was scared that we'd get lost in there or something bad would get me, but we didn't have to go in very far. My father chose a dark green tree that seemed extremely tall to me, and he made me stand back farther than I wanted. Never very practical or handy, he had brought a carpenter's crosscut saw, but it seemed to work all right. I can still hear it gnawing at the trunk and see the yellow sawdust spurt out in the snow and hear my father cry, 'Timberrr!" The tree tipped and fell with a rush and snow flew off in all directions. In the soft silence afterward, a chickadee sang somewhere. My father hoisted the tree up on his shoulder, and I wallowed along behind, up toward the red sheds and the house with sweet smoke curling from the chimney and the woodpile high as the house. Inside, there was laughter and old people with white hair who spoke Swedish and gave me sheets of brittle flatbread and a mug of hot milk.

I'm not so much for New Year's resolutions anymore, but I remember that scene from my boyhood, way back there when my father was a giant, and I remember what my encyclopedia told me, that my ancestors once worshiped trees, and I resolve that this coming Christmas I will go into the woods to cut my own green tree.

*Crosscountry skier, northern Minnesota, 1965*

· · ·

# Cold Feet

## Emily Carter

*"Home" is not a single, familiar spot on the map, peopled by a fixed cast of characters. Emily Carter reminds us that home is wherever we accidentally—or providentially—find acceptance, kindness, and even redemption. First presented by its writer on National Public Radio on Christmas Day, 2001, "Cold Feet" is published here for the first time.*

Samuel Kaminsky stalked out of the December 25th 9:00 A.M. gratitude meeting, holiday breakfast to follow. A flush of hot righteousness initially kept him from realizing how cold a Minnesota winter could actually be. Every step he took, however, was an icy lesson in how not to dress in December.

At the treatment center up north, he had spent the entire month of November inside. Besides, how exactly was a restaurateur, late of Tullio's, one of Miami's finer purveyors of fusion cuisine, supposed to know what it was like walking down an empty street in Minneapolis when single digits were dropping into the double negatives? . . .

Since he'd been court-ordered into treatment, he'd been mostly living an indoor life. Kaminsky had never even thought about winter beyond dislike of the term "white Christmas," which also happened to be the brand name of a particularly potent strain of freebase cocaine that had led to his presently reduced circumstances. He only knew that he had his own perfectly valid reasons for walking out of the warm little recovery circle in the church basement.

First and foremost. . . . there was the concept of gratitude. Should he be grateful for his room in the sober house on 16th Avenue South, a part of Minneapolis so bleak that it didn't even merit the word "ghetto," since ghetto implied at least community, for the money he'd spent? Should he be grateful for the unrelenting, unrelieved grayness of the sky, which he'd heard on good authority lasted until the middle of May? Should he be grateful for the so-called friends that didn't call just because he'd borrowed money from them and forgotten to inform them about it? Should he be grateful for his mother, who did call not to wish him joy of the season but to explain the lack of a Christmas check in the mail? "I can't enable you anymore, Sammy."

"That isn't love," he mimicked her, in a simpering, mocky, wheedle that male stand-up comics use when putting on a woman's voice. "Merry Christmas," he said, implying vicious air quotes around the word "Mom."

He was just about to kick a clump of black, hardened snow when he remembered his shoes—the good ones, with the butter-soft oxblood uppers and hand-crafted insoles, made in a small *bottega* in Tuscany and available nowhere else. He thought they'd be OK with a pair of thick socks, but the water was seeping right through them and showing his feet. He watched as he walked how the snowflakes landed on the tops of his shoes and disappeared. His mother had failed to be impressed with the purchase even when given its provenance. "They make your feet look small," she'd said. "Besides, who spends that kind of money on a pair of loafers?"

Stamping his feet to circulate the blood back into them, Kaminsky forgot to watch where he was heading and he lost the sidewalk, nearly walking into the sound wall that bordered 35 North. The shortcut, he thought, his sponsor Larry's favorite saying, turns into a dead end, as usual. He observed without much interest as a car came slowly down the street, coasting as if empty or out of gas. The noise it made when it crashed into a signpost startled Kaminsky out of his dishwater-colored daze, and he watched slack-jawed as a figure in bright red, its sleeves trimmed in white fake fur, came staggering out and sat down under the signpost. When he bent down to see if the man was OK, exhaust fumes of cheap vodka smacked Kaminsky's face. "Sir," he said, and touched the man's shoulder.

The man answered by pulling aside his white Fiberglas beard and vomiting. "Ha," he said, apparently pleased with his foresight in pulling aside the beard. Then his blue eyes rolled back in their red sockets and, looking unexpectedly comfortable, the man began to snore. Shaking him only made him swing his arms in belligerent circles.

Kaminsky retreated toward the car and turned off the still-running engine reluctantly because he savored its warmth. The glove compartment yielded nothing more in the way of ID than an empty pint bottle of Georgi. His gaze snagged on a large bag in the backseat. It was full of boxes wrapped in shiny paper, each box with a name on it. Attached to the bag was a card with an unfamiliar address. Someone's Christmas party. Clearly, they'd used the wrong agency.

Perhaps, Kaminsky thought, the address was for one of the gracious lakeside manors—in the Kenwood area where the kids, already sated with Playstations and roller-sneakers but still in need of entertainment, would be getting whiny and intrusive, pestering the caterer and interrupting the conversation of adults trying to sip their single malts in front of the high, many-paneled windows looking out over the lake. There would be discussion of politics and real estate deals, revenue bonds and rollovers—the things that made a city work. The men would lift their drinks with the well-lubricated motions of power-greased players, and the women would gleam in the burnished gold light of the enormous flagstone fireplace. Then the doorbell would ring, and standing there would be a young, sophisticated individual with a smile so infectious and a story so charming that one could only give him a seat by the fire, a slice of duck breast drizzled with white truffle sauce, and upon hearing of his admittedly somewhat intimidating East Coast background, a restaurant to manage. After all, any kid who could walk a mile in those shoes and not get them ruined had to know what he was doing. In any case, why go back to the green, mildewed smell of his so-called sober house. He hoisted the sack and went to wait for a bus, walking quickly to keep the cold off and trying to avoid the patches of ice and gravel, which would, he was sure, be the death of his leather shoe soles.

On Franklin Avenue, the street was empty, except for a few stray crackheads, disheveled and desperate. The only sound: the wind's invisible, monotonous whisper. He looked at the schedule on the bus shelter, but he didn't know what time it was and so had no way of knowing if he had just missed a bus, one was about to arrive or if he was stuck in between. It seemed as if he had just missed one because the next one wasn't anywhere in sight for a long time. His feet were getting damp and chilled; the socks, no protection. "Should I be grateful for my cold feet?" he muttered. His sponsor Larry's midwestern accent poked around inside Kaminsky's head: "You should be glad you have feet."

"Even if they're freezing?"

"You should be glad you're not in jail."

"For a few unauthorized advances?"

"You know what they do in jail? First thing, they take your shoes."

To keep himself from curling up inside the bus shelter, he pictured his triumphal entrance in the arched foyer, but the compassionate cooing of a hundred imagined trophy wives couldn't drown out the chattering of his teeth. Kaminsky was beginning to lose the feeling in his feet. The pain was receding, replaced by a cool absence. He was shivering, almost seizure-like, no hat on his head. But even if he'd wanted to turn back, he was as far from the boarding house as he was from his destination.

His teeth were clattering so loudly that he almost didn't hear the yellow cab pull up. "OK, man, get in. Merry Christmas." Kaminsky didn't have to be asked more than once.

"No money," he said.

"Like I said, man, OK, my one good deed. Besides, is no business today at any rate."

Kaminsky fell back into the intoxicating warmth of the car. It was like getting into bed after a bath, innocent, unafraid, someone coming to kiss you good night. The driver headed south for about 10 minutes. He wasn't sure of the address, but he told

Kaminsky it was far, almost Richfield. Kaminsky wanted to inhale the heat inside the cab, wanted to tuck his feet up under him and never, never leave.

Too soon, however, an unintelligible squawk came over the call box, and the driver leaned over to answer it. "OK," he said, "I've got to go to the airport, but you're very close—five blocks." Kaminsky checked the guy's hack license and imagined the check he would send him when he got back on his feet. The guy trying, say, to bring his mother to the States for surgery or his kids wanting piano lessons, and it looking like there was no way, suddenly a check arrives in the mail signed only "A Passenger."

"You're welcome," the driver said, laughing as if Kaminsky was some kind of good-natured fool for having forgotten the proper response to an act of kindness. Kaminsky began to walk. Five blocks would have passed in a moment in South Beach, but here, the blocks were long and wide, and the wind was slamming into his face. After three blocks, his feet inside his once-beautiful shoes began to fail him, as if they were rubber things, not his at all. He stumbled and didn't even bother to turn the collar of his jacket up. He let the needles of snow prick his neck. With the sack he was carrying, he could only get one hand in his pocket at a time, so he switched the bag from side to side. This was tiring but not tiring enough that he wasn't aware of the street he was walking down: distinctly unpatrician, lined with mock Tudor cottages and respectable limestone bungalows.

By the time Kaminsky got to the door of the house and double-checked the address, he'd abandoned his original scenario. The door would either be answered or he would have to go from house to house begging someone to call 911. That was the situation. He leaned on the bell with his elbow; hands were useless. After a taut, elastic moment, the door swung open.

A round, adult face, with the unmistakable small eyes of Down syndrome, shouted, "Santa's sick." A woman's voice called out, "Let him in please."

Kaminsky stepped inside the small, low-ceilinged house. To the right was a living area with pleather couches, armchairs and an old Zenith TV. The carpet was gray, and everything was soothing, clean and somehow generic. There were no knickknacks or picture frames that Kaminsky could see, no personal touches of any kind. On the couches, four or five men, all exhibiting varying degrees of mental disability, sat around in freshly laundered sweaters. They looked warm and well fed and, at the moment, much healthier than Samuel Kaminsky. The woman's face floated toward him. "The agency said you were unreliable. They didn't say you were an idiot. What did you do? Take the bus?" Kaminsky fainted.

Drifting back into consciousness, Kaminsky found himself looking at the star of

Bethlehem. It twinkled and shot out rays of light before resolving itself into a diamond nose stud on the face of the woman smiling above him. Ridiculously out of date, a nose stud, clearly not a diamond at all; still, he found himself drawn to its sparkle. Ten minutes later, the woman, having calmed her charges, was sitting next to him on the couch, while his feet soaked in a bowl of room-temperature water. Above his head, bolted to the wall, Kaminsky was reading the rules of the house. "Rule number one," it said, "respect." The woman kept laughing, even when the feeling came screaming back into Kaminsky's feet, and he moaned and winced and was generally anything but cool.

The woman, Linda, was not the glossy-haired creature he had imagined listening to the tale of his travels, but for some reason, perhaps because he couldn't think of one, he wasn't tempted to give her a less ridiculous explanation of his presence. "Wrong neck of

*Brothers watching daytime television, and perhaps some special holiday programs, 1954*

· · ·

the woods," she giggled when his imagined destination came tumbling, against his will, out of Kaminsky's mouth. "Welcome to the Olson Family Style Community Home."

"Linda," James called out from the kitchen, "is Santa too sick to give presents?" Some of the men looked at him. Some ignored him, rocking and humming to themselves. Kaminsky himself looked at Linda. She wore cat's-eye glasses, a homemade knit cap and, of course, the extremely out-of-style nose ring. Her whole look, in fact, could be summed up in the word "alternative." He and his friends had used this word with each other as a sort of code to mean "loser," implying hapless guys with rock star dreams or chicks with too many tattoos and non-aerobic midriffs. But Linda's laugh had a magic log effect, instantly whooshing the room into fire-lit coziness. He watched as she moved around the living room picking things up. He forgot for the moment that he prided himself on dating only resilient actress models and was struck by a longing to make a good impression on her. Perhaps by paying her a compliment, but what? He didn't think his usual line, "Your hair looks very expensive tonight," would impress her.

"You're like a server at a five-star joint," he observed. "You can take care of eight things at once without looking rushed."

"Yeah, but I don't get paid like one," she answered. "Now waiters make some good 'ching." She took away a can of caffeinated soda from one of the men saying, "Three's your limit, Scott. Anyway, do you think you could?" she asked Kaminsky. "The presents?"

"I don't have a costume," Kaminsky murmured.

"No problem," she said and tossed him a hat. Kaminsky put it on, the red tail of it flopping in his eyes, the base crushing the well-moussed and individually fussed-with strands of which, he had to admit, he was rather proud.

He looked around at the developmentally disabled men, the Mongoloids, the artistic rockers, the pudgy, strangely formed and utterly unglamorous guests at the party he had pictured all wrong. Samuel Kaminsky began to hand out presents. "Ho, ho, ho," he said.

When he picked out a present, he called their name out. Sometimes they needed help from Linda. They lunged at the gifts like cheerful Rottweilers after pork chops. They got three presents apiece, immediately discarding the socks and scarves without so much as a glance. But James got a wind-up, furry toy that squeaked and sent him into spasms of silent laughter. He wound it over and over again, until Linda put it away before he broke it. One guy, who resembled no one so much as Popeye, had gotten a small tape deck and some batteries. He immediately assembled it and began wrapping it with masking tape. Over this, Linda wrote in big block letters, with an exclamation point at the end, the name Bill. Bill hugged the cassette player to his chest, glaring, implicitly daring anyone to come and take it. Kaminsky couldn't remember when he'd seen anyone like their presents so well. Still, the entrepreneur, fallen on temporarily hard times, was finding reason to sulk. Linda was paying far too much attention to what she called her clients and not quite enough, in Kaminsky's opinion, to him, who had nearly died of hypothermia as a result of his heroic efforts to bring Christmas to their humble home, asking no reward except perhaps the phone number of the home's chief of staff, who was busy throwing away wrapping paper and whose nose ring was perhaps not out of date but merely classic.

Also, although he didn't like to mention it, Kaminsky hadn't gotten a present, not even a plate of homemade chocolate chip cookies, which was, he understood it, within his rights to expect pursuant to his job description.

"Are you bummed?" Linda looked at him, clearly amused. "Nothing for Santa?"

"Don't be crazy," Kaminsky said. He immediately regretted his word choice, not polite in the circumstances.

"I know. Scott, go into Andrew's old cubby." Here, she began to whisper.

"Really," Kaminsky demurred, "you're very"—he looked for the word—"thoughtful, but totally unnecessary." But by the time he had finished his sentence, Scott come lolloping out, holding a pair of snow boots. Kaminsky shrank. They seemed large and unruly, the linings frothing grungily over the tops, a myriad of eyelets and laces, latches and tongues boisterously flopping around everywhere.

"What happened to Andrew?" Kaminsky whispered. Linda whispered back, "Aneurysm."

"I don't know," he said.

"No," Linda assured him. "You lucked out." In almost a reverential tone, she added, "They're Sorels." Kaminsky dried his feet, grabbed some of the rejected socks and tried on the boots. His feet were instantly warm. He pressed his hand over his face, as if the light hurt him.

"What are you crying for?" Linda asked him.

Kaminsky couldn't think of a cover. "I'm crying," he said, "because these are such beautiful boots."

*Christmas dolls made this St. Paul girl happy, about 1903 (Sadie M. Ray)*

· · ·

# · 4 ·

# The Giving Season

———•———

## The Gift of Oranges

### BEATRICE FINES

*Oranges, unexpectedly, loom large in many holiday memories. Maybe it's because they were a rare treat, playing a once-a-year cameo role in the toe of a Christmas stocking. Beatrice Fines shares here a tender story, told by her grandmother, of kindness, gratitude—and oranges.*

His name was Peter Slevska, but we called him "the Galician." He lived alone in a cabin banked and chinked with manure about two miles from our homestead in northern Minnesota. When the other neighbors came in their wagons and sleighs for Sunday visits, I often heard them discussing the Galician's "outlandish" ways with Father and Mother, so I was a little afraid of him until a day late in November the year I was seven.

Father invited my sister Jennie and me to go to town with him. He did not often go to town, a distance of seven miles over a rough road. Even less often would he take any of us children. But this day he said Jennie and I could go. Still more wonderfully, he gave us each a shiny nickel to spend.

My little brother Jim cried at being left behind. "The girls will have to run behind the sleigh when they get cold," Father explained. "Your legs are a mite short for that."

"Don't cry, Jimmy," said Jennie, who was nine years old. "We'll bring you something special; wait and see." With that, Jim rubbed the tears away.

When we got to town, choosing something to buy wasn't easy. We stood with our noses pressed against the glass of the showcase in the General Store and gazed long and thoughtfully at the peppermints, licorice, and maple sugar bars. Then I noticed some fruit piled high on the shelf behind the counter.

"Look, oranges!" I said.

"Oh, I love oranges," said Jennie, "but those don't look as bright as the ones we had last Christmas."

"Don't they?" I asked. It was hard for me to remember.

"Perhaps they are a different kind," said Jennie. "You know, like Winesaps are different from McIntosh Reds."

"That must be it," I agreed.

When the storekeeper came we pointed to the fruit and asked him how much it cost. He answered, "Three for ten cents."

We looked at each other with glee. Three for ten cents! One for Jennie, one for me, and one to take home to Jim. We each gave him our nickels.

Father was still loading the sleigh, so after the storekeeper handed us the fruit, we sat down on a bag of feed near the door and started to eat our oranges. They would not peel, so we sank our teeth through the thick skin and bit a hole to suck them. They were unaccountably sour and bitter.

Our disappointment was too painful to face, so we tried to find a liking for the taste. But finally I said, "These are not good oranges at all."

Jennie nodded soberly. "Jim will be very disappointed."

Just then a pair of huge legs in rough trousers came into view. They stopped directly in front of us and we looked up into the wind-reddened face of a gigantic man. It was the Galician. Though he was smiling at us as timidly and shyly as a small boy, I felt a thrill of fear at being so close to him. He continued to smile at us for a moment and then pointed to the fruit in our hands.

"Why eat lemon?" he asked in his halting English. "Too sour."

Lemons! Of course, lemons! How could we have forgotten this bitter cousin of our favorite fruit? We stared at him, speechless for a moment. Then I confessed.

"We thought they were oranges. We had oranges last year at Christmas, and they were so good." I turned to Jennie in dismay. "Oh, Jen, what will we do? We can't give them back; we've bitten two of them. And what will we take back to Jim?" We couldn't ask Father for another nickel; money was much too scarce.

The Galician was still standing in front of us. He didn't understand all of our words, but he could read much from our stricken faces. Suddenly he reached into his pocket and drew out a small paper bag, twisted tightly at the top. He held it out with a bright, friendly smile.

"I trade you. Candy for lemon. Lemon I like. He smacked his lips loudly, convincingly. We gazed into his wise brown eyes. Then slowly Jennie reached out her hand, and Peter Slevska dropped the little brown bag into it. He picked up Jim's lemon, polished it on his sleeve and turned it this way and that, grinning.

"I got little girl like you," he said softly. "Little girl, little boy, too. Some day, I get money. They come live with me. Then you play with them, eh? You play with?"

It was then that Jennie gratefully made a promise that became a burdensome secret to both of us.

"We sure will, Mr. Slevska. We'll play with your little girl and boy all the time when they come. And Mr. Slevska, at Christmas you come to our house. We like company at Christmas."

Mr. Slevska's eyes glowed, and he nodded and bowed to us as he left. "Ya, ya, I do it," he said.

Just then Father came in and hurried us out to the now loaded sleigh.

Each night after that, snuggled together under our feather comforter, we discussed our invitation in hushed whispers. "If it were somebody else I'm sure Father and Mother wouldn't mind us doing the asking," Jennie would say, "but you know how they feel about the Galician."

"If we tell them how kind he was maybe it would be all right, but I don't want to tell about the lemons, do you?"

"Father would say we shouldn't have traded. He would say Mr. Slevska didn't really want the lemon."

"Do you think he did?"

"Well, at first he said they were too sour to eat. Then he said he liked them. I don't know," said Jennie.

Three days before Christmas the wind began to howl down the chimney in a particularly ominous way. Jennie and I pressed our hands against the frosted window and thawed a little place to look out. Plumes of snow were lifting from the fields near the house and swirling along with hard-driven flakes from the sky. We watched with heavy hearts. There would be no oranges for Christmas this year if the storm persisted. Father would not be able to get to town. But we were comforted by the thought that Mr. Slevska would not be able to make his promised visit, either.

The wind howled and the snow fell without ceasing all that night and all the next day. It stopped at last before dawn on Christmas Eve. The sun rose, sparkling off drifts that were piled high and deep around the buildings. We knew Father would not attempt to go to town.

In the afternoon he brought in the tree, a fragrant balsam from our own bush, and we decorated it with paper chains, apples, and popcorn. The next morning there were gifts: new knitted scarves and mittens for Jennie and me and a homemade sled for Jim. Mother had made Christmas pudding weeks before and we had a roast goose, but there was a kind of hush all through the house that was not in keeping with Christmas. Even Jim was subdued and quiet. About noon Mother paused during her preparations for dinner and stood, head raised.

"I keep listening for sleigh bells," she said. "It just doesn't seem like Christmas with no one calling around. I know we should all be thankful that we are snug and safe and have lots of provisions, but I keep wishing for company."

At that moment the dog growled softly in his throat, and a second later we heard a knock on the door. We all started in surprise. Father's face had a comical look of doubtful pleasure when he opened the door and there stood Mr. Slevska. Though his moustache was rimed with frost, he was beaming. He held out his hand to Father and his voice rang gleefully as a child's as he said, "Hello, hello. I come for Christmas."

Father opened the door wide but was still unable to find his tongue. Mr. Slevska came in, brushing snow from his trouser legs and taking off his heavy cap. He saw Jennie and me standing shoulder to shoulder behind the table and his big voice boomed.

"Ah! The little girls. Look!" He reached into his capacious pockets and began pulling out oranges, piling them on the table in a glowing heap.

"Too hard for you to go to town. But I go. Get oranges, my gift."

At last Father could speak. "How did you manage?" Mr. Slevska grinned proudly, rubbing his hand over his rough black hair. "Snowshoe. Strong, me." He patted his chest with both hands. "Long way from town. Keep oranges here in coat so don't freeze."

Father placed a chair for him. Mr. Slevska sat down, and after a while he began to speak wistfully of his family and his plans for them, touching our hearts with his unconscious revelation of a loneliness that was deeper than any we could ever know. If Father and Mother wondered what had prompted his visit and why he brought oranges, they did not ask. When the snow had blued with the coming of dusk, he struck off across the fields on his snowshoes, and we all stood in the doorway and called after him to come back soon.

Later, as I held my orange in my hand, not wanting to spoil its perfect beauty with any mark of tooth or fingernail just yet, I caught Mother watching me with a gentle, almost dreamy smile. "What a wonderful gift Mr. Slevska brought us," she said.

I knew even then that she did not mean the oranges.

———•◦•———

## "I was delighted with my presents"

*For many decades Anna Ramsey, wife of Alexander Ramsey, Minnesota's first territorial governor, wrote frequently to family members back East, including her daughter Marion and her grandchildren, Ramsey, Anita, and Laura Furness. Anna's Christmas letters suggest the relentless socializing and gift-giving required to maintain status amidst well-to-do Victorians. Today the Ramseys' fifteen-room mansion in St. Paul's Irvine Park neighborhood is a popular historic site, especially at Christmastime.*

*Nineteenth-century ornaments, some handmade by Alexander Ramsey's family*

* * *

*Anna wrote to Marion on December 29, 1875:*

My Dear Daughter,

Your box arrived safely on Monday morning: and the contents examined and admired. I was delighted with my presents and thank you very much. Shall do as you wish: Use them daily. That is the water-pot and coffee cup. Your Papa hesitates about using it daily: fearing some mishap may befall it: but I tell him the care I take of it: there will be no dangers.

Your letter of this morning gives me a full account of your doings on Christmas: your presents etc. I think you were highly favored: and should feel very happy to be so kindly and affectionately remembered

*To her granddaughter Anita, in boarding school in Paris, Anna wrote on December 23, 1894:*

How funny that I should have sent Mrs. Goodrich the same book you have sent Ramsey. For curiosity tell me how much you paid for it.

Packages have come from Aunt Helen—Chicago & New York. The first containing a pair of silver sleeve links for Ramsey fortunately, as he has broken one of those I gave him, & a silver belt pin for Laura. From Chicago—a "Delft" china animal for Laura & Harvard College for Ramsey. From N.Y., Washington Irving's *Sketch Book* & *The Alhambra* for Ramsey from Uncle Dawes, & from Aunts R & L a handsome striped silk sash from London. For Laura a little pin with an enameled bird, one of those Italian silk striped caps and some pretty colored bordered handkerchiefs with embroidered initials. I think a book from Uncle Dawes will come for her tomorrow. Aunt Hannah sent her a long silver chain for her watch. For Ramsey, she sent an imitation diamond pin, which I shan't let him wear, and I don't know whether to tell her or not. She may want to give it to some one else.... It doesn't seem more than half like Xmas without you. I can't tell you how I miss your suggestions about things.

Excerpts from Anna Ramsey letters
in the Alexander Ramsey and Family Papers,
Minnesota Historical Society

# Betsy, Tacy, and Tib Go Christmas Shopping

## Maud Hart Lovelace

*"We go shopping to shop." Not such a modern, mall-driven concept after all. It's what moti-vates a foursome of preteens in the Christmas season in this excerpt from one of Maud Hart Lovelace's stories about girls growing up in Mankato ("Deep Valley") in the 1900s.*

School closed for the Christmas vacation. That meant that Betsy, Tacy, and Tib had an important engagement. For years on the first day of Christmas vacation they had gone shopping together.

"Let's take Winona this year," Tib suggested.

Winona had come to be quite a friend of theirs. They often stopped after school to slide down her terrace, a particularly steep and hazardous one, or to play show in her dining room. Winona loved to play show; she was always the villainess.

"I'd like to take her," said Tacy. "She'd be pretty surprised, I guess, at the way we shop."

"She certainly would be," said Betsy, and all of them laughed.

"You see," Betsy explained to Winona when they invited her, "we usually make our Christmas presents, or else our mothers buy them for us . . . the ones we give away, I mean."

"Then why do you go shopping?" Winona asked.

"We go shopping to shop," said Tacy.

The three of them smiled. Winona looked mystified.

"We've done it the same way ever since we were children," said Betsy. "We always take ten cents apiece, and we always buy just the same things."

"What do you buy?"

"You'll see," said Betsy, "if you want to come along."

They liked to tease Winona because she was such a tease herself.

Winona's black eyes snapped.

"I'll come," she said. They made plans to meet the next day at a quarter after two. . . .

Winona was waiting in front of her house wearing a crimson coat and hat. She looked like a rakish cardinal against the snow.

"Does it matter," she asked, swinging her pocket book, "if I take more than ten cents?"

"Of course it matters. It isn't allowed." Betsy, Tacy, and Tib were noisily indignant.

"That's all I've got anyway," Winona grinned. "Just asked for fun."

"You go way back and sit down," Tacy said.

They started off down town.

The fluffy white drifts had packed into hard ramparts guarding the sidewalks. The four had to keep to the sidewalks after they passed Lincoln Park. The streets were crowded with sleighs and cutters. Chiming bells added to the Christmassy feeling in the air.

Front Street was very Christmassy. Evergreen boughs and holly wreaths, red bells and mistletoe sprays surrounded displays of tempting merchandise in all the store windows. In one window a life-sized Santa Claus with a brimming pack on his back was halfway into a papier-mâché chimney.

"Look here!" said Winona, stopping to admire. "This will tickle the little kids."

"The *little* kids?"

"The ones that believe in Santa Claus."

"Gee whiz!" said Betsy. "I didn't think we were *little* kids any more. I thought we were twelve years old; didn't you, Tacy?"

"I was under that impression," said Tacy.

"Why, we are! What do you mean?" asked Tib.

Winona knew what they meant.

"Are you trying to tell me," she asked, "that you believe in Santa Claus?"

"Certainly, we do!"

"Well, of all . . ." began Winona. She stopped, words failing her, and looked at them with a scorn which changed to suspicion as she viewed their broadly smiling faces.

"I expect to believe in Santa Claus when I'm in high school," said Tacy.

"I expect to believe in him when I'm grown up and married," said Betsy. "I hear him on the roof every year; don't you, Tacy?"

"Sure I do. And I've seen the reindeer go past the bedroom window, lots of times."

"You see," explained Tib. "We've made an agreement about him. We've crossed our hearts and even signed a paper."

"You three take the cake!" said Winona. "All right. I believe in him too."

They came to Cook's Book Store.

"We start here," said Betsy.

"Is that where we spend our dimes?" asked Winona.

"Mercy, no! We don't spend them for hours yet. We just shop. Choose a present."

"I know what I'm going to choose," said Betsy. "*Little Men*. I got *Little Women* last year."

They went in and said hello to Mr. Cook. His bright eyes looked out sharply under his silky toupee.

"You never pass me up, do you?" he said. He said it good naturedly though.

"This year we brought Winona Root. She's another customer for you, Mr. Cook," said Tib.

"Customer!" said Mr. Cook. "Customer! Oh well, look around."

They looked around. They looked around thoroughly. They read snatches in the Christmas books. They studied the directions on all the games. Tacy chose a pencil set, and Tib chose colored crayons.

"Choose! Go ahead and choose! Choose whatever you like," they urged Winona hospitably.

Winona chose a book about Indians. . . .

They went next door to the harness and saddle maker's shop. There wasn't much to choose here, just whips and buggy robes. Getting into the spirit of the game, Winona cracked a dozen whips before she chose one. Betsy and Tacy chose robes, with landscapes printed on them.

There was a tall wooden horse standing in the window. It was almost seven feet tall, dapple gray, with flashing glass eyes and springy mane and tail. Every year the harness and saddle maker let Tib sit on the horse.

He looked at her sadly now as she put her foot in a stirrup and swung nimbly upward.

"If the horseless carriages keep coming to town, I'll have to take that fellow down," he said.

That gave Tib an idea.

"I know what *I'll* choose then," she cried. "I'll choose this horse. I'll put him up in our back yard and all of us can ride him."

"Tib! What fun!"

"I wish I'd thought to choose him."

"It's a spiffy idea, Tib!" Betsy cried.

Winona had an idea even spiffier.

"Let's go choose horseless carriages," she suggested nonchalantly. "The hardware-store man sells them."

For a moment Betsy, Tacy, and Tib were dazzled by this brilliant plan. Then Tib scrambled down from the horse. Saying good-by to the melancholy harness and saddle maker, they raced to the hardware store.

Sure enough, there was a horseless carriage on display there. They inspected it from every angle, and the curly-haired hardware-store man let them sit in it for awhile. He was very obliging. All four of them chose it, and while they were in the store they looked at skates and bicycles.

"I could use a new sled," said Winona.

So they looked at sleds too.

At the Lion Department store they shopped even more extensively. There were many departments, and they visited them all. The busy clerks paid little attention to them. They wandered happily about.

They chose rhinestone side combs, jeweled hat pins, gay pompadour pouffs. They chose fluffy collars and belts and pocket books. They chose black lace stockings and taffeta petticoats and embroidered corset covers.

It was hard to tear themselves away but they did so at last. They went to the drug store where they sniffed assiduously. They sniffed every kind of perfume in the store before they chose, finally, rose and lilac and violet, and new-mown hay.

"I want new-mown hay because it's the kind Mrs. Poppy uses," Betsy said.

"Mrs. Poppy!" exclaimed Tacy. "That reminds me of her party. We'd better go to the jewelry store and choose some jewels."

"Goodness, yes!" said Betsy. "I need a diamond ring to wear to that party."

They hurried to the jewelry store. The clerks there weren't very helpful, however. They wouldn't let them try on diamond rings, or necklaces, or bracelets. They wouldn't even let them handle the fat gold watches, with doves engraved on the sides, which looked so fashionable pinned to a shirtwaist.

"They act this way every year," said Betsy to Winona. "Let's go to the toy shop. That's the nicest, anyhow."

The toy shop was what they had all been waiting for. They had been holding it off in order to have it still ahead of them. But the time for it had come at last.

At the toy shop it was difficult to choose. In blissful indecision they circled the table of dolls. Yellow-haired dolls with blue dresses, black-haired dolls with pink dresses, baby dolls, boy dolls....

Betsy, Tacy, Tib, and Winona had stopped playing with dolls, except on days when they were sick, perhaps, or when stormy weather kept them indoors. Yet choosing dolls was the most fun of all. They liked the dolls' appurtenances too.

They inspected doll dishes, doll stoves, sets of shiny doll tinware, doll parlor sets.

There was one magnificent doll house, complete even to the kitchen. Winona asked the price of it.

"Twenty-five dollars? Hmm! Well, it's worth it," said Winona thoughtfully, swinging her pocket book.

When they were through with the dolls they began on the other toys. Trains of cars, jumping jacks, woolly animals on wheels.

"Gee!" said Winona at last. "I'm getting tired. When do we spend our dimes?"

"Dimes!" said the clerk who had told her the price of the doll's house. "Dimes!" She settled her eye glasses on the thin ridge of her nose and looked at the four severely.

When she had turned away, Betsy whispered, "Right now!"

"I hope," said Winona, "we spend them for something to eat."

"We don't. But after we've spent them, we go to call on our fathers. And you can't call on four fathers, without being invited out to Heinz's restaurant for ice cream."

"I suppose not," Winona agreed. "Well, what do we buy then?"

Betsy turned and led the way to the far end of the store.

There on a long table Christmas tree ornaments were set out for sale. There were boxes and boxes full of them, their colors mingling in bewildering iridescence. There were large fragile balls of vivid hues, there were gold and silver balls; there were tinsel angels, shining harps and trumpets, gleaming stars.

"Here," said Betsy, "here we buy."

She looked at Winona, bright-eyed, and Winona looked from her to the resplendent table.

"Nothing," Tacy tried to explain, "is so much like Christmas as a Christmas-tree ornament."

"You get a lot for ten cents," said Tib.

They gave themselves then with abandon to the sweet delight of choosing. It was almost pain to choose. Each fragile bauble was gayer, more enchanting than the last. And now they were not only choosing, they were buying. What each one chose she would take home; she would see it on the Christmas tree; she would see it year after year, if she were lucky and it did not break.

They walked around and around the table, touching softly with mittened hands.

Betsy at last chose a large red ball. Tacy chose an angel. Tib chose a rosy Santa Claus. Winona chose a silver trumpet.

They yielded their dimes and the lady with the eye glasses wrapped up four packages. Betsy, Tacy, Tib, and Winona went out into the street. The afternoon was drawing to a pallid close. Soon the street lamps would be lighted.

"Which father shall we call on first?" Winona asked.

"Mine is nearest Heinz's Restaurant," said Betsy.

They walked to Ray's Shoe Store, smiling, holding Christmas in their hands.

# What a Christmas Shopper Saw

## An Anonymous Lady

*In 1915, downtown St. Paul was a consumer's mecca. With department stores, furriers, a music shop, jewelers, a rug merchant, an electrical appliance store—Sixth Street was the city's Mall of America. Little of it remains, but you can still find Borup's candies and Keljik's rugs elsewhere in the city. "An Anonymous Lady" dispensed Christmas shopping advice in this newspaper article.*

An especially good place from which to start a busy day is the Minnesota Phonograph Company's store at the very top of business Sixth Street. You can buy either a Victor or an Edison machine for a sum beginning at $15, and as for new records for the old machine—they are supplied to meet the needs and tastes of every one. There is a special list of records for this season, in English and in German—one double-disk record of the Westminster Chimes holds the very heart of Christmas. Especially for children is Eugene Field's "Jest Fore Christmas," together with two more Field poems. Lovers of the voice of John McCormack will want his superb rendition of "Adeste Fideles" this month. . . . And if you want a new and also extraordinary dance record, get "Ragging the Scale," a fox trot. It is a musical oddity in which the scale contrives to be a tune—a fascinating, infectious, keep-on-dancing tune. . . .

My stay in the gray and violet tearoom known as the "Violet Way," at 52 East Sixth, was too brief to tell me more than that the management believes in goods backed by personality, for the things sold for holiday remembrances are all known by the name of the maker, Mrs. Baldwin's fruit cake and mincemeat, Miss Burns' marmalades, and Miss Borup's candies, those names being guarantees of quality in all of us.

Victor Ekholm, 62 East Sixth, has all the other furs you may want to see, but what I am most interested in is his bear. It sounds rather a coarse, harsh fur, but nothing could be softer and silkier than a set of Russian silver bear, which is a real silver in color, with just a faint hint of the classroom brown closer to the skin. . . .

Just sixteen years ago, the firm of Keljik Bros., 64 East Sixth, came into existence, and today is the largest exclusive Oriental rug store in America. There isn't any sort or size of Oriental rug you can't buy there, and speaking of size, Mr. Keljik says the largest one he ever sold was an Ispeban rug from Constantinople, which weighed 410 pounds, the price of which he preferred not to tell at all. . . .

The T. V. Morean Co., 114 East Sixth Street, wants to sell you Flint River pecans for your dinner table and holiday greeting cards for your friends, but their real interest is in seeing that every one that has any need for glasses has his eyes fitted with the new Crooks' lens. This is an invention of Sir William Crooks of the X-ray fame, and is a chemical glass of a scarcely perceptible wine tint which shuts out all ultra violet rays, these being harmful to the eye. . . .

In the office of the St. Paul Gas Light Co., the big white enamel gas range which won the gold medal at the Panama exhibit generates enthusiasm of its own self, and to any woman who saw the electric bulb which lights the interior of one of its four ovens the sigh which greets the ultimate would come. Its cost? One hundred and fifty dollars. . . . If the bride be without a maid, she may serve her beloved his favorite breakfast, pancakes, without absenting herself from his side or filling her sitting room with smoke if some one gives her the new electric griddle, made of a composition metal which does not smoke and to which the cakes won't stick. If he prefers toast, she can have a toaster which automatically turns the slices, saving her from scorched finger tips. It also provides a place on which the coffee may be kept hot.

Electricity seems to be woman's particular servitor, for aside from all the devices by which it saves her labor, there is a set, comprising hair dryer, curler, and waver, guaranteed to help her be beautiful to Edison, a suffragist.

Directly as I entered the big department store of Mannheimer Bros., at Eighth and Robert, I saw a purple dog. Not a cow—but a dog. It has brilliants for eyes and a pearl pendant from its golden collar. Why a purple dog? I don't know, and I went immediately up-elevator to escape the haunting question. I met a French skating blouse of white washable satin with chiffon sleeves. It has moleskin collar, belt, and buttons, is meant for wear on the artificial ice rinks which are usurping the dance floors in Eastern hotels and cafes. Worn with it should be white kid boots with fur tops to match, and I hope Saint Paul opens its indoor skating rink soon. . . .

So many things I saw were for the use and adornment of women only that I asked to see articles of interest to men when I went into Bullard Bros. at 95 East Sixth. The newest and most useful of these is an auto cigar lighter, a vest pocket contrivance of silver in which a steel wheel against carborundum ignites an orange-colored cord. Any man, motorist or not, would value it for another use. Army men wear wristwatches and Mr. Bullard expects their use to widen—though slowly. . . .

There is only one place where more money can be spent in a given time than in a jeweler's, and that is in a furrier's. The firm of F. Albrecht & Son, Sixth and Minnesota streets, shipped out $12,000 worth of furs the day before I visited their Fur Shop, and you couldn't hardly notice it at all. . . . I gloried in fox for almost an hour, genuine silver fox, Arctic white fox, natural blue fox, red, taupe, gray, blues, London smoke, ash rose and pointed fox, as well as many other shades.

There was juvenile week in the St. Paul Book and Stationery Co., at 55–59 East Sixth. Fostered by the Y. M. C. A., the schools and some ministers revealed a book display for youngsters from the Mother Goose age, up through fairy tales and Boy Scout books to college stories—everything any child could or should have is featured. . . . And paper dolls, what little girl would enjoy a Christmas with no paper dolls in it?

Miss Berkheimer, 49 E. Sixth, looked up from fondling a wee jade elephant, which means luck, to say that plumes can't properly reappear until the vogue of small hats for all occasions is over. . . . Oddest concern I've seen yet is the corsage bracelet in whose clasp flowers, natural or artificial, may be held on the arm. I know that anklet bouquets are in vogue in some circles in New York, but the arm bouquet seems to me to be more apt to please St. Paul.

Of all the thoughtful little things I ever met, the after–9 P.M. street car schedule pasted inside the door of the cigar and confectionery shop of Philip Claus at Sixth and Wabasha is about the nicest. You get courtesy and careful service in this place always, and that makes all the nicer the good things to eat you can buy. I had a Claus luncheonette at a table while I waited for my box of pomegranates and kumquats to be packed. Just now nearly all the fruit comes from California, next month it is from Florida.

Schuneman and Evans is the last doorway into which I turn. I went downstairs to the basement here, on my way stopping to investigate a pile of gay color, which proved to be chopsticks, in celluloid, to be used as hair ornaments. A pair in jade green in black hair—I would like to wear them. Have you seen the glass baking dishes? Through their transparent sides you can see the condition of food as it cooks. It's a find to give to an ardent housewife.

———————

# "A day of excitement, of joy"

## HARRISON SALISBURY

*Veteran journalist Harrison E. Salisbury grew up in the now-vanished Oak Lake neighborhood of Minneapolis. Christmas meant visits to the fabulous Donaldson's Glass Block department store, as exciting as a trip to an amusement park, and to Holtzermann's, the "most German of German stores." Holtzermann's changed abruptly in 1917, when American soldiers began shipping out to Europe to fight in the Great War.*

Christmas was the event of the year for me. I don't know how old my sister and I were before we broke the custom of getting into one or the other's bed together trying to keep ourselves awake all night long on Christmas Eve, telling endless stories and waiting for the noises of the adults behind the closed door of the bedroom finally to cease so that we might silently slip out, hand in hand, through the mysterious heavy-scented darkness, through the dining room with its dimly gleaming silver and porcelain, through the living room where stockings hung bulging at the fireplace, and into the parlor—now a place of strange shapes and imponderable riddles, a Christmas tree silhouetted against the bay window, the scent of spruce mixed somehow with other fragrances—then tiptoeing back to bed, promising each other not to take another peek until the loud-ticking cuckoo clock struck three; probably sinking back into sleep and not awakening again until—horrors!—six o'clock, time to tumble into our parents' bedroom and wheedle them into staggering up, heavy-lidded, to set the fires going in the fireplaces, to shake up the furnace so that hot air began to billow up through the open registers and then, but only then, in heavy woolen bathrobes and fleece-lined bedroom slippers, to begin the ritual of the presents.

Yes, Christmas was *the* day of my childhood—a private day, really. Just the family. My aunt and uncle and cousin. Sometimes another aunt and uncle and cousin—if they were in Minneapolis. A day of excitement, of joy. Usually either my sister or I got sick. Sometimes both.

For weeks we had been building up to it. The anticipation started immediately after my birthday in mid-November. There were not-too-subtle warnings that Santa Claus was observing the conduct of young children with special care. And if one wanted his full attention and kind response, one had best give him no cause for displeasure—that is, eat your meals quietly and leave nothing on the plate, no joking or playing at the table;

go to bed swiftly at the appointed hour, no "five minutes more"; do your chores without being told; pick up your boots, don't leave them strewn about the kitchen; see that your toys are in their places in the cupboard or the window seat, and don't leave the building blocks scattered around; and don't complain about errands to the basement and the woodshed.

Well, there were many more admonitions and they changed a bit, year by year, but that was the start of Christmas. Then came the composition of the letter to Santa Claus, a serious occupation which required much thought. One should not ask for too much—that would certainly cause him to think he was dealing with a greedy child. But, on the other hand, one should try to remember to put on the list the things one really wanted—otherwise how could he know what presents were the most essential? The list was usually completed just after Thanksgiving Day. Then the pace began to quicken. There were visits downtown, perhaps to Donaldson's Glass Block, the nearest thing to Brighton which Minneapolis boasted. A sight of Santa Claus with his bell and his chimney (soliciting alms for the Salvation Army or the Volunteers of America). Sometimes—heavens—two Santa Clauses were spotted and that required a bit of explanation. But the climax of the pre-Christmas activity was the visit to Holtzermann's store. I don't know how I managed to square this most wonderful of institutions with my deep-seated germanophobia. Holtzermann's was the most German of German stores. It had been transported direct from the Black Forest. It was crammed from top to bottom with German toys (and there *were* no other toys in the years coming up to World War I). Somehow, possibly through Captain von Boy-Ed and his U-boat, or more likely by prudent advance buying, the stock of German toys, the mechanized animals, the Anchor blocks, the miniature trees, the small chimes which played "Stille Nacht," the lebkuchen, the pfeffernüsse, the gilded angels, the shepherds, the golden stars, and the crimson ornaments with German Christmas mottoes on them did not vanish in 1914. They went on through 1915 and 1916. Only in 1917 did Holtzermann's become more of a ghost than a store, with Japanese trinkets replacing the Black Forest music boxes and cuckoo clocks, but, miracle of miracles, the great basement bins of Dutch wooden shoes were somehow still filled to the brim. But no tin soldiers, no Prussian horsemen with their lances, no small leaden cannons, no banners and flags of grenadier regiments, no flaxen-haired dolls with slow-closing blue eyes, no stuffed animals with genuine leather hides. I did not cry on that wartime visit to Holtzermann's. I was too big a boy. But I felt like it. It was a dream vanished. A world that was never to return.

---

## "Can't fool Santa"

*The* Minneapolis Journal Junior *published articles and letters by young writers, including this 1901 Christmas memory.*

When I was but a small boy, I thought a great deal of Santa Claus. Christmas eve before I went to bed, I thought of a plan to get many presents. I found a stocking of large capacity and made a hole in the foot of it. Under the stocking I put a good sized box, thinking the toys would fall through into the box, and therefore it would take a great many toys to fill it.

The next morning I awoke early to see what Santa Claus had brought me. To my great surprise I found the box half filled with potatoes and turnips. For the first time I found out that it does not always pay to be greedy. But although I did not have the benefit of my peculiar present in one way, I did in another. I gave the vegetables to a poor woman living across the street who thought it a better present than the box full of toys would have been to me. So, I was satisfied.

Ike Swiler, eighth grade, North High School,
*Minneapolis Journal Junior*, December 21, 1901

*Children's letters addressed to Santa Claus, 1959*

· · ·

# "I dreamed I was in New Ulm"

## Celia Tauer

*Among many other, more pleasant things, Christmastime usually means a lot more kitchen work. For a servant in 1910 in a Summit Avenue mansion, household duties at Christmas expanded considerably. Celia Tauer, second cook on the James J. Hill household staff, wrote frequently to her beau, Henry Forstner, back home in New Ulm about her holiday workload— and the generous gifts she received.*

Saturday Eve 12–18–1910

Dearest Henry—

Your welcome letter reached me yesterday morning and see how you are coming a long these nice days. The weather up to now certainly looks more as if Easter was coming instead of Christmas, but I expect it'll turn suddenly and be bitter cold for Xmas.

This week we put in a good week's work. Wednesday evening the blowout came off. We had dinner for 44 and after that a dance for 75.

Tuesday we worked pretty steady as we had to make soup for that bunch for dinner and supper. Wednesday Mrs. Farley and Mrs. Miller came in so we tried to duck out of the worst parts. They had the rugs taken up in the music room & drawing room and also in the hall. As the two rooms are opposite each other, they dance from one to the other across the hall. After the tables were cleared in the big dining room, we cleared out a little bit, turned out the lights, pulled the drapes and started to waltz in there. Kept it up till one o'clock when it was all over.

Thursday Eve, 12–23–1910

Dearest Henry—

Received your letter yesterday morning and I guess I better get busy to get it in place before Xmas. Axel has to take some letters out for the ladies & he gave me 15 minutes time, then mine will go too. Don't think I'll do it quite as fast but he's got to wait that's all there is to it. . . .

And you think you was real good for the past year as you got a Xmas present a week a head of time. Well I got a package Tuesday so I must be pretty good too.

I sent you a little remembrance by registered mail Tuesday night but I imagine it reached you by this time. . . .

Wednesday Aft 12–30–1910

Dearest Henry—

Received your letter this morning and was patiently waiting for it. See where you got Xmas off & get a chance to go home and not dig all day. I guess as far as work was concerned I got my share. Saturday afternoon & evening Lena got off & Mrs. Farley came in to get the children's supper & dinner for the family. That of course she did but no turn more, so it left me quite a bit of extra work & kept me going till 9, but Axel helped me with the dishes & carried things in the ice box for me. Miss Rachel gave Lena leave to stay [away] all night & of course in the morning she'd miss the car & there I was left all alone again to all the breakfasts & having the Slades here too. Then I got mad & disgusted & didn't get in good humor till I got out in the afternoon. We had quite a big dinner for 11 & Saturday Lena thought I'd have to come home but I changed my mind by the time Sunday came. I thought who ever had a good time last night will have to work to-night & I get my share of good time too & so I did. I never before spent a more disgusting Xmas than this trip. But it's all over now.

Your package reached me Friday forenoon and it was just the thing that I needed and I'm very much pleased with it & ever so many thanks for the same. As a whole I was treated pretty good by dear old Santa. Got $15.00 from Mrs. Hill, a $4.00 glove board [?] from Miss Rachel, silk for a waist from Miss Clara, and $5.00 from Mr. Louis Hill, 2 corset cover, 2 boxes of chocolates, 2 aprons, a hat pin holder, a muffler and a dozen handkerchiefs, counting from 5 different parties. Besides I'm promised an emerald ring and Mrs. Blockle told me she had a package at her house if I call for it, so I guess it'll be tomorrow. I think that's about as good as he could have done with me. Everyone that went out to-day was chewing the rag to blow in their 10 spot, so I spose I'll do the same tomorrow if bargains suit. . . .

Xmas morning I dreamed that I was in New Ulm, but only had a few minutes time, and I met you on a bridge and I was going to speak to you. The alarm went off & that was the last of it. That's the way it goes when ever I have a civilized dream. Guess that's all for this trip.

Wishing you a Happy New Year. With deepest love
Your true loving Celia

## For their pleasure and amusement

*Literary critic and professor James Gray described the sad fate of his handmade Christmas present to his children on January 2, 1930.*

The holidays, conducted with a proper Rooseveltian strenuousness, end as always with the feeling that there is something rather wrong with sentiment in general or with the native interpretation of it. I am feeling particularly thwarted because the doll house which I, with unaccustomed patience, devoted the evenings of several weeks just before Christmas to making for the children has already been removed to the attic in such a state of ruin as never befell a French farm house during the war.

I had completed it in a high state of ecstasy, amazed that I had actually done it and feeling that at last I had found my creative level. The children immediately fell upon it with what seemed to me an especially revolting imitation of German Kultur and ripped apart the enchanting pieces of early American furniture that I had made out of the cardboard that comes in shirts from the laundry. I suffered in silence because after all I had theoretically been working for their pleasure and amusement. But yesterday the end came and in high dudgeon I carried it away to the attic where I shall probably retire from time to time to play with it quite peacefully and nicely by myself.

Letter, January 2, 1930, James Gray and Family Papers, Minnesota Historical Society

*Papa's Christmas—The Youngster: "Boo-hoo-ooo!*
*I want to play with my too-too-cars!"*

• • •

*Minneapolis Journal*, December 25, 1902

# Daddy's Gift

## EVELYN FAIRBANKS

*Evelyn Fairbanks, who grew up in St. Paul's oldest African American neighborhood, recalled yearly Christmas presents from an unknown friend of her father. "Daddy was gone," as she writes, but these generous gifts brought him back.*

I woke up to the sounds of Daddy. He would either be making a fire in our wood-burning cookstove, running water in the bathroom, or filling the coffeepot from the kitchen tap. When he got the fire going and the coffee on, he'd come back to bed for our morning talk.

It seemed to me that we talked about everything, but now that I think back, I know we really only talked about my life. I could tell Daddy all the things that I kept secret from Mama. Like about the time Donald Callender and I lay down on one of the pews in the back of the church whispering quietly so his sister, Danetta, couldn't find us. Of course, she started crying, and pretty soon we heard Reverend Callender calling Donald. Well, that was the end of that, but I sure was mad at Danetta and I told Daddy so. He thought it was funny. He must have thought a lot of things were funny, 'cause he laughed a lot. Except when he said, "Ba,"—I was nicknamed for Mama's sister Alice, who was known as Babe—"Ba', your Daddy sure loves you." I'd always frown and say, "I *know* that, Daddy." I acted as if it made me angry, but a warmth filled me every time he said it. And it still does, just thinking about it.

After a little while, we got up and Daddy went off to work at the commissary of the Great Northern Railway Company, where he was a janitor. When he came home from work, Daddy and I still talked a lot, but Mama was there, too.

This routine went on every day until one evening in January 1935 when I was six. Mama and I finished setting the table for supper and sat at the kitchen table looking out of the window for Daddy, because it was dark already. Daddy always got home before dark, even in the wintertime.

"Wonder what's keeping Mr. Edwards?" Mama said, more to the window than to me. (Mama always called him Mr. Edwards.) I started to worry then, not because Daddy wasn't home, but because Mama was worried.

We heard a sound on the front porch, and both of us turned that way, but then she said, "That's not your Daddy, your Daddy always comes in the back door. Must be somebody going upstairs. They sure are noisy."

Someone knocked on the door, real loud, and Mama said to me, "Ba', go tell those folks they knocking on the wrong door." Mama kept looking out the window for Daddy and I ran through the house, out into the hall. It seemed as if the entire porch was full of people, but the street light was in back of them and I couldn't tell who they were. When I opened the door I recognized Mr. Kaelble, our insurance man, with two other men. Mr. Kaelble and one man had their arms around the man in the middle. They started to follow me down the hall with me backing up in front of them. And when they got in the house, I saw the man they were holding up was Daddy.

Mr. Kaelble was talking and I was screaming for Mama. Then Mama was there asking questions. Mama told me to get out of the way and they took Daddy to his room and put him to bed. The other man went to the store to call the doctor.

While we were waiting for the doctor to come, Mr. Kaelble told us how he had found Daddy staggering and falling on the corner of Mackubin and Rondo, with a group of people standing around making fun of him because they thought he was drunk. Mr. Kaelble told them that Daddy didn't drink and that he must be sick and asked someone to help him get Daddy home. Mama kept getting up and going into Daddy's room and coming out again. I didn't say anything because I was scared, and pretty soon Mr. Kaelble stopped talking too. We just sat there and waited for the doctor. . . .

Daddy was gone, but he had left me a legacy in the form of a friend. The Christmas Eve after he died, right after dark, someone knocked on our front door. As usual Mama said, "Wonder who that is?" and I gave her my standard answer: "I don't know, Mama."

Mama opened the front room door and looked down the hall to the front door, but whoever was knocking was on the front porch, at the outside door. That meant it was a stranger. Everyone who wanted to see us came into the entryway and knocked on our hall door. And everyone who was visiting the people who lived upstairs went all the way up the stairs and knocked on that door.

Mama went down the hall with me right behind her and opened that door and called through the outside door, "Who is it?"

"Is this the George Edwards residence?"

Mama frowned as she stepped into the small entryway between our hall door and the outside door. I stayed in the hall.

She opened the door. A white man stood there in a dark coat covered with large snowflakes.

"Mrs. Edwards?"

"Yes, I'm Mrs. Edwards. But my husband passed on earlier this year."

"Yes, I know. Do you have a daughter named Evelyn?"

"Who are you?"

"I was a friend of your husband. He and I worked at the Great Northern commissary together."

"Oh, my goodness! Won't you come on in. No need to stand out there in the snow and cold."

"No, my wife is waiting in the car. I just wanted to drop this off for Evelyn. Her father talked about her all the time. I know that my coming doesn't replace him, but since he's not here . . ."

"Well, tell your wife to come in too."

I had just noticed that the man was carrying a bag when he handed it to Mama and said, "No, we've really got to go. This snow is really coming down and it's a long way home from here. Merry Christmas, ma'am."

"Merry Christmas to you, sir. And God bless you."

The man turned to go and then turned back.

"Tell Evelyn Merry Christmas, too."

Mama stepped aside to reveal me standing in the hall.

"Tell her yourself. Did you say what your name is?" Without waiting for an answer she said to me, "Evelyn, this is a friend of Daddy's."

"Merry Christmas. Your Daddy spoke of you often."

And I said, "Merry Christmas."

As the man left, we walked back in the house.

"What's in the bag, Mama?"

"How do I know, Ba'?"

"Open the bag, Mama!"

"Don't get so excited." Mama set the bag down on the front room table. I could see apples on the top, those big Delicious apples Mama loved.

"These sure are some nice apples."

"What else is in the bag, Mama?"

Mama took the apples out, and then an envelope. It was sealed.

"This has got your name on it."

She handed me the envelope. I just looked at it. I didn't ever get sealed envelopes.

"Well, open it, Ba'!"

While I was opening it, Mama said, "Mmmm, look at these big pretty oranges."

"Mama, there's a dollar in the envelope. A whole dollar!"

I had never had a dollar before, either. I didn't know what to do with it. So I just held it in my hand. Mama took the oranges out and then handed me a bag of hard Christmas candy. Christmas was about the only time Mama bought candy. Now we had two bags.

Then she took a package out of the bottom of the bag. When Mama unwrapped it we saw it was a chicken. So the man became "my chicken friend."

That was the first of nine times he showed up at our door on Christmas Eve, always with a bag holding the same contents. We found that he raised chickens, that he lived in White Bear Lake, and that his name was Anderson.

During my sixteenth year he didn't come and we thought he was sick. But the next year he didn't come either. By this time, I was old enough to realize I had never properly thanked him. And so I tried to find him. I called all the Andersons in White Bear Lake, but none of them was him. Or none of them admitted to being him. And so he left my life. His going had been as sudden and unexpected as his coming. But he had extended Daddy's love nine more years.

---

# "One more saving grace"

## CHERI REGISTER

*The world turned upside down for union meatpackers in Austin, Minnesota, during the protracted strike of 1959. The strike affected everybody and everything, including holiday celebrations. Christmas in that bleak year was especially memorable for "packinghouse daughter" Cheri Register, and it bequeathed her "a priceless souvenir."*

Throughout this commotion, Albert Lea was pelted by a driving rain that froze on the trees and road surfaces. On the wettest, most bone-chilling night, the National Guard opened the plant for several hours so that a contingent of strikebreakers, management personnel, and union observers could go in and finish processing perishable meat. TV newsfilm of officials ducking in and out of the plant, while thunder rolled and the rain refracted the lights outside, looked like a scene from a Frankenstein movie. The packinghouse made an appropriate house of horrors.

When the rain turned to snow and the snow softened the lay of the land again, life resumed something like a normal rhythm. I went to school, relished French class, tolerated algebra, and passed notes and flirted in science. I gave up *American Bandstand* long enough to practice a play in which Kathy Wicks and I played twins named Flora and Dora, roles that required us to dye our hair flaming orange. One day after play practice, I spotted Mom sitting in the Pontiac outside the door nearest the school's theater. "You have a brand-new nephew," she announced. Joey had given birth in a hospital in Mankato, and she and Rodger would be bringing little Jeffrey Alan to Albert Lea for Christmas vacation.

The shortage of Christmas presents would be more than offset by a new baby, the first member of the family's next generation. Nancy and Rog came home from Michigan, too, and the tension in the house was broken by baby cries and adult laughter. The guys spent much of their time hanging out at the Union Center, listening to stories over glasses of tap beer, while we females indulged ourselves in our new baby, whose downy little raisin face made sucking motions even while he slept. Visitors appraised him with the odd but familiar line, "He's so homely he's cute."

There was yet one more saving grace in our strike-burdened Christmas. Local 9 in Austin had collected the names and ages of all the children in Albert Lea's striking families and distributed them among its members. Each of us—1,700 kids in all—was to get one Christmas gift from a Hormel worker's family. They were delivered and sorted at Skateland roller rink, where we were to come on the Tuesday before Christmas to claim them.

I had never been to Skateland before. Much as I would have enjoyed roller skating, I understood that hanging out at a roller rink would taint the good reputation I needed to do well in school and to win the scholarships that would help me out of town. Skateland, a huge room with a chicken-coop roof, was now aflutter with noisy little kids. My friend Mimi and I stood in line, trying to maintain our fourteen-year-old dignity and feeling a bit miffed about being counted as children. Union sons and daughters fifteen and up had been offered a much better deal—one five-dollar bill apiece—and their line moved quickly because there was no matching to do. Mimi and I groused about our bad luck in being born too late and worried aloud about what strangers might choose for us. With a five-dollar bill, we could at least buy something we really wanted.

We had checked in at the door and been handed slips of paper with numbers that corresponded to our names on the list. At the head of the line, I handed over my numbered slip, now curled and sweaty, and the man who took it headed toward a pile of gifts along the wall. He returned with a rectangular package about five inches by three inches and I clutched it in my hand while he found a bigger present for Mimi. We carried our gifts off to a corner to open them. Hers was, as we feared, a poor choice. The single man who had signed the tag on her gift was obviously unfamiliar with teenage tastes and sizes. He had bought her a butterfly-bedecked sweater in a child's size fourteen. I ripped at the flap on the end of my present with growing apprehension. My heart thudded to my stomach when I saw what it was: a blue jewelry box with gold embossing on the top. Green, blue's mismatch, was my favorite color, and I seldom wore jewelry. I carelessly flipped open the lid. Inside was a five-dollar bill.

That moment of grace, an undeserved act of generosity from a family whose name I believed, in my youthful complacency, I would always remember, has stayed with me throughout my life as a restoration of faith in goodwill. It shocked me then that such kindness could come to me from Austin, the town we had learned to distrust. It surprises me now to think how little we teenagers expected from the common bonds of work and social class and union membership.

The jewelry box has stayed with me, too, a priceless souvenir of that long strike and a symbol of solidarity and compassion. In it I keep my other childhood treasures: the watch Grandpa and Grandma Petersen gave me for Confirmation the following spring, the one remaining cuff link from the beautiful melon-and-rust plaid dress my mom sewed me for the ninth-grade party, my first two-dollar bill, my high school class ring, my school honor pins, and the mink earrings Joey let me wear when I played dress-up. Whenever I open the lid, the memory spills out, and I am always pleased to relive it.

The Associated Press sent out a wire about the Christmas gifts at Skateland, and a file in the UPWA archives contains clippings of the AP story from around the country. The 1,700 names had been snapped up in less than an hour at Local 9 headquarters. The cost of each gift was to range from four to six dollars, and I doubt I was the only child whose benefactors broke that rule. "This act of human kindness will never be forgotten by these children," the Austin *Unionist* newspaper reported. This is one assertion I will not submit to fact-checking, but take as given on the strength of my own experience.

———◆•◆•◆———

*A familiar annual sight during the season for giving, 1956*

• • •

# In Stitches

## Sam Cook

*It's nice to get a homemade gift at Christmas. More often than not, this category of gift comes from a child of our acquaintance, and involves red construction paper, glitter, and a mess. But in this reminiscence, the fumble-fingered amateur craftsman is a married grown-up, and his wife is the warmly appreciative recipient.*

The frumpy old booties sag against one another in a corner of the closet. Once their ripstop nylon shells were orange and bright. Now they are smudged and torn. Once their goose-down filling was full of puff and bounce. Now it's droopy and matted. They should have been chucked long ago, I suppose. But to understand why they haven't been, you have to go back to the Christmas of 1974.

When the booties arrived in the cardboard box, they weren't booties at all. They were a few pieces of ripstop nylon, some clumps of goose down sealed in plastic, a couple of knit cuffs and a sheet of instructions. The box had come from one of those sew-it-yourself kit companies. To a guy who didn't know his bobbin from his zigzag. But I was excited. I was going to make my wife a pair of booties for Christmas.

I had time, plenty of time. I started in November.

I had moral support. A couple of women at work and the wife of a friend said they'd give me any tips I needed.

What I didn't have was skill. I found out fast that I wasn't a seamstress—or seamster—whatever you call it.

I set up a card table in an extra room, shut the door to keep Phyllis—the intended receiver—at bay, got out all my booty ingredients, and uncased the sewing machine. From the very beginning, that machine was The Enemy. And this was supposed to be a decent machine. Lord knows, Phyllis could run it. She could make that thing hum. She made herself all kinds of clothes that looked just like store-bought.

Throughout the ordeal Phyllis knew I was making her something, of course. So she'd stand outside the door and try to guess what it was. I'd sit inside answering, "No . . . no . . . no . . . How do you thread a bobbin?"

Like the tower talking to a pilot in an emergency, Phyllis tried to talk me through it from the other side of the door. When I realized it was useless, I put away my booty stuff and let her come in. We got the bobbin threaded.

Out with booty stuff again, on with the project. First, you singe the edges of the nylon with a candle flame to keep them from fraying, the instructions said.

"What's on fire in there?" the voice outside the door would say.

"Hey, get outa here!" I'd say. "Did Betsy Ross have to put up with this?"

Giggles.

Eventually I got the fabric singed.

Then we got down to the needlework. That's when The Enemy got vicious. It would miss stitches. It would refuse to penetrate a glob of material. Or it would run amok, like a car with its accelerator pedal stuck.

I broke needles. I broke out in a sweat. I said bad words.

It wasn't all my fault. If ever a machine was made that was sexist, it was a sewing machine. They're built for slim little woman fingers with nice, pointy fingernails. Ever try to run one with pudgy little boy digits and smushed, bitten nails? Hopeless.

Each night I'd come home, eat supper, and report to my cell. I hated those booties. I hated that machine. Finally, I could stand it no more. I boxed up my booty stuff, cased up The Enemy and drove directly to the sewing machine store. I told the man what I was up to. I told him my problems.

"Hmmmmm," said the sewing machine man. He looked at the machine for a long time. "Tell you what," he said. "Why don't you trade this unit in on a new one and give your wife a real nice present?"

I nearly took his head off. I'm sure he meant well, but at the moment it just wasn't what I wanted to hear. When I calmed down, we talked rationally again. Something about a good cleaning and an alignment.

"Now we're talking," I said.

Back to the cell.

Finally, The Enemy and I began to see eye to eye. The machine was less belligerent, and I had decided to give it another chance. We had become friends, a team. We drilled those little stitches, 10-to-the-inch just like the instructions said. Make a seam. Stuff in the down. Make a seam. Stuff in the down.

I quit sweating. I quit swearing.

The booties began to look like the ones in the instructions. Finally, we stitched on those knit cuffs. Ta-dah!

It was still a few days before Christmas. Not since I was a kid had I waited with such anticipation for the day to arrive.

I was squirming when Phyllis began tearing the wrapping off the package. I relived the entire process as she stripped the paper off: the initial excitement, the frustration, the hate, the success.

She popped the lid off the box and stared at the booties. She loved them.

Never, before or since, has the giving of any gift thrilled me as much.

Every winter evening, Phyllis padded around the house in those things. Her feet were even warm when she got in bed at night. She wore them until they were tattered and battered, and she got another pair for a gift, fancy blue ones with padded soles and drawstring tops.

She still keeps the old orange ones in the corner of her closet. Both of us know why.

———————◆—◆—◆———————

# A Cut-Glass Christmas

## SUSAN ALLEN TOTH

*Christmas can be exhausting. Joyous, gratifying, uplifting—yes. But exhausting, too. Writer Susan Allen Toth admits that the season wears her out, but she can't bring herself to ignore its many demands. A memorable childhood Christmas stands out in her mind and reminds her of the holiday's true meaning and value.*

The December after my father died, when I was seven and my sister was nine, we worried about Mother. We knew she was going to feel bad on Christmas Day, and we wanted to do something special but we didn't know what it could be. We huddled in the bathroom, whispered in corners, argued intensely in our bedroom after lights out and—unusual for us—at last came to an agreement. We would be Mother's Santa; we would fill a stocking for her just as she did for us. How surprised she'd be on Christmas morning to see her very own stocking hanging there on a drawer pull of the maple bureau in our living room! We felt sure that would cheer her up.

A week before Christmas we emptied our piggy banks and set out for Woolworth's, where we always bought our presents. Woolworth's was the Santa-Claus-and-

Christmas-tree part of Christmas. It blazed with lights in the after-school dark, smelled of peanuts and popcorn at a counter heaped for the season with chocolate-covered cherries with cellophane-wrapped, red-and-white candy canes, rang with "Jingle Bells" and "Hark! the Herald" on a radio turned up loud near the cash register. Every year we each were allowed to pick out one new ornament from the tree-trimming counter, where we fondled brilliant glass balls, folding tissue-paper bells, and colored electric lights that bubbled when you plugged them in. No other store . . . had the glitter and gleam that Woolworth's had at Christmas.

First we headed for our two traditional counters for Mother's presents—cosmetics and kitchen utensils. Although Mother never wore make-up, I wouldn't give up hope, encouraging her with a fake tortoise-shell compact of red rouge or a tiny bottle of Evening in Paris perfume or a set of mascara brushes. My sister was fond of small silver funnels, metal straining spoons, glass measuring cups. But this Christmas we felt none of our usual gifts would be quite right for a special stocking. We wandered up and down the rows, pondering pencil sharpeners, packaged stationery in floral cardboard boxes, little china dogs that were really salt and pepper shakers. We rejected a card of assorted needles from England, a fat red pincushion with an attached strawberry-shaped emery ball, an earring tree. The tree was gold-colored metal and spun on a plastic base, but unfortunately, our mother did not wear earrings.

At last we found ourselves together, discouraged, at a back counter, hidden behind toys and semidarkened under a burned-out fluorescent light, where Woolworth's kept its glasses, dishes, pots and pans. We knew we couldn't afford a teakettle or a frying pan. Mother used empty jam jars for glasses and she didn't need any more silverware. But suddenly we both saw at the far end of the counter a section of cut-glass dishes—not just plain round cereal bowls, but jagged and deeply carved, dark-green glass. Small bowls were ten cents; a size big enough for soup or oatmeal was 20. I hurried to the end of the counter, where it was brighter. How the glass shone! My sister agreed that the fancy dishes were unlike anything Mother had. With our allowances pooled, we could buy six small bowls and two big ones. The clerk at the front packed the dishes carefully in newspaper and warned us to unpack them gently. The edges were sharp, she said. We hurried home in the dark, happy and warm inside with our secret. Eight cut-glass bowls! Mother would never have had such a Christmas!

On Christmas Eve my sister and I faced our only other problem—what to use for Mother's stocking. We each had a red felt Christmas stocking, hung year after year, but we hadn't had enough money to buy one for Mother. While she was washing dishes after supper, we tiptoed down the hall to her room and began to rummage through her dresser drawers. . . . Mother had several pairs of sensible cotton and wool anklets, but none of them seemed big enough. We could barely fit one small bowl into each sock. My sister lifted out a cardboard packet. "What about these?" she said. We looked at each other, then at the beige nylon stockings, never worn, folded neatly around the cardboard. Mother didn't have many nylons; this was just a few years after the war and they were still expensive. But we knew these stockings would be big enough to hold our dishes. "I think if we're careful, it'll be okay," I said. We tiptoed out of the bedroom with the nylons hidden under my sister's skirt.

Early Christmas morning we crept quietly out of our beds, scarcely breathing as we passed Mother's door, desperately hoping she wouldn't hear our feet on the creaky wooden stairs. In the living room we hurriedly stuffed her stockings, using both nylons, yanking them wide to accommodate the jagged edges of the cut-glass bowls. We didn't try to hang them up. They were too heavy. Instead we propped them against the bureau that we used for Santa in the absence of a fireplace. Then we looked at the bulging stockings, grinned with pleasure at each other, and ran to call Mother.

When she sleepily entered the living room, her eyes were immediately riveted to the bureau. Two green cut-glass bowls hung precariously over the tops of her stretched, snagged, new nylon stockings. "My!" she said. "Did you girls do all this?" There was something odd in her tone, but she quickly recovered. "What absolutely beautiful bowls!" she said admiringly, sitting down on the floor and taking them out one by one, setting them in a row on the floor for us all to enjoy. She hugged us both. We were so proud we had pleased her. "You are wonderful girls to have thought of this, and I love you both very much," she said. She ignored the empty stockings on the floor beside her.

Now a mother myself, living alone with a nine-year-old daughter, at Christmas I think of many things, but always I remember that Christmas of the cut-glass bowls. To me it shines as a beacon my mother has left me, a beacon to guide me through the maze of conflicting feelings, emotional demands, free-floating guilt and worry that afflict me at this time of year. When my mother looked at those ruined stockings and ugly cut-glass bowls, which eventually disappeared into the deep recesses of her bottom shelves, she knew what Christmas was all about. "I love you both very much."

I am always tired after Christmas. Sometimes I get cranky, catch cold, come down with a headache—signs of stress, I do not need to be told. It may be foolish to try to cram so much into an already bursting schedule, to sandwich concerts around exams to be graded, plum pudding between cards to be answered, a long walk under starlight when presents are waiting to be wrapped. But I cannot bring myself to give up any more of Christmas than I am absolutely forced to. I fervently pack it all in as my sister and I stuffed those glass dishes into Mother's stretching nylons so many Christmases ago. Like my mother, I want to set out the tokens of love on the living-room floor, look past their gaudy color and cut-glass gleam, ignore the ruined stockings that held them, and remember why they are there.

———◆◆◆———

*Bustling shoppers at the Golden Rule department store, St. Paul, 1961*

◆ ◆ ◆

# Gifts

## Maura Stanton

Lilac, lavender, lily of the valley—
I lift the soap up to my face.
I'm Christmas shopping for my aunt,
forced to discontinue chemo,
hardly able to keep food down.
I used to send her panettone,
boxes of glazed apricots,
or lavish travel books on Ireland—
things I thought a nun would like
to unwrap after midnight mass.
But the many worldly objects
I've fingered in a dozen shops—
hand-blown glass, engagement books,
tote bags stenciled with sleeping cats—
seemed so wrong I stepped into
this fragrance store for inspiration.
And yet a wave of guilt chokes me
as I give my credit card to a clerk
for this little stack of boxes,
wildflowers sealed in glycerin,
hand-milled distilled carnations,
lanolin ovals of English violet.
Is this to be my final gift?
The clerk hands the card back.
My thumb runs over the numbers
embossed on the slick front,
and with a tingle I remember
stroking my aunt's holy cards
enclosed with childhood birthday presents,
pictures of Mary dressed in blue

bending over the swaddled child,
or martyrs smiling serenely
from the rack, their legs broken.
My favorite scene was Jesus
surprising his mother in the Temple,
his expression rapt and tender
as he taught the amazed elders.
I'd stroke the textured halos
around the sacred heads, as if
sanctity might rub off on me
absorbed through my human skin.
Now it's only money's ghost
I touch, slipping my card
back with others into my wallet,
before I grab the paper bag
off the glass counter, hoping
in spite of my devouring gloom
that my aunt's face is shining
like the saints, that this soap
smells to her of heavenly gardens.

---

# "Promises of bright, warm days coming"

## SAMUEL HYNES

*After his family settled in Minneapolis, literary critic Samuel Hynes attended staid Christmas morning services at the Presbyterian church prescribed for him by his father, not the Catholic services of his stepmother, Nellie, and his brother, Bill. Reflecting on "the other part of Christmas—the part that was Jesus' birthday and a winter festival, too, the feasting and present-giving part"—he concludes that "in childhood, all Christmases are one."*

Worship at Aldrich [Avenue Presbyterian Church] was a wintry duty; even Christmas was a bleak occasion there. Nellie and Bill and the girls would go to Midnight Mass on Christmas Eve; I'd hear them coming in late long after I was in bed, laughing and chattering. But there was no Midnight Mass for Presbyterians. Our service was early on Christmas morning, so early that we trudged to church in darkness, hunched in our mackinaws, woolly hats pulled down against the wind's sharp edges. Up ahead we could see the church windows casting their paleness across the snow, the only lights in the dark street. Inside, as we sat in our pew, the windows were still night-colored and opaque, and shadows gathered in the corners of the room and under the high roof, in spite of the hanging lamps.

The Christmas service was always the same: the familiar carols, the manger story from Luke, a sermon that was last year's sermon. The Reverend Nelson must have felt the worn familiarity of what he was doing; one year he tried to give the service new life. At the end, after the sermon and the collection, he asked us all to stand in a circle round the aisles and then to come forward in turn, receive a small candle, and light it from a big candle by the pulpit. Slowly the rotating circle of the congregation became a circle of little lights, shining up into faces and making them warm and bright. When it was complete we stood holding our winking candles and sang "Silent Night." It was pretty, but it was something more—it was a kind of ceremony, a ritual such as I had never seen in that church before. For a moment, we had made our Presbyterianism beautiful.

By then dawn was breaking, leaking into the church through the tall windows; I could see the ascending Christ floating grayly against the cold half-light. Reverend Nelson stepped into the pulpit. "These candles," he said, "are the light of the Christmas spirit. Take them out of this church into the world to spread that spirit wherever you go." We filed obediently to the doors at the back, holding our little flames, and out into the winter grayness. Every candle was immediately blown out by the whipping wind. We walked home toward the morning, each carrying an extinguished candle stub.

The other part of Christmas—the part that was Jesus' birthday party and a winter festival, too, the feasting and present-giving part, the part that chooses the dark time of winter as a day when winter-dwelling folks can turn to each other and say, "Eat, drink, this won't last forever, spring will come," and give each other presents that aren't birthday presents but promises of bright, warm days coming—that part began as we walked home. The sun was up by then, and the sky was a cloudless palest blue. Through windows along the block I could see lighted Christmas trees; in our house a fire would be burning in the living-room fireplace. As we came in, stomping the snow from our feet, noisy with expectation of presents, Nellie would say firmly: "Breakfast first, everybody needs a hot meal in the morning!" One more duty before pleasure, adults making kids wait. But endurable, because from the dining room I could see the presents in a drift of bright paper and ribbons under the Christmas tree.

There are no particular Christmases in childhood, all Christmases are one, all happy in the same way: the same excited anticipation, the same joys of having on this day more than you expect or really want—more presents, more food, more affection (that's what the presents and the food express in reticent families). For one day the make-it-do-or-do-without rule doesn't apply. In one long tinseled, colored-lighted, tissue-paper-wrapped morning I am given: a toy furnace that melts lead and casts toy soldiers, a chemistry set, Tinkertoys, Lincoln Logs, an Erector set, Big Little Books, Tootsie Toy cars, a dump truck that really dumps, skates, crayons, a magic blackboard that erases itself, a Lionel train, skis.

The skis are special: long, grown-up skis, so special that Nellie takes my picture with them, and notes on the back: "Sam Jr., Christmas 1936. New 7 ft. skis." I stand by the front steps, dressed for skiing—knitted hat, warm jacket, wool knickers, mittens. The bright winter sun casts shadows of tree trunks across the snow. With my right hand I hold the skis upright, the tips two feet higher than my head. They are of dark wood, and heavy looking, with a leather toe strap to hold them on my feet. I will cut two thick rubber bands from an old inner tube and run one under each toe in front of the toe strap and around my heel, and these will be my bindings. With them on I will ski the slopes of Powderhorn, and try the lower, easier jumps. But for the moment of the picture I stand, proud and determined, older and more courageous than I was before Christmas because I own seven-foot skis.

When the Reverend Nelson preached to us about Christmas, he got one thing wrong, I thought; Christmas isn't a time of giving, it's the year's great feast of getting, a day when things pile up around you, more than you can ever play with, or read, or eat. Of course you have to give presents or you won't get any, I could see the justice of that. But buying presents was easy, you just gave people the same thing you gave them last year: bottles of Evening in Paris perfume from the drugstore for my stepsisters, a Big Little Book for Chuck, a tie for my father, a handkerchief for Nellie. It didn't matter what you gave them, a present was a present.

One gift I gave that Christmas when I was twelve was different. I didn't buy it in a hurry, any old-way, I *chose* it, and took pleasure in the choosing. And it was a grave misjudgment. Walking through Dayton's in the present-buying season, I wandered into the picture department and was struck by a framed motto:

*A friend is not a person*
*Who is taken in by sham:*
*A friend is one who knows your faults*
*And doesn't give a damn!*

The special beauty of it was in that "damn!" Frank, blunt, a little daring—like Nellie. Just the right present for her, I thought, and I bought it. On Christmas morning she opened the package, read the motto, thanked me, and went to hang it on her bedroom wall. It hung there for a day or two, or possibly three, and I went up to admire it. Then it was gone, and in its place was a motto that my stepsister Rose Marie had given her:

*A mother's love is like a precious rose,*
*With sweetness in every fold.*

That, I saw, was what you did with a present you didn't like; it was how natural kindness dealt with mistakes.

After the presents, after the blizzard of torn tissue paper ("save that piece, we'll use it next year"), after the carrying off of new possessions to bedrooms to be gloated over, Christmas dinner: turkey with bread stuffing and giblet gravy, mashed potatoes, candied sweet potatoes, cranberry relish, watermelon pickles, pickled peaches, pickled crab apples, homemade rolls. No green vegetables, of course, and no salad: it's winter, and this is farmhouse winter food—at its grandest, but still farmhouse, still winter. My father sits silently for a moment gazing down at the turkey, thinking perhaps how much it cost, or how he'd like a drumstick this time, just for a change, or maybe that this is how life should be all the time, this generosity, this bounty that loads our table. He looks round at the faces of his family, shining with gifts received. Then he launches into his grace: "Lord, we're here today . . ." I lower my head as I'm supposed to, but peep out at the steam rising from the dishes, the turkey and the gravy, the potatoes (two kinds), the rolls. He finishes his prayer, waits while Nellie rattles through hers, then stands, solemn as a preacher in a pulpit, and begins to carve. I am very happy: happiness is this rich having; having is happiness.

By now it is midafternoon, the sun low in the elms on Pillsbury Avenue, the shadows on the snow blue cold. Adults go to their bedrooms for a nap; children run out into the fading day to try out skis or skates, or up into the attic to put the train together, or into the cellar to make lead soldiers and chemical stinks. Christmas has passed its highest moment, gone beyond the excitement of expectation to the diminished, because real, excitement of fulfillment. What I wanted, I have. But having is never as good as wanting, I know that by now. The day will end soon, the last light will fall into darkness; there will be another meal—the same food, but less wonderful now because it isn't Christmas dinner anymore, it's only leftovers—and then something on the radio, or a family game in the living room, and then bedtime, the year's best day done. But not completely, the happiness still floating in the air, the day's special affection still enclosing us. We have had another Christmas, just like the other ones, or so nearly like as to be indistinguishable in memory, a ritual that will be performed again next year, and every year. I take it for granted that this is the right way to celebrate Christmas, the only way there is to act out with food and gifts what we feel, or ought to feel, for each other.

*Several generations of families, with hired help, gathered to open presents around the tree, 1910*
*(Chester S. Wilson)*

· · ·

## A Juvenile Delinquent's Christmas

*William Cummings, age 16, had a tough December holiday season in St. Paul.*

Monday, Dec. 10, 1934. Went to school today. Got caught [by] special dicks [detectives] for lifting overcoats. Got expelled from school. I got put in jail (East Side Jail, Minneapolis) at 2:30 P.M. Didn't have a good supper. Called up Mother to tell her where I am.

Tuesday, Dec. 11. The cops took [me] in a police patrol car to the Hennepin County Jail at nine A.M. I stayed there until 5:30 P.M. Then two St. Paul police came to get me. They took [me] to the St. Paul Jail. Had a good cell.

Wednesday, Dec. 12. Sat around all day in my cell with Bruce Crosby, a 17 year old "gangster." We just talked & read. Hedsnicker & his assistant took me around to get all the overcoats I sold. The food is rotten here.

Thursday, Dec. 15. Hedsnicker & his assistant took [me] around to get some more coats. In the afternoon they took me to the court house. Hedstrom my probation officer took me home.

Christmas, Dec. 25. Received presents from:

> Grandma Gold—shirt, socks, hankie,
>     diary & key case.
> Grandpa Cummings—handkerchief.
> Lola Jean—fish.
> Ann—snail.
> Art Oltman—socks.
> Daddy—skys [skis].
> Mother—pen.
> Jimmy Hadlow—tie.
> Jeanette Cummings—tie clasp.
> Jeanete Joachum—tie.
> Aunt Peg—handkerchiefs.

Excerpt from diary, William M. Cummings Papers, Minnesota Historical Society

# The Gift

## KEVIN KLING

*Humorist, playwright, and Osseo native Kevin Kling is justly celebrated for hilarious stories about his childhood, but this is a Christmas story about grownups and the gifts—the real and the not-so-real—that we give each other.*

In "A Child's Christmas in Wales," Dylan Thomas said that he can't remember whether he was six and it snowed for twelve days or he was twelve and it snowed for six. I know the feeling. Often when I ask my memory to serve me, it doesn't always bring what I ordered. But luckily I'm from Minnesota so I figure it's probably what I really wanted anyway.

One December a few years back I was flying home to Minnesota from a whirlwind European romp. After dancing in the all night discos of Barcelona, a sudden discovery of my recessive Latin genes, I badly needed some rest from my vacation. The plane circles St. Paul, and a familiar sight welcomes me; a white blanket of snow covers the earth. I'm home.

Next to me on the plane are two Spanish women who are looking out the window at the frozen landscape and talking in very concerned tones. This is not home for them. I assure them there is nothing to worry about, it's just weather. The plane lands, and as we wait to file out, the rear door opens and in steps a large human form, covered from head to foot in a snowmobile suit, scarves and mittens. He's there to collect the garbage. There is a white frost circle where he has been breathing through his mouth and the only exposed flesh is the end of his nose, and it is white, frostbitten, a gonner. His presence has taken the European women aback. One woman asks, "Is it cold?"

"Well," says the form, "I'd wear a coat."

I'm home.

I get in a cab. Instead of going directly home, I tell the cabbie to take me to the Uptown bar, and see what the lads are up to. As we drive I mention it's great to see snow. The cab driver sarcastically tells me to feast my eyes. His cab driver identification badge says his name is Said, he's Egyptian, so I ask if he ever gets homesick. "Oh," he says, "very much." I ask him what he misses most, and he says his language. He says, "Our language is like music." I ask him to speak for me and he's right, it is music and Said is a wonderful performer. I tell him our language is like music, too, not English per se, but the Minnesotan dialect to me is music.

In the rearview mirror I can see in his eyes a clear look of disbelief. So I decide to help him out, teach him to speak like a Minnesotan. It's a technique based on the method devised by Henry Higgins to help Eliza Doolittle learn proper British in *My Fair Lady*. Dr. Higgins has Eliza repeat, "The rain in Spain falls mainly on the plain." In this case the dialect is Minnesotan and the sentence is derived from a conversation overheard in a convenience store. It goes like this: "I ain't gonna pay no dollar for a corn muffin that's half dough." Say that five times and you're on your way to speaking with the nuanced rounded *o*'s of a true northlander.

We arrive at the Uptown, in those days a truly working class establishment. B-girls still sat up at the bar—women, who for a drink and a couple bucks, will tell you how interesting you are. They are true sirens and few can resist their art of conversation. One time a B-girl told me in confidence that she liked her men like her coffee . . . stupid. Behind the bar is a cash register decorated with bad checks, tickets to a meat raffle, and a jar of pickled eggs that are old enough to vote.

The clientele at the Uptown is for the most part on the wide end of the economic pyramid. Troubled men and women who sat over their highballs staring into the glasses like ice fishermen waiting for a bite. The Uptown bar is a hub of contemplation more designed for the incubation of ideas than the actual hatching.

I sit at the bar. Next to me is a guy named Larry. I've been going to the Uptown for years and I've never been in there without seeing Larry. Sometimes I'll be driving past and wonder if Larry is in there so I stop and peek. He is. One time I accidentally saw Larry outside. It was a horrible sight, Larry in daylight. He looked lost and like the sun was trying to kill him. I wanted to throw my jacket over him and breathe smoke on him until we could get back into the bar.

Larry turns to me, points to the waitress, and says, "I've got fourteen personalities"—he did, easily—"I got fourteen personalities and each one is in love with her." He points to a waitress. She smiles and it's obvious she's in love with all fourteen of him. I decide to fade into the woodwork and leave the two lovebirds alone.

I sit at another table and take out my Christmas list and run down the names. I want to get my brother-in-law something good because every year, whatever I get him, he says, "Well, that's different." "Different" is Minnesotan for "what are you thinking?" This year I decide to get him something that actually is "different" so when he says it I won't feel so bad. For instance, I saw this bird feeder in a magazine that is shaped like Prometheus. You put him on a rock and the food goes on his liver and every day the birds come and peck it out. Or there is a bumper sticker I saw with a picture of the Pillsbury doughboy and an inscription in gothic letters, "He is Risen." I feel guilty I've put this off 'til the last but "Guilt is the gift that keeps on giving."

My favorite gift-giving story is from my friend John Van Orman, who is an ethnomusicologist. It involves a group of aboriginal people in Borneo. John told me of an anthropologist who lived among this group in the wilds of Borneo. They gave dances as gifts—dances to each other, to other villages, to their wives or husbands and children—to show their love. This anthropologist lived there for two years and when it came time to leave they performed a dance especially for him. It was incredible, unlike anything he'd ever seen and he was very moved. He decided to return the favor. It happened he was quite a virtuoso on the violin and he'd brought his instrument along, so he took it out and played the most difficult piece he knew. When he was done the people were ecstatic, they loved it, but they wondered if he "could do it again only this time without making that hideous noise?" I guess that's their version of "Well, that was different."

Larry is now watching TV. On the TV is the news. An old guy from up north, International Falls, is saying, "Yeah, fifty-two years ago I moved up here for arthritis and this year I finally got it."

I look around the bar and spot an elderly woman sitting by herself in a Naugahyde booth. She must be in her eighties or nineties, and very dressed to the nines, pink and black Jackie O suit and a matching pill box hat and drinking tea. Tea. Very out of place in the Uptown bar. Our eyes meet but instead of looking away, like I usually do and perhaps due to the recessive Latin gene, I walk up to her. When she looks up at me, her eyebrows disappear under her wig. She feels this and gently and very delicately pulls the wig back. I ask if I can join her, and she says, "Of course," like she has been expecting me. As I take a seat across from her she tells me her name is Rose, we pass the next two hours talking about everything under the sun. I tell her about my trip to Spain, she tells me about her travels and how her husband invented the Frisbee—but back in the 1930s it was called a saucer-tosser, and she has the prototype hanging in her bathroom. I tell her one time on a train I met the guy who invented the fragrance for Halston perfume and Rit Dye number three. "Well," she says, "don't we have interesting lives." I agree, "Yes, Rose, we do." At one point I noticed Rose has a brooch on her lapel shaped like a lamb. The fleece is rows of pearls. In the middle of the lamb one of the pearls is missing. I ask Rose about her brooch. "Oh," she says, "this is my lucky pin." She says, "Whenever something terrible happens to me I take out a pearl." I say, "Rose, there's a pearl missing." She smiles and says, "Yes, but look how many I have left." When her tea is finished, she tells me she must be getting home. I help her to the door while Larry bursts into "Blue Christmas."

One of his fourteen personalities is Elvis. Rose says, "He's very good" and he is. I walk Rose to the bus stop and we wait together in silence. When her bus comes I help her aboard. Suddenly she turns and says, "I live in a residence home and I go out maybe twice a year. Once a year during Hanukkah, I make a deal with myself. I won't go home until I have made a new friend." She smiles and says, "And now I can go home." I watch her as the bus pulls away and walk home where I take out my tuba and practice my gift for my brother-in-law.

*Christmas dinner at the Wilson home, Stillwater, 1914*

. . .

# ⬩ 5 ⬩

# Eating and Making Merry

———◆———

## "A Christmas for their souls"

### Vilhelm Moberg

*The tastes and smells of Christmas meals pull us back into our pasts with an irresistible force. Even in their first impoverished year in Minnesota in 1850, Vilhelm Moberg's Swedish immigrants can taste their homeland in a simple Christmas porridge. This excerpt is from the second book,* Unto a Good Land, *in Moberg's quartet of novels.*

Yuletide was near—a strange Yule for Kristina, a Christmas in another world, a Christmas without Yule chores. No pig to butcher, no ale to brew, no great-bake to bake. But they must nevertheless celebrate the holiday and honor the Saviour's birth like Christian people. She said to Karl Oskar, this year they must not think of the outside—food, drink, and material things. They must celebrate Christmas in their hearts; this year must be a Christmas for their souls.

She scoured the cabin floor until it was shining white, she washed their underclothes in ash lye, so that all could change for the holiday, she hung fresh pine boughs on the walls and decked the cabin inside as best she could. Of a pine top with upright branches Karl Oskar made a five-armed candlestick, an ingenuity which his wife praised greatly. He had promised they would celebrate Christmas at a table, and he kept his promise: on Christmas Eve itself he gave the table the last finishing touches with his plane. He was proud of his handicraft, the first piece of real furniture he had ever made, particularly when, at the final inspection, Kristina said: This sturdy oak table would undoubtedly last so long that not only they themselves but their children and grandchildren as well could eat their meals at it throughout their whole lives.

While they had eaten their meals at the chest lid Karl Oskar had felt like a pauper sitting in a corner of someone else's house, eating handed-out food. Now, as he put his feet under his own table, his self-confidence increased: Now he had settled down, now he had become his own master in the new land.

They used their new table for the first time at the Christmas Eve dinner. And Kristina too was pleased—to gather for a feast around a table was something quite different from sitting down to a meal at the old chest lid. The five-armed candleholder was put in the center of the table; they had saved only three candles for Christmas, so two arms were left empty, but the three burning candles spread Yule light in their house. They had bought a pound of rice for the Christmas porridge, and with it they used sweet milk. It was their only Christmas dish, but they ate it with a deep sense of holiday spirit. Its smell and taste brought to their minds recollections of this Holy Eve's celebration at home. Long ago Christmases now entered their cabin, Christmas Eves with the whole family gathered; and their thoughts lingered on those who at other Yuletides had sat down at table with them. Relatives at home in Sweden tonight seemed more alive than ever, and they spoke of the letter from Sweden which they had been waiting for so long. How much longer before they would hear from parents and relatives? The expected mail from Sweden had not had time to arrive before the river froze and the packets stopped coming for the winter. Now it could not arrive until spring, and that was a long time to wait.

Tonight Karl Oskar remembered his parents as he had seen them that last morning—when he had looked back from the wagon seat for a final glimpse of them as he left the old home: father and mother, looking after the departing ones, standing on the stoop close together, immobile as two statues. To him they would always remain in that position; they could not move or walk away; they stood there, looking after their departing sons; they stood like two dead objects, hewn in stone. His parents could never again resume life in his mind's eye. Perhaps this was because deep within him he knew he would never again meet them on this earth.

A thought came to him—it remained a thought only, which he would not utter: his father and mother might already be dead and buried, without his knowledge. . . .

After the meal Kristina opened the Bible and read the second chapter from St. Luke which in her home had always been read by her father on Christmas Eve in commemoration of the Saviour's birth:

"And so it was, that, while they were there, the days were accomplished that she should be delivered.

"And she brought forth her first-born son, and wrapped him in swaddling clothes, and laid him in a manger; because there was no room for them in the inn. . . ."

Kristina read the Christmas Gospel for all of them, but after a few verses she felt as though she were reading it for herself only: it concerned her above all, it concerned her more than the listeners. Mary's delivery in the stable in Bethlehem reminded her of the childbed she had but recently gone through. It seemed that Mary's time too had come suddenly and unprepared for, even though her days were accomplished: Mary had been on a journey, and perhaps they had been delayed, unable to reach home in time. And Mary had been poor, even more impoverished than she herself. Kristina had borne her child in a human abode, in a well-timbered house—Mary had lain on straw in an animal shelter, in a stall. Kristina had enjoyed the comfort of a kind and helpful midwife, but the Bible said not one word about any help-woman for Mary in the stable. And she wondered whence the Saviour's mother had obtained the swaddling clothes she wrapped about her child before she placed it in the manger. Had she prepared them in advance and brought them along on the journey to Bethlehem? The Bible was so sparing with details that she often wondered and questioned while reading. She guessed Mary must have had as much concern about the clothing of her first born as she herself had had for her child. Perhaps Mary too had been forced to cut up her petticoat to prepare the swaddling clothes for Jesus.

For the first time in twenty years Kristina slept on Christmas morning; ever since early childhood she had gone with her parents on this morning to the early service, which took place hours before daylight, the church illuminated with many candles. But here also they would revere Christmas Day, and Second Christmas Day: all work in the house ceased. They had carried in enough firewood before the holiday, all they had to do was to tend the fire and prepare food. On Third Christmas Day they had unexpected guests. Swedish Anna and Samuel Nöjd came driving a team of oxen and a dray which they had borrowed from the lumber company; holidays were the time for visits among their countrymen, and they were eager to see the first child born to Swedish settlers in the St. Croix Valley. The boy was now seven weeks old, he was in splendid health, he nursed heartily and cried for more. The mother had enough milk for him, and he was hungry—both facts made Kristina's heart glad. What more could she ask? Suppose she had been without milk, or the child without appetite?

Swedish Anna looked at the tender child as if beholding a miracle of God; she wanted to hold the baby in her arms the whole time she was there. And for luck each of the guests gave the child a coin—a whole silver dollar each!

*In the following passage (from* The Settlers*), some time has passed, and Ulrika Jackson, a Swedish immigrant married to an American minister, is giving a party at their home in Stillwater. As smell, taste, and memory collide over the Christmas table, time and distances vanish, and past collapses into present.*

Ulrika offered her guests old-fashioned Swedish Christmas dishes: boiled pig's head, preserved and rolled pork, stewed pork, meatballs, chopped calf liver. She had made sausage of lamb and veal, prepared sweet cheese and cheesecake. This was not ordinary food, it was holiday abundance, not meager, everyday fare but sumptuous Christmas dishes—the Christmas delicacies of Sweden served to the Swedes in the St. Croix Valley.

The guests helped themselves from the smorgasbord and found places to sit down with their overflowing plates. They ate in silence. The fat rolled pork melted in their mouths, their tongues savored the aftertaste, the jellied pork from the pig's head trembled on their plates, the smell from the sweet cheese penetrated their nostrils. It was a revelation: they had forgotten this taste. They had forgotten how wonderful all these dishes were. But after a few bites memory returned and they ate in silence and reverence; it was the taste of Christmas in Sweden!

Only a few times had they eaten these dishes since they left their homeland. After having been away for so long this feast became to them a return home, as it were. They saw, they tasted, they smelled Christmas in the homeland. It penetrated their eyes, mouths, and noses. The Christmas fare they devoured affected them more than physically—it penetrated the souls of the immigrants.

Memories from that land where they had eaten these dishes every Christmas filled the minds of the guests. A vision of that land suddenly fled before them with Christmas tables and festivities, with close relatives, intimate neighbors, forgotten friends. In their vision, they sat down with people they would never again see; they were sitting in a company who no longer belonged to the living. They remembered *that* year, and *that* Christmas, and *that* party—what festivity and hilarity! But she? She was at that party, and she is dead now. And he? I'll never see him again.

To the Swedish settlers in Minnesota Territory, Ulrika's party became a party of memories; their old-country past caught up with them in the new, dwelt with them in this room. Ulrika's table brought back their homeland in concrete reality. They had left that country, but the country was still with them.

Here they sat at memory's table, in the company of the living and the dead. And they talked of the country they never again would see.

———•◦•———

# "Strange and unusual holidays"

## CIVIL WAR SOLDIERS

*Being away from home at Christmas for the first time is difficult—but for soldiers fighting in a war, the absence can be especially painful. Christmastime diary entries, letters, and reminiscences by Minnesotans in the Union Army show them covering their homesickness by attempting to recapture familiar traditions, including holiday foods. Many oysters are sacrificed in the process.*

*In 1861, Samuel Bloomer of Stillwater, Company B, First Minnesota Infantry Regiment, performed picket duty along the Potomac River and wrote in his diary.*

December 25, 1861—This Morning dawned very pleasant and the whole day, but it was a very dull Christmas to us. Last night our sutler had a lot of goods come, with all kinds of marks on them. Some were marked Knifes and forks, boot blacking, pepper &c. But our *Col* smelt a rat and had the wagon taken up to the guard house, and this morning had the boxes opened and *lo* and behold they contained choice Whiskey & Brandy, which to his surprise were taken up to Poolesville to the hospital department, to be used in that institution. During the day 2 or 3 kegs of beer were got and some boys began to feel rather light headed. Had no drills, nor even dress parade. I suppose the reason was it was Christmas and it don't come but one in a year. I for one wish that we had Christmas every day on the drilling account, not because we had such a good time, for it was the dullest Christmas that ever I spent in all my life and hope I never shall again. Being a soldier is not like being at home on that day. The boys in my mess got a lot of oysters and good fresh milk and made a good Soup of them. But I had to look on and see them 'go in right' . . . as I am no oyster eater. I could not stand it to look on, so I pitched in and eat a lot of bread and molasses, for a substitute of the oysters.

• • •

*Young Knute Nelson, later governor and U.S. senator from Minnesota, wrote about the three Christmas Days he spent in the Union Army.*

Sundays and Christmas days are not much different from other days in respect to military routine and military duties, especially if not confined to a permanent camp. On the march, in bivouac, in skirmish or battle, no heed is given to the character of the day, and even in a transient or permanent camp there is usually no change in food or other incidentals, except as eked out by the soldier's own scanty means.

Three Christmas days have I passed in the Army as an enlisted man. They have been strange and unusual holidays to me, not indeed like those at home, but not entirely unhappy. They have had a sobering effect on a wild, wayward, and enthusiastic boy.

*Norwegian immigrant Knute Nelson*

· · ·

The first Christmas we spent in Baltimore, at Patterson's Park, in old leaky tents, with straw on the ground for beds, with a scarcity of fuel, money, and with rather poor army rations.

It would have been a very dull and dreary Christmas for us, if it had not been for the kindness of Mr. Leach, a strong Union man, of Scotch descent, who resided a short distance from our camp and had often visited us. He invited our entire company (B, 4th Wis.) to his home for a Christmas dinner.

He gave us a fine Christmas turkey dinner. After dinner his wife and daughters sang, and played on the piano many fine national and patriotic songs. Some of our boys joined in the singing, and were all greatly cheered and enthused. It expelled the lingerings of homesickness, and turned our thoughts to our work of saving and preserving the Union. . . .

The next Christmas was spent at Baton Rouge, the capital of Louisiana. It was a sad, dull, and dragging day, only relieved by a very badly cooked dinner of geese, supplemented with army rations of the usual kind, with black coffee in large tin cups.

To make it specially discouraging and disagreeable to me, I had been on picket duty the night before, was drowsy and sleepy, with a bad headache. A quart of the black coffee revived me and in part dispelled the headache.

This Christmas [1863] has not been quite so barren and lonesome as the last one, tho inferior to the Baltimore Christmas in many respects. The breakfast was of the usual army kind, bread, fried salt pork, and an ample supply of black coffee made of yellow Mississippi water.

At this time I was a corporal stationed as an orderly at regimental Headquarters, and in consequence I was invited by the quartermaster to partake in a dinner which he gave to some of his friends at headquarters.

We had roast goose and turkey, hot biscuits and butter, potatoes, cookies, sugar loaf cake, and coffee with sugar and condensed milk. A most wonderful dinner for us soldiers in those days! Some had liquors and cigars, but I neither tasted the liquor nor touched the cigars, and I was all the better for it.

♦ ♦ ♦

*William Bircher, a young drummer boy with the Second Minnesota Infantry Regiment, spent Christmas 1864 near Savannah, Georgia.*

December 24: As rations were yet very scarce, we were informed that a short distance below Savannah were several large oyster-beds. A detail of men and two teams were sent down to see if it was possible to procure enough for a Christmas dinner for the regiment.

On their return we found they had succeeded in filling one wagon-box; but they were of a very inferior quality. The natives call them the "cluster oyster." There were two to five in one bunch, and hard to get out. So our Christmas dinner did not consist of turkey with oyster filling and cranberry sauce.

What a glorious camp-fire we had that Christmas eve of 1864! It makes me rub my hands together to think of it. The nights were getting cold and frosty, so that it was impossible to sleep under our little shelter-tents with comfort; and so, half the night was spent around the blazing fires in front of our tents. I always took care that there should be a blazing good fire for our little squad, anyhow. Hickory and white-oak saplings were my favorites, and I had them piled up as high as my head on wooden fire-dogs. What a glorious crackle we had by midnight!

We could go out to the fire at any time of night we pleased (and we were pretty sure to go out three or four times a night, for it was too cold to sleep in the tent more than an hour at a stretch), and we would always find half a dozen of the boys sitting about the fire-logs, smoking their pipes, telling yarns, or singing snatches of old songs. . . . It looked quite poetical in the retrospect, but I fear it was sometimes prosy enough in the reality. . . .

It was Christmas eve, and here we were with no protection but our little shelter-tents pitched on the hard, frozen ground. It was hard to be homeless at this merry season of the year, when folks up North were having such happy times, wasn't it? But it was wonderful how elastic the spirits of our soldiers were, and how jolly they could be under the most adverse circumstances.

◆　◆　◆

*Faithful correspondent Thomas Christie, who enlisted with his brother in the First Battery of Minnesota Light Artillery, wrote to his father, James Christie, from Vicksburg, Mississippi, in 1863.*

We are all busy these days making fireplaces and chimnies in our tents, for the weather is getting cold. I have been more than usually busy the past week, making out Muster-out Rolls, each of them 3 feet long, in quintuplicate; muster-in Rolls in quadruplicate; Descriptive Lists; Discharge papers; Clothing accounts, etc. etc. Everything about our reenlistment has to be done right, or it might as well not be done at all; there is an immense amount of writing required about each man. . . .

Yesterday being Christmas some of us had a very nice dinner together in honor of the day, Southwick being the cook. Just think of it! We had oysters, soda-crackers, bread and butter, sardines, raspberry sauce, oranges, and apples! You may imagine how we enjoyed the feast; and you may imagine also how we talked about our friends in the North, and many a bygone Christmas.

# "Come and eat, eat"

## OTIS TERPENING

*Men working in isolated lumber camps away from families and city pleasures celebrated Christmas as best they could. Food and music helped ease some of the loneliness. This 1931 recollection (retaining the original spelling) by Otis Terpening details a typical lumberjack Christmas in the north woods.*

As the day drew near the real Cristmast Spirit seemed to pervail, And in the snatches of song that we would hear in the woodland during the day their was a real ring of joy

*Breaking from the work routine in a Grand Rapids lumber camp, 1903 (John Runk)*

• • •

in them, And in the voice of the Jacks on Cristmast morning as they wished one an-other Merry Christmas, And to hear one Jack say "Thanks Pal. I hope you live forever and I live to see you die." We seldom ever worked on Cristmast, but the day was spent in visiting, darning our socks and mittens. While some spent their time in playing cards, And listing for the cheerie sound of the dinner horn, saying Come and eat, eat. The cook would always have something extry, and plenty of it.

Dinner—The old horn at last was heard, and was answered with a cheer. . . . Their was roast beef brown gravy, Good home made bread, Potatoes, Shiny tins heaped with golden rings called fried cakes And close to them a punkin pie baked in a ten inch tin about one and a half inch deep, And cut in four peaces. Any other day to a Jack it was one peace but today it was Cristmas, It only came once a year and help your self if you wanted a whole pie you was welcome, And rice pudding black with rasns, Drid prunes or the old fashon dried apple for sauce, Black coffee sweeten with brown sugar, And tins full of sweet cookies, They were white and had a raisen in the center of them. Did we eat I will say we did. I have eaten many a Cristmast dinner in camp. And some here on the farm, but the best was in camp. Just one more with a jolly crew, And I would be willing to say, Life is now complet. Let me go.

---

### Italians prepare to dine on eel in 1908

The Italian colony in Minneapolis will not be compelled to rely on common everyday turkeys for their Christmas feast this year, for the large shipment of fresh eels, ordered by merchants for the occasion, has arrived.

The eel is said by the Italian residents to have it on the turkey or any other winged edible in several respects. In the first place it makes no difference whether the eel is young or old so long as he is an eel. Then he isn't half bone, and when the father of the family takes up the carving knife on Christmas he isn't watched by critical eyes. A few strokes of the blade is all that is required and everyone is served. The eel is also said to create a much better thirst than can be obtained by eating turkey and the man who has received a present of some choice Christmas beverage can know no end of enjoyment if he eat eel instead of fowl.

Of course there will be side dishes that go well with baked eel, such as imported macaroni and tropical fruits, but the eel will be the king of them all.

*Minneapolis Journal,* December 23, 1908

# "Celebration and saunas"

## Shirley Schoonover

*Not for this crowd a sedate Christmas party of punch and cookies. No, the hard-living Iron Range Finns of Shirley Schoonover's autobiographical novel* Mountain of Winter *sit down to a three-hour dinner amply fueled by spirits and beer, followed by sweat and soul-baring in the sauna, in turn followed by more raucous partying. Presided over by a colorful matriarch, Anni, these people knew how to have a good time.*

Christmas Eve was a time for celebration and saunas. Anni ordered Ava and Mummu to come and visit. "Yas, you come over," she said on the telephone. "Or I'll come and haul you out by the toes. You ain't a bear that's hibernating. Waller'll be glad to give you a ride over."

Ava and Mummu rode with Waller in his truck, bringing a change of clothes to wear after the sauna. They arrived at Anni's in the early afternoon and shared a dinner of fish soup, roasted ham, venison steak, potato balls, butter and onion sauce, raisin pie and sour cream custards. Anni presided grandly on a high stool at the table. "Hey, you, Eino," she scolded a child. "Get your fist out of the custard." "Mamie, you better get a corset. Your rump's too big. Like two watermelons in a sack." To Ava she said, "You and 'Riika'll sauna with me."

Dinner lasted three hours and toward the end of it there were quantities of beer, ale, homemade brandies and whiskey. Anni drank beer and ale, belching robustly. She laughed and rubbed her stomach. "Listen to my big wind."

"Anni, when are you and Waller gonna get married?" one of the daughters-in-law asked.

"That's for me to know and for you to find out." Anni cocked her head, "I don't think winter's a good time. Too cold. And he ain't courted me enough yet. We still have to drive down to the cities for a big weekend. I wanta see color television."

"Be cheaper to buy you a TV set," Rikku advised.

"Nah, not up in these mountains. Don't worry, Waller'n me'll get married when we're ready. You young folks always rush into marriage, like you didn't have enough time. We got plenty of time yet." Anni nodded to Ava. "Come. Let's sauna now."

"I'm tired of living alone," Anni confided to Ava and Mummu in the steam room.

"I get too bossy with my kids. They're grown, they don't need me. Time I had a life of my own." She sloshed water into a pail and sat down on a bench to beat herself with a bath whisk. . . .

Anni stopped swinging the bath whisk. "You ain't said what you think about my getting married."

"I think it's fine," Mummu replied. "You'll do fine with Waller."

Anni nodded. "You think so?"

"*Kyllä.*"

"You know, I got to thinking it over after I said yes. I ain't no bargain anymore." Anni's shoulders slumped, "I'm past the rosey-posey age. If you look at me straight on, I'm even homely."

"Oh, Anni." Ava shared a look with Mummu. "You don't have to worry about looks."

"Heh, I guess you're right. He's known me all these years, even before I got these store teeth. You don't think it's funny, old folks loving together?"

"I think it's fine." Mummu smiled at Anni.

"You know what we're gonna do? I'm moving down to live with him in back of his store. Rikku needs this house for his family. And we already ordered from Monkey-Ward a king-sized bed. I figured no sense in scrimping on room. Anyway, I 'most fill up a regular bed. Oh, I don't figure it'll be the hotblooded nights like when we were young. But I don't expect to sleep alone, neither." Anni scratched a thigh. "No, it'll work out fine."

The three women went back to the house. Someone was playing a guitar and singing. An accordion wheezed from another room and feet began tapping. Children ran in and out between the adults' legs, tipping chairs over. The Christmas tree stood in a corner of the parlor, burdened with lights and glass ornaments, an angel leaned from the tree top. Popcorn and cranberries strung from branch to branch as did striped candy canes and frosted cookies. Anni handed out plates of fruitcake, raisins, and plumcakes.

Old Crow gurgled and brimmed over in the glasses, the family grew hot and affectionate, kissing and swearing of love. Anni was kissed, pummeled, embraced, and adored. She was red with joy and perspiration, her dress wilting and wrinkled. She led the family into a schottische, careening around the crowded room, yelling, laughing, hooting, and stamping her feet. The rooms grew warm, small, overcrowded with bodies and the breath of celebration. The Christmas tree was jostled, the angel leaned still further, holding its china arms out in benediction. A child squalled, lost and hurt amid the forest of legs; then was found and put to bed with the coats, boots, mittens, and wool scarves. A string of cranberries broke to roll under the dancing feet, crunching crimson juice into the wide floorboards. Someone swung a fist, blood rose to anger, blue eyes searing for the bastard that struck out on Christmas Eve. Anni bullied her way between the antagonists, swearing, "Hey, you bung-holes. *Hauska Joulu!* Merry Christmas!" She clamped the fighters together in her warm embrace. "We love each other in this house. *Hauska Joulu!*"

Ava and Mummu were swept into it, kissed and mashed against cousins, uncles, the whole family. Ava loved them all, returning kiss for kiss, drenched with Christmas and Anni's huge affection.

Four o'clock in the morning and Anni said, "All right. Go home. Cows to milk. Church is at seven." She tossed coats right and left, bundled children into mittens and scarves. Cars were started, motors roaring up into the silent bell of the sky. *Hauska Joulu!* rang over and over as the family dispersed to their various homes.

"That's some woman," Waller commented as he drove Ava and Mummu home.

"She is. She's full of life," Mummu agreed.

"Ah-hum." Waller drove into the farmyard. "*Hauska Joulu.*" He waved to them.

"*Hauska Joulu!*" Ava said, waving back at Waller.

When Waller had driven out of the yard, Mummu went into the house. Ava remained outside to stretch her legs and to look at the sky. The night was starless, still it glowed from the pale-brilliant snow cover. Old Big stood to the north, mantled in black and silver. Only the Pole Star shone from beyond Old Big, and from the east the Aurora Borealis spangled in carnival colors. A cold night, and Ava's breath hung frozen in the air, a million particles of her life suspended in the silent air.

# The Kookie Never Krumbles

## Nick Fauchald

*"I remember making Christmas cookies with my . . . ." The person who usually fills in that blank is "Mom" or "Grandma." But here's a story where "Dad" is the one who's in charge of the cookie assembly line.*

Say what you will about Norwegian cuisine. It doesn't involve a lot of fancy ingredients. The finished dishes aren't very pretty—most assume a grayish matte finish resulting from hours of slow cooking. Plus, making Norwegian food usually involves some inane piece of equipment—a paddle or hammer or iron of some sort—that must be resurrected from a box in the basement, used for an hour, and returned to its box, where it waits for another year with all the other unwanted kitchen gadgets. And—let's be honest—most of the food doesn't taste very good.

Most of the world's cuisine is rooted in necessity; a particular food can be traced back a few hundred years to the kitchen of a peasant woman, the best of whatever meager ingredients she could gather. Where most of the world updates its cuisine, we Norwegians have decided to cling to our ungentrified peasant food, thank you very much. We're fully aware there are new ways to preserve cod, but stick with our lye.

Now, before you smack me with your lefse sticks, let me name the one thing Norwegians excel at: pastry. Kringler, rosettes, sandbakkeler—all are gorgeous desserts and pretty dang tasty.

But my favorite Norwegian pastry, krumkake (pronounced "KROOM kah kah," the oft-anglicized "crumb cake"), is also one of the simplest—a very delicate cone-shaped cookie made from eggs, sugar, flour, butter, and some vanilla or cardamom, if you want to get fancy. Krumkake is my favorite for the same reason that thousands of Minnesotan families break out the old family recipe book each December and stumble through Grandma's secret sandbakkel recipe or Aunt Ingrid's "Scrumptious Swedish Meatballs" every holiday season: tradition.

Every year, a few days before Christmas, my family transforms our kitchen into a Norwegian pastry shop. My mom and sisters hunker down on one side of the kitchen, making sandbakkeler and frying rosettes and squeezing butter cookies through a cookie gun. My father and I tackle the krumkaker, which, on paper, seems like a simple three-step process: make batter, cook batter, roll cooked batter on a wooden cone.

But somehow Dad elevates this process to a complicated ritual, not unlike the lowering and folding of the American flag. First, he diligently covers every available surface with aluminum foil, turning our half of the kitchen into what looks like a postmodern art exhibit. Then, using his mother's recipe, he beats eggs with equal parts of sugar, butter, and sifted flour until it hits the correct consistency. ("No lumps. Not one. None.") Then he heats his six-inch Nordic Ware stovetop krumkake iron (which looks like a flat, circular waffle iron) over medium-low heat and smokes a cigarette until it heats up.

He drops the batter, a half-tablespoon at a time, onto the hot iron, closes it, and gives it a little squeeze, enough so "if it were a bird, it couldn't fly away, but you wouldn't hurt it." The batter hisses and squeaks (much like Dad's analogous bird would if it was squeezed between two discs of hot iron). Exactly 28 seconds later, he flips the iron and cooks the opposite side for 24 seconds.

He separates the two halves of the iron and carefully coaxes the krumkake off the top half and onto the foil-covered counter in front of me. I must now take the piping-hot disc and roll it around a wooden cone before the krumkake cools and hardens into a misshapen cone. And I must perform this task knowing full well that my fingers will burn in the process and the next hot disc will arrive in exactly 52 seconds.

My father could perform both the cooking and rolling process by himself, but, just like hanging Christmas lights, it's always better to have an extra pair of hands and ears around, absorbing the delicate intricacies of holiday tradition that fathers pass down to their sons.

Over the past 20 or so years, I've made hundreds, perhaps thousands, of krumkaker. I think I've eaten four. They don't taste like much, really, thin, crumbly, under-sugared cookies that are best masked by melted chocolate. But all those hundreds of uneaten krumkaker play a more crucial role than mere gustatory satisfaction. They fan the family flame, a cultural tradition. So Dad and I continue burning both batter and fingers, interminable soldiers of the Norwegian heritage army. Just don't ask us to eat it.

# Dinner Guests

## Helen Hoover

*Few places in America are as remote—or as Christmassy—as the north woods of Minnesota, way up by the Canadian border. A chemist and self-taught naturalist, Helen Hoover moved there with her husband, Adrian, in 1954, bringing Christmas traditions with them. Their birch wood–fired stove yields up a turkey that you can almost smell coming through the type on these pages.*

On a Christmas Day, in the kitchen of our summer cabin . . . I popped a length of split birch into the purring range, saw that its somewhat doubtful oven thermometer still indicated a proper temperature for turkey roasting, and took the coffee pot from its place on the ring of iron warming trivets that surrounded the stove pipe. As I settled down in the low walnut rocker with my black coffee, I decided that the kitchen would have pleased my Great-aunt Anne, who died in 1932 at the age of ninety-four. The walnut pie safe with sides perforated in patterns, the dry sink with its washpan and dishpan, the oil lamps waiting for the dusk—even the fragrance of wood smoke belonged to her era. . . .

Christmas is for dreaming, but not at the expense of letting the cooking fire go out, especially when we were expecting Jacques Plessis for dinner at four o'clock. . . . He is an old-time lumberjack, slow and quiet of speech, with the size and strength of these now almost legendary men, and an appetite developed in the days when trees were cut with handsaws. Jacques would lean back in his chair and politely starve if dinner were late.

I knelt by the big oven and poked the bird with a fork. It was time to remove its cloth covering and let it brown. I thought wistfully of the foil I had forgotten to have mailed to us from town, then soothed myself by recalling that Great-aunt Anne had done very well without such luxuries. The turkey would be done on time. I wondered how Ade, a hundred yards away in the winter log cabin, was getting on with his voluntary job of peeling the potatoes and grinding the carrots for salad. I was meditating on the importance of cooperation in small things as well as in large if two people are to live happily in as nearly complete isolation as Ade and I when I heard branches snapping in the woods, loud as little firecrackers in that stillness. I stepped outside.

The sun, below the tops of the great spruces, reached pale fingers between the trees to draw their shadows long and blue across the little clearing. Last night's snow, wind-rippled on the ground and weighing down the branches, sparkled like chips from a star.

Here and there clumps of snow slid from their precarious support of needles, separated, and drifted away like steam. Under the blue of the sky, opalescent with falling frost, the silence waited—until branches snapped again. I tried to look into the leafless maple brush that covered the hill between the house and the little side road. Did one shadow move among others in the thicket? Probably not. The temperature was beginning to drop as evening approached, and trees and branches pop and crack as their freezing increases.

The heat from the stove was melting the snow on the kitchen's slanting roof and icicles dripped as they formed on the eaves. Two chickadees, puffed into black-and-white feather balls, flew down to hang upside down on the edge of the shingles and drink from the unseasonable drops of water. Some blue jays squawked in the treetops and I scattered cracked corn on the snow, then went inside to watch them drift down to eat. Suddenly they flew away, startled by the voices I heard from the woods.

I opened the door as Jacques and Ade stomped from the edge of the trees, beating the snow into a wider path and puffing clouds of frosty breath ahead of them. Jacques peered over a heaped-up double armload of stove wood and Ade dragged a toboggan, on which was the oval shape of a burlap-wrapped platter, a large sheet of plywood, a black iron spider, and three pails. All I needed was a Paisley shawl and a long, full skirt to turn the scene into something by Currier and Ives.

Amid shouts of "Merry Christmas" and "How's the turkey?" the latter even more enthusiastic than the former, we crowded inside. Ear-flapped caps and heavy gloves flew here and there and I pointed to the stove and said: "Ten minutes." Ade began to unwrap the platter and Jacques leaned against the pie safe. Tall, broad, bronzed, and heavy, he filled the kitchen. Ade, who is slim and wiry, once said that when he stands beside Jacques he probably gives the impression of a side view.

"I thought you were cutting timber to keep your figure," I said to Jacques, "but you look as if you've gained."

Smiling, and with the air of an indulgent uncle, he removed from his mackinaw a box of chocolate-covered cherries and the largest buttercup squash I ever saw.

I was so tickled that I sat crooning over the squash. We had no car in those days and brought staple foods by boat down the lake. When it froze over, supplies had to be gotten by mail and had to be carried in Ade's packsack for the last three miles along the side road. Store candy was excess baggage and fresh things were out. Even a squash would freeze after an hour at thirty below.

Beaming because his presents were a success, Jacques, who likes to know everything but who is too polite to ask questions, said casually: "I was surprised to see smoke over here as I came along the road. Didn't know you used this house in winter."

I pulled the turkey in its pan out onto the open oven door.

"Take a look at this brute. I asked for a big one, and when this twenty-six-pound bird came it wouldn't go into the oven next door. By pure luck we kept this range. We'd have gotten rid of it if there'd been any way to move it up the hill. I've been very cozy while cooking. Thirty-five degrees on the floor and ninety-seven at head height. The bird is done—if anybody cares."

While Ade and Jacques maneuvered the turkey onto the platter, I set out flour and seasoning for gravy. Jacques, pouring drippings into the iron spider, said tentatively: "Nice you had a pan to hold it."

Ade laughed. "As you can plainly see, that is a piece of galvanized sheet iron, dug out of the snow, cleaned with gasoline, scrubbed with a brush, and cut and bent to fit both bird and oven. You will note that I made a nice little pouring spout at one corner."

I tipped the gravy into a kettle and covered it. Jacques smothered the fire with ashes to safely smolder out. Ade slid the turkey platter onto the plywood. A few moments later we marched through the woods, Ade carrying the turkey triumphantly, I stumbling in his too widely spaced footsteps with the gravy in one hand and a book I had not opened in the other, and Jacques, behind me, candy and squash again under his jacket, hauling the toboggan on which the pails of unbreakables bounced and clattered.

Rough-barked pine boles, standing apart from us with the dignity of their two centuries, spread their lowest branches fifty feet above our heads. The dense boughs of balsam fir and spruce shut out the sky, and their seedlings stood beside the path, living Christmas trees. The light was pale and diffuse, scattered from the minute crystal facets of the snow. And from all around wild dark eyes watched, wary and hidden, the watchers ready to fly or run if we should prove hostile as well as strange. But one watcher knew us and had no compunctions about approaching. From the top of a spruce a gray jay glided on spread wings, lit on the plywood, snatched a loose flap of lusciously oily turkey skin, and flashed away.

An hour later, when half the turkey was a handsome ruin, we sat around the drop-leaf table in the log-cabin living room and considered whether any more mashed potatoes, sweet potatoes, beets, peas, cranberries, raw carrot salad, watermelon-rind pickles, Anadama bread, or chocolate-coconut pie could safely be consumed. I was as stuffed as the turkey had been. . . .

---

# Coins of the Realm

## SUSAN HAUSER

*Christmas cookies barely rate a mention in food reminiscences from territorial-era Minnesota. But for most of the twentieth century and in more recent traditions, cookies and cookie-making are as vital to the holiday as Santa Claus and evergreen trees. For essayist Susan Hauser, they are "coins of the realm," icons of Christmases past.*

New snow today. How I love to watch it fall. It lazes down from the sky, the way I would like to move through my life, taking my time, and riding a little now and then on a warm updraft that passes by.

*Stylish homemakers baking
Christmas cookies, 1954*
· · ·

Gradually and thoroughly, it covers the ground, at first filling up all the tiny spaces between the browned grass blades, then moving up to surround fallen leaves. Finally it overcomes the twigs and branches blown down by the last dry wind. By tomorrow it will *be* the ground and we will measure the winter by its depth.

Now that the scenery is right, I can begin to think more seriously about Christmas. It is the last obstacle to the fine silence and solitude of mid-winter. In an intense two weeks of glorification, gifting and gregariousness, we will fill ourselves with the company of others. And when the door of December closes and leaves us locked in the new year, we will, like animals fattened for hibernation, be able to live off the accumulated chaos and good feelings for a good eight to ten weeks.

As every bear and chipmunk knows, the gluttony necessary to a safe passage through the dark caves of January and February requires dedicated preparation. We have enough instinct left to understand that and, being closer to our nature than we readily admit, food becomes the focus of our campaign to consort with our species.

Cookies are the touchstone for me: icons of Christmases past. Their making was itself part of the festival. For a week my sisters and brothers and mother and I gathered in the kitchen after dinner and worked dough. Each night was devoted to a different kind of cookie. For Russian tea cakes we stood at the table and rolled little balls of dough in our hands. Then, after baking, we rolled them in powdered sugar, then rolled them in powdered sugar again. Spritz were the easiest, and caused the most trouble. We fought over the cookie press . . . at first for the right to use it, then for the right to rest our broken fingers.

Rosettes were the scariest. We took turns standing on a chair in front of the stove, dipping the long stemmed iron butterfly into batter and then into a sinister kettle of simmering oil. Sugar cookies were the hardest . . . because they took the longest: rolling, baking, cooling, decorating. By the time the last silver bead blessed the top of the last Christmas tree, everyone was ready for cool air and solitude.

We found both out on the lake, on the black disc of ice that we kept clear of snow. We pushed ourselves around in little circles, not talking, not touching. Sometimes, far out where the water is deep, the ice would crack. The sound exploded in the dark and echoed across the waste of snow, making us glad for the light from the house.

We never stayed out long. The cookies still had some power over us, and when the ice yelped a second time, we let ourselves be drawn back to the kitchen, where we sneaked one last handful of our favorites and went our separate ways.

However much the initial pleasure gave way to the pain of an overdone passion, the cookies paid off. Coins of the realm when company came by, they bought a spontaneous chorale of oohs and ahs from grown-ups who remembered. Children liked them, too, because they tasted so good. And there were enough to last right through to New Year's Day, when no one wanted to cook any more. In fact, no one wanted to even talk to anybody else. In my memory, it was always a bright, bright day. The sun shone hard on the snow. The wind had come the night before and stolen our tracks from the lake. Nobody called on the phone. There was nothing much to watch on TV. One at a time, we would rummage through the ravaged cookie tins and boxes, cleaning out the last broken pieces of the holidays. I took my share back to my room, closed the door, and let myself down into the pages of a new book. When I came out again, it would be spring.

———•◦•———

## "It took my breath away"

*When sickness prevents us from being where we want to be at Christmas, we appreciate special acts of kindness. George E. Gilbertson recalled a young woman whose energy brightened his polio ward.*

About two hours before our nurse's shift was over, she came into the ward with a shopping bag filled with tree trimmings. She walked around and let us choose one. I was in my "armor" that year so she chose a sparkling bunch of tinsel and put it in my right hand. Then this little lady went back to the first bed, pulled it from its place, and ran the length of the ward with it. She skidded to a stop and then moved the bed in so that the kid could hang the trimming he had chosen. She went back to each and every bed, and for two hours

she ran that floor and gave each of us the same thrill ride. I was in the last bed and the anticipation of the ride had made me so excited that my tinsel resembled a shiny bird's nest. She grabbed the bed, spun it out to the middle of the floor, and started to run. . . . It took my breath away. We reached the tree and found just the right spot for a bird's nest. I couldn't reach so I asked her to place it for me so that I could see it from my last bed in the row. When she realigned my bed she stepped to the middle of the doorway, still smiling, bowed and quietly walked out.

Letter in Steven E. Koop,
*We Hold This Treasure: The Story of
Gillette Children's Hospital*

# Mickey's Diner

### COLLEEN KRUSE

*Comedian and columnist Colleen Kruse would readily admit that she has been around the block a few times, or—put another way—she has had some "diverse life experiences." These include an immense variety of Christmases and Christmas dinners, one of which she recalls in this reminiscence, published here for the first time.*

I have been a waitress for over twenty years. More than half my life. And let me tell you something about that. No one ever starts out thinking that they are going to be a waitress for twenty years. It just sort of sneaks up on you.

You strap on an apron your first year thinking, "Hey! This'll be kinda fun for like, a *summer*. Then I'll figure out what it is I really want to do for a living." Then the next thing you know, your co-workers have nicknamed you "Mom," it's twenty years later, and all you've figured out for sure about what you want to do for a living is that it probably doesn't involve hairnets and polyester.

I knew I wouldn't want to work in a fancy place. I'm not a fancy person. I got a job at Mickey's Diner, a real diner in downtown St. Paul on the corner of Seventh and St. Peter. You should go sometime, it's still there.

On the outside, the diner looks like a little toy train's dining car; streamlined, neon and deco. On the inside, it's all gleaming stainless steel and red vinyl, easy to clean, and homey.

Pat, short for Patricia, was my boss. Boss of the whole place. Not the owner, big difference. I'd say she was around fifty years old, but I don't know for sure. That's just not the kind of question you ask your boss. Howie the dishwasher was thirty-five years old, with the mental capacity of a twelve-year-old. But I'm not so sure. How many twelve-year-olds do you know that could work a forty-hour week and pay their bills on time?

I was seventeen, almost eighteen years old when I started working at the diner. I had quit school the year before and though my family didn't much approve of the path I'd taken, they figured at least my job at the diner kept me off the streets. I lived by myself in an efficiency apartment about five blocks away from the diner.

The winter of 1984 started in mid-November. Bitter cold, no snow, no ice. Painful searing winds whipped through the downtown grid this way and that, making the five-block walk to the diner from my efficiency apartment an endurance test.

I'd found the answer to my prayers at the St. Vincent DePaul shop up West Seventh. I'd gone in looking for a parka but came out with a full-length black fur. Who knows what beast shed its skin for that coat? Gorilla, maybe? I put it on and it covered me from the tips of my ears to the tops of my shoes. The pile on that coat was so deep, if I turned up the collar, it blocked out all sound. I went to Woolworth's and bought a hat to go with it, a blaze-orange bank-robber ski mask with black stitching around the mouth and eyeholes. My walk to work was now toasty and amusing, since people saw me coming and bolted out of my way.

I worked second shift, 3 P.M. to 11 P.M., which meant no late nights and—more important to me—no early mornings. The diner was open 24 hours a day, 365 days a year. That means Christmas, too.

When I found out that I was scheduled to work Christmas that first year, I called my Ma to tell her I wouldn't be making it to my sister's house for dinner. The news went over a lot easier than I expected. Surprisingly so. As we resumed small talk, I scanned my mother's voice for something that sounded like disappointment. I couldn't find it. During that phone call, I keyed into a lot of things. Weariness, fear, and anger were the top three. Love was in there too, but I had to look for it.

*St. Paul's downtown with holiday lights and shoppers, 1967*

· · ·

On Christmas Day, we had the first real snow of the season. Grand, showy flakes, but no accumulation. Just swirly, snow-globe snow. I slept till noon, and drank coffee and watched my little black-and-white TV until it was time to go. At 2:30, I stepped into my uniform and big gorilla coat. I left the TV on so I'd have something to come home to. I stepped out the door.

You've just never known quiet until you've walked downtown St. Paul on Christmas Day. No people, no cars, all that decoration just for me. Twinkle lights framing every skyway and spindly boulevard tree. You could hear the traffic lights click. This wasn't just downtown St. Paul on a Sunday quiet, this was a higher grade of silence, like the difference between gold and platinum. It was ominously beautiful, like an act of God or something. Like the Rapture. I could see the diner up ahead, glowing dimly in the snow, the Pancake House of Purgatory.

When I got there, Pat said. "Go ditch your stuff in the back room and get out here; I've got some cleaning for you to do." In the back room, Howie was quartering chickens at the prep table, singing and dancing and slipping around on the chicken guts that had fallen on the floor. I wrapped a clean apron around my middle, and took my station behind the counter.

It never dawned on me that Christmas might be dead on top of everything else. It was weird to see the place empty, no regulars even. Pat slapped a Phillips-head screwdriver in my one hand and a bleach-soaked towel in the other. She said, "No way you're gonna sit on your rear all day and moan, kiddo. We all got other places we'd rather be. Your gonna take apart the pie case and scrub it down." This is a complex task on a par with disassembling a triple-decker aquarium.

Three hours later, Howie had moved on to chopping onions, I had the pie case put back together, Pat had the meat cooler sparkling, and we got our first customer.

Al Venutti was a big, fat cab driver who worked through Cityside. Venutti ordered everything from the diner in double, like James Bond ordering a martini, except with Venutti it was ham and eggs. He always carried his own insulated gas station coffee cup with him. That thing was like an ice cream bucket with a sippy lid and a handle on it. The cup suited the scale of his body. If Venutti tried to drink out of one of our coffee cups, he would have looked silly, like a fairy tale giant.

Venutti came in wearing a fuzzy red Santa hat and ordered a double patty melt to go on the double. "I'd love to stay and talk, but I got volleys all day between the senior high-rises and the suburbs." I handed him his Styrofoam box of food, and Venutti peeled the cheesy bun off his sandwich and upended a bottle of ketchup over it. It was a new bottle, and the ketchup wasn't pouring so Venutti pounded his meaty hand on the bottom of the bottle, sending a good sized splat on his patty melt, and a fair sized one on my clean pie case. Before he left, I saw him sneak a small brown paper bag to Pat.

Pat told me I might as well order my shift meal as long as the grill was dirty, so she wouldn't have to clean it twice. She yelled at Howie in the back room to do the same. Ten minutes later, she told us to have a seat in one of the back booths. "Today, we can eat like human beings at the table at least." I dug the buck that Venutti gave me out of my apron and plugged it into the mini tableside jukebox.

Christmas dinner 1984 was a burger and cole slaw for me, a hot turkey with mashers for Pat, and a malted waffle sundae for Howie. When Pat sat down with us, she brought over three cups of coffee laced with Wild Turkey. When I smelled the whiskey, I looked at Pat in surprise. Pat smiled, a curling flutter played over the edges of her lips like bacon thrown on a hot grill. "Don't you know that Santa always comes on Christmas?"

Pat bent her head to pray. I thought it was a joke at first, what with the unexpected whiskey and all. Howie followed her lead, bowed his head, and clasped his hands together with his eyes shut. I admit, I kept mine open. But I still heard the words.

"Heavenly Father, thank you for this day, and this good food."

The whipped cream on Howie's sundae smelled wonderful, and was melting into the waffle squares.

"Thank you for our families. At home, at work, and in Christ your son our savior."

I looked from Pat's strong face to Howie's earnest one, and I felt as close to them as anyone else in my life.

"Search our hearts, God, and please bless and keep us in the path of your everlasting light. Amen."

There was an instant, before either of them opened their eyes and we began eating. At that moment, I felt if God had searched my heart, he would have found it as spotless as the pie case. It felt new, and shiny.

In the past twenty years, I've had family Christmases and orphan Christmases. Work Christmases, hospital Christmases, Christmases when the tree fell down and the turkey caught fire in the oven, and Christmases when everything went just right.

My Christmas at the diner taught me that Christmas is transferable. The only responsibility you have to Christmas, wherever you are, whoever you're with, wherever you're headed, is to put it in a to-go box.

# A Minnesota Christmas Eve Feast

---

### Glüh Wein (German mulled wine)

*Serve this popular hot beverage, a standard drink at outdoor Christmas fairs, around the fire.*

1 slice lemon or orange

4 whole cloves

1 stick cinnamon

2 dashes ground cinnamon

½ tsp. sugar

glass of red dinner wine

In a stemmed mug, mix fruit, spices, and sugar. Top with well-heated but not boiled wine. Stir and serve.


### Ribbe (Norwegian Spareribs)

*Norwegians make enough Christmas Eve ribbe to provide leftovers for buffet meals on the festive days that follow.*

4½ pounds spareribs

2 tsp. salt

1 tsp. pepper

2 cups water

Cut a pattern of 1-inch squares in rind. Rub with salt and pepper, cover and let the meat steep refrigerated for 2 to 3 days. Heat oven to 350°. Pour 2 cups water into the roasting pan and add the roast with the rind facing down. Bake for 20 to 30 minutes. Remove roast, rub with salt and pepper, and place on a rack in the roasting pan with the rind facing up. Roast for 1½ hours or as needed. The ribs are ready when the bones loosen easily from the meat. To crisp the rind, leave in the oven with the door open for 10–15 minutes.

SOURCE: Kathleen Stokker, *Keeping Christmas: Yuletide Traditions in Norway and the New Land* (Minnesota Historical Society Press, 2000)

## Minnesota Wild Rice Dressing

*Wild rice, the kernel of a wild aquatic grass, is harvested in autumn from shallow lakes and paddies.*

| | |
|---|---|
| ⅔ cup uncooked wild rice (4 oz.) | ½ pound fresh mushrooms, sliced |
| ½ pound breakfast sausage | 2 cups bread crumbs |
| 4 slices bacon, cut into 1-inch pieces | 1 tsp. dried oregano |
| 1 cup chopped onion | ½ tsp. teaspoon dried sage |
| 1 cup chopped celery | Salt and pepper, optional |

Cook wild rice. Brown sausage, breaking up chunks with a spoon. Preheat oven to 325°. In medium-size skillet over medium heat, fry bacon until almost crisp. Add onion, celery, and mushrooms; continue cooking until vegetables are tender. In large bowl, combine the bacon mixture, wild rice, bread crumbs, sausage, oregano, and sage. Season to taste with salt and pepper. Spoon dressing into lightly greased 2-quart baking dish. Bake covered for 35 to 40 minutes, or until steaming hot. Serves 8 to10.

SOURCE: Adapted from a recipe by Marilyn McAlpine, Turkey Growers Association, in Ann L. Burckhardt, *A Cook's Tour of Minnesota* (Minnesota Historical Society Press, 2004)

## Rutabaga Casserole (Lanttulaatikko)

*Finns served a version of this golden dish every Christmas dinner, and many more times throughout the year.*

| | |
|---|---|
| 1½ cups mashed potatoes | ¼ tsp. black pepper |
| 1½ cups mashed rutabagas | 2 eggs separated |
| 1 T. packed brown sugar | 2 T. butter |
| ½ tsp. salt | ¼ cup breadcrumbs |

In large bowl, mix mashed vegetables well, using a masher. Add sugar, salt and pepper and mix well. Beat egg whites until stiff peaks form. Beat egg yolks for 2 minutes. Stir yolks into rutabaga mixture. Gently fold in egg whites. Spoon into buttered 1½ to 2-qt. casserole. Dot with butter. Sprinkle breadcrumbs over top. Bake 1 hour, or until lightly browned, at 325°.

SOURCE: Anne R. Kaplan, Marjorie A. Hoover, Willard B. Moore, *The Minnesota Ethnic Food Book* (Minnesota Historical Society Press, 1986)

*The Barilla Family gathers in the kitchen at Christmas, St. Paul, 1953*

• • •

## Anise Cookies (Italian)

*A favorite sweet at Christmastime. This recipe is from Mama D (Giovanna D'Agostino) of the former Mama D's restaurants in the Twin Cities.*

| | |
|---|---|
| 4 eggs | 2 T. anise seed |
| 1 cup sugar | 3 to 4 cups flour |
| 1 tsp. vanilla | 4 tsp. baking powder |
| ⅓ cup milk | 1 cup shortening |

Preheat oven to 375°. Beat eggs well. Add sugar, vanilla, milk, and anise seed. Mix well. In another bowl, mix 3 cups flour, baking powder, and shortening. Add liquid mixture.

If necessary, add more flour or milk to make cookie-dough consistency. Roll out and cut into shapes on a lightly floured board. Bake on greased cookie sheets for about 12 minutes. Makes 6 to 8 dozen cookies.

SOURCE: Giovanna D'Agostino, *Mama D's Homestyle Italian Cookbook* (Golden Press, 1975)

## Buñuelos

*A traditional Mexican Christmas dessert similar to a deep-fried flour tortilla.*

| | |
|---|---|
| 1½ cups flour | ⅓–½ cup milk |
| ½ tsp. salt | vegetable oil for frying |
| ½ tsp. baking powder | ½ cup sugar |
| 2 T. lard | 2 tsp. cinnamon |

Sift together flour, salt, and baking powder. Work in lard with fingers or pastry blender until like coarse meal. Stir in milk, adding only enough to make dough that will hold together for kneading. Knead on lightly floured board for 2 minutes. Divide and form into 20 small balls. Roll each into very thin 4–5" circles. (If dough does not roll easily, allow to stand, well covered, for 15 minutes.) Place in a single layer on plastic wrap while making other circles.

Heat oil, at least 2 inches deep, to 375° in fryer or deep heavy pan. Carefully stretch each circle gently in all directions, beginning at center and retaining circle shape. Fry 1 or 2 at a time until light brown, turning once. Drain on paper towels. Mix sugar and cinnamon in a paper bag and gently shake buñuelos to coat. Makes 20.

SOURCE: *Minnesota Ethnic Food Book*

## Shortbread

*An adapted favorite from the St. Paul kitchen of territorial governor Alexander Ramsey and his wife Anna.*

| | |
|---|---|
| 2 cups unsalted butter | TOPPING: |
| 1½ cups powdered sugar | ⅛ cup sugar |
| ½ tsp. salt | ¼ cup sliced almonds |
| 2 tsp. vanilla | |

Cream butter. Add powdered sugar, salt, and vanilla. Blend well. Add flour one cup at a time to form a stiff dough. Pat evenly into a 10-by-15-inch pan. Press edges with tines of a fork and prick dough with fork at 2-inch intervals over the entire surface. Sprinkle surface with sugar and almonds. Press into dough by running a rolling pin over the surface. Bake at 350° for 30–35 minutes until firm and light brown. Cool 5 minutes and cut into 1½ inch squares or diamonds. Cool completely before removing from pan.

SOURCE: Alexander Ramsey House collections, Minnesota Historical Society

## Cranberry-Apple Pie with Crunch Topping

*A favorite from Betty's Pies on Lake Superior's north shore.*

1 lightly baked pie crust

FILLING:

| | |
|---|---|
| ¼ cup gingersnap cookie crumbs | 1 cup sugar |
| 4 medium tart green apples (Granny Smiths), sliced thin | 2 T. flour |
| | 1 T. cornstarch |
| 1½ cups frozen or fresh cranberries | 2 tsp. grated lemon peel |
| ½ cup raisins | ¼ tsp. nutmeg |

TOPPING:

| | |
|---|---|
| ¾ cup old-fashioned oatmeal | 6 T. butter |
| ½ cup chopped pecans | ⅓ cup flour |
| ⅓ cup packed brown sugar | ½ tsp. cinnamon |

Preheat oven to 375°. Sprinkle cookie crumbs in bottom of partially baked crust. Combine apples, cranberries, and raisins in bowl. Add sugar, 2 T. flour, cornstarch, lemon peel, and nutmeg. Toss to coat fruit. Put in shell and press to compact.

TOPPING: Mix oatmeal, pecans, brown sugar, butter, ⅓ cup flour, and cinnamon. Mix until moist clumps form and sprinkle over filling, covering completely. Bake at 375° for about 40 to 45 minutes.

SOURCE: Betty Lessard, *Betty's Pies Favorite Recipes* (Lake Superior Port Cities, 2001)

## Pepparkakor

*A spicy cookie that is part of traditional Swedish American Christmas celebrations.*

| | |
|---|---|
| ½ cup sugar | 1 tsp. ground ginger |
| 1 egg, beaten | ½ tsp. ground cloves |
| ¼ cup molasses | ½ tsp. ground cinnamon |
| ¼ cup shortening | ½ tsp. ground nutmeg |
| ¼ cup butter, at room temperature | ¼ tsp. salt |
| 1¾ cups all-purpose flour, spooned into cup | ¾ tsp. crushed cardamom seed |
| 1 tsp. baking soda | ½ tsp. grated orange rind |
| | ½ tsp. grated lemon rind |

Combine sugar, egg, molasses, shortening, and butter. In a separate bowl, mix flour, soda, ginger, cloves, cinnamon, nutmeg, salt, cardamom, orange rind, and lemon rind. Slowly add to sugar-egg mixture to make a smooth, soft dough. Chill, covered with plastic wrap, for at least 24 hours. Preheat oven to 350°. Lightly grease baking sheets. Remove ¼ of dough from refrigerator. On a lightly floured or cloth-covered board, roll out dough ⅛-inch thick. Cut shapes such as traditional Swedish hearts, pigs, or horses. Place cookies on baking sheet and bake for 6 to 8 minutes or until cookies are firm but not browned. Remove immediately from sheet and cool on racks. Can be decorated with white icing. Makes 48 to 60 cookies.

SOURCE: *Minnesota Ethnic Food Book*

*North shore of Lake Superior, about 1875.*

· · ·

## Norwegian Rice Pudding (Risgraut)

*Rice pudding is traditional at Christmastime; the person who finds the almond is guaranteed a year of good luck.*

½ cup uncooked long-grain rice
1 cup water
½ tsp. salt
2 cups milk
1 cup whipping cream
½ cup sugar

2 eggs, separated
½ tsp. almond extract
½ tsp. ground nutmeg
1 whole almond
2 T. sugar

Cook rice in water and salt over low heat in a heavy 3-quart saucepan until all water is absorbed, about 15 minutes. Heat together 1 cup of the milk and ½ cup of the cream. Do not boil. Stir in ½ cup sugar until sugar is dissolved. Add to rice, mix well, and cover pan. Cook over low heat for at least 1 hour or until most of liquid is absorbed.

Beat egg yolks and mix with remaining milk and cream. Stir into rice. Cover pan and continue cooking rice mixture for 15 to 20 minutes or until most of liquid is absorbed. Mixture will be creamy. Add almond extract, nutmeg, and the almond, stirring in gently. Remove from heat. Lightly butter 8-by-12-inch pan or baking dish with 1½ to 2-inch sides. Preheat oven to 350°. Beat egg whites and add 2 tablespoons sugar to make a meringue. Pour rice mixture into prepared dish and spread meringue over top.

Bake for 10 minutes or until meringue is lightly browned. Cool at least 1 hour before serving. Traditionally served with rich cream or whipped cream. Serves 6 to 8.

SOURCE: *Minnesota Ethnic Food Book*

*Several generations of a Minneapolis family opening gifts around the tree, 1957 (William Seaman)*

• • •

# ◈ 6 ◈

# Family Matters

————◈◆◈————

## Santi Claw

### SYL JONES

*Here's a family Christmas reminiscence that combines elements of an African American folktale, a ghost story (warning: there are scary parts), and a little bit of the getting-of-wisdom genre. It's from the memory and vivid imagination of playwright Syl Jones.*

For us "colored" folk, the great trick of life in a newly integrated society was to master several different speech patterns, each one appropriate for some race or class. We didn't know it then, but we were practicing multiculturalism. In this context, my father's use of the term "Santi Claw" to describe St. Nicholas was little more than an assertion of his own roots. His people were from Arkansas, where nicknames were considered signs of affection.

As children we knew little about that tradition, so the appellation became our only point of departure for the myth. With a flick of his vocal chords, the old man managed to change jolly St. Nick into a kind of nightmarish creature who slid down chimneys in the middle of the night to snuff out wicked little children. I knew, of course, that I was wicked because my father told me so.

Around the first of December, he'd start to sing the song as only he could, and I would lay awake at night trying to fathom the mixed messages:

*You better watch out,*
*you better not cry,*
*you better not pout,*
*I'm telling you why—*
*Santi Claw is comin' to town!*

There was no escaping the menacing imperative "better." Christmas was not optional. A fat white man in a red suit was coming, and if you didn't act just right there would be hell to pay. My father sang it with a half smile, leering the lyrics as if they contained some terrible secret only he understood. In that smirking grin lay the mysterious truth about Christmas, a truth that explained why the holiday contained the seeds of melancholia. The truth was revealed by my father's tone of voice and by the words themselves:

*He's making a list,*
*he's checking it twice,*
*he's gonna find out,*
*who's naughty or nice—*
*Santi Claw is comin' to town!*

It was Santa as Hired Gun, a cool but jovial fellow who took notes on offending children, passed judgment and executed the wicked. Those who were good received toys. The ones in between, neither good nor bad, got nothing except a reprieve from death. Santa as avenging angel. Somehow in my eight-year-old mind, it all made sense. During the Christmas season, there were more fires than at any other time of the year. People committed suicide, little children turned up on street corners frozen to death, people felt lonely even in the midst of their families. Of course! Why hadn't I made the connection before? It was Santi Claw—the serial killer. "Is Santi Claw a white man, Daddy?" I had asked some years earlier, and this had brought a puzzled look to his face. "'Course he's white," he'd replied disdainfully. "If a colored man wore a suit like that out in public, don't you know the po-lice would put him up under the jail!"

That Christmas Eve brought a storm of ice crystals against my bedroom window. Like hail, the crystals made noises as they fell, a hard rain of ice that left invisible patches of treachery on the highway. Grandma had taken an awful skid in her new cordovan-colored Ford several days earlier.

"I couldn't see nothing on the ground—no ice, no nothing," she'd told my mother. "Seemed like the Devil himself reached up and grabbed the car. Lord, Lord, Lord!"

Grandma's imagination quickened in wintertime. That's when she told us all about the 'Haint who walked through the wall and into her bedroom every night, and about the time Christmas came around, she would lead me in the time honored tradition of speculatin' on the personal characteristics of Santi Claw.

"Wonder do he ever get cold?" I'd ask, and although she appeared to be ruminating, Grandma always knew what she wanted to say and how to say it.

"'Course he don't get cold. He from way up there at the North Pole . . . near Minndianapolis," she claimed. Geography had never been our strong suit as a people. We were happy to be anywhere and still be alive. But Minndianapolis?

"You mean Minneapolis, Grandma?" I queried, and her reply, "I mean up there where the icicle peoples be dwelling," formed the foundation of my view of Minnesotans for the rest of my life. For years when I went to bed in wintertime trying to keep warm under my flimsy blanket, I imagined the "icicle people" in Minndianapolis having a picnic in the snow, looking a lot like Eskimos, eating the ice cream treats that bore their name.

*A young boy keeping his eye on Santa,*
*about 1940*

• • •

At 4 A.M. on Christmas Eve, unable to sleep soundly for fear that Santi Claw might be lurking about, I sat up in bed like a startled buck and sniffed the air. The bright moonlit night hung perfectly framed by the crystaled glass that separated me from the world's reality. Outside, the harsh and bitter wind blew, bending small trees in its path. Inside, whispered voices floated up from downstairs. In a six-room, termite-infested house, noises were the norm, but this was different. It sounded like someone I knew, but the girl-like giggle was unfamiliar. Then came the rustle of heavy paper, scurrying, and finally a pronounced "Shhh!" from a male voice.

Suddenly, the stairs leading to my bedroom began to creak. I could tell by the cracking of the wood what stair the intruder stood on. Swallowing hard, I leaned back with one arm extended and felt beneath my bed. Behind the cigar boxes containing my baseball cards and hard earned paper route cash, I felt for my Frankie Robinson model Louisville Slugger, a formidable piece of lumber that I kept well positioned for just such occasions. I closed my hand around the throat of the bat and gently lifted it into position. No light, except that of the moon at the foot of my bed, could be seen in any part of the house.

"Creeeeeeeeeeee," moaned the third stair softly. "Croooooook," groaned the fourth stair. "Craaaaaaaaacka," the fifth stair protested. Then came a long, pregnant pause. "What we sneaking for? If they ain't 'sleep by now . . ." It was my father, king of the stage whisper, talking to my mother. For a moment I was confused. I sat on my haunches holding the bat in the air, ready to hit a home run, when suddenly the creaks turned to heavy thuds as my father's footsteps fell naturally on the stairs, followed by my mother's shuffling gait. (Because she never put her feet completely inside her shoes, she walked with her heels exposed, dragging leather and wood across the floor, leaving a distinctive sound in her wake.)

They reached the top of the stairs and stood in the darkened landing like two thieves. The bat now replaced beneath the bed, I lay supine on top of the covers, fighting the impulse to turn over and hide my face. But not a movement or a sound did I make.

I was a master at feigning sleep. Many times I had dodged a whipping by pretending to be safely tucked away in the lap of the Sandman. Now, with the stakes not quite so high, I relaxed into position, fixing my face in an idyllic pose intended to communicate the innocence and wonder that transfixed all parents in the middle of the night.

The sound of my sister's sudden, pig-like snore in the next room nearly convulsed me, but I fought off the laughter by thinking about hitting a baseball: eyes steady, hands held high but level, back shoulder upright, seeing the seams, waiting, waiting, then—Pow!

He stood at the foot of my bed, in the dark, unconvinced. I heard his labored breathing, caused by the protracted stair climb, and I wondered what was different this time. He seemed to be studying me hard, and as I tried to relax by concentrating on another ball, a curve this time, which I took to right field—Cracka!—I was swamped by a sudden sickening feeling. So, this is why he leered when he sang the song. Santi Claw and my father were one! Santi Claw, the serial killer, had come to murder me in my sleep. Finally, I thought. He'll kill me and I'll be happy.

"The girls are dead out," my mother murmured from the hallway, but Santi didn't respond. He was still watching me. Carefully, I cracked one eyelid. Now he stood at the side of my bed, leaning over me, the silence weighing down like lead. They both stood there for what seemed like hours, tilting their heads, listening to my too measured breathing, until my father's right hand shot up quickly, pulling the string that triggered the overhead light.

I froze in terror. I could not have moved a muscle if I had wanted to. I saw a slider dipping toward home plate at 60 miles an hour. Planting my back foot, I swung easily and caught it with the fat part of the bat, snapping my wrist on impact and shooting the ball through the gap in left field. I rolled over, snorted, and began to breathe regularly again.

"Ohhh . . . he's dreamin,'" came my mother's angelic voice. Snap. Out went the light. There were few pauses now as they hurried downstairs believing we were fast asleep. I could hear them digging out boxes, tearing wrapping paper, fighting gently over which ribbons and bows to use for which presents.

Finally, the mystery of Christmas had been solved. So, this is how it really is, I thought. Outside, the cold wind whipped across the main highway as tiny snowflakes dipped and danced on the blacktop, buffing it to a high gloss. Inside, my stomach churned as I contemplated the world and my darkening awareness that it could never, ever be fully understood.

———◆———

# Carol's Christmas

## SINCLAIR LEWIS

*In* Main Street *by Sinclair Lewis, Christmas proves to be a tearful disappointment for his heroine, Carol Kennicott, recently wed to the complacent Dr. Will Kennicott of Gopher Prairie, Minnesota. The holiday becomes just one more reminder of how out of place she feels in Will's suffocating hometown and how she misses her own family and its traditions.*

Kennicott was heavily pleased by her Christmas presents, and he gave her a diamond bar-pin. But she could not persuade herself that he was much interested in the rites of the morning, in the tree she had decorated, the three stockings she had hung, the ribbons and gilt seals and hidden messages. He said only:

"Nice way to fix things, all right. What do you say we go down to Jack Elder's and have a game of five hundred this afternoon?"

She remembered her father's Christmas fantasies: the sacred old rag doll at the top of the tree, the score of cheap presents, the punch and carols, the roast chestnuts by the fire, and the gravity with which the judge opened the children's scrawly notes and took cognizance of demands for sled-rides, for opinions upon the existence of Santa Claus. She remembered him reading out a long indictment of himself for being a sentimentalist, against the peace and dignity of the State of Minnesota. She remembered his thin legs twinkling before their sled—

She muttered unsteadily, "Must run up and put on my shoes—slippers so cold." In the not very romantic solitude of the locked bathroom she sat on the slippery edge of the tub and wept.

## A season, not a day

In the week or two before Christmas, Mexican Americans observe *La Posada* (the Inn), a reenactment of Mary and Joseph's search for shelter. Children carry a tableau with figures of Mary and Joseph from door to door and sing songs requesting a place to rest. When they find shelter, families gather to break a piñata and eat Christmas sweets. *(Photo 1971, St. Paul)*

Swedish Americans celebrate Lucia Day on December 13. Girls wearing white robes and light-ringed crowns, symbolizing the return of longer days, serve breakfast with saffron buns and ginger cookies to their families. *(Photo 1951, Minneapolis Swedish Institute)*

Many Orthodox Christians, including Russians and Serbs, celebrate Christmas at the end of the first week of January, a date in accordance to the traditional Julian calendar. *(Photo 1960, St. Paul's Holy Trinity Orthodox Church)*

Santa Lucia ceremony

• • •

Posada celebration (Morton)

• • •

Orthodox Christmas mass

• • •

# An Adolescent's Christmas

## Carol Bly

*Carol Bly describes coming home to Duluth for Christmas from her boarding school in the East. The year is 1944. Her mother had died, and several brothers are away fighting in World War II. But the family prevails, managing to maintain some holiday traditions and to pull together a stoical kind of happiness.*

In my family the extroverts were courteous to the introverts! I especially noticed our family courtesy at Christmas, because Christmas is a season when outward-going people, at least in ordinary places like Duluth, Minnesota, most tend to be cruel to private people. In *A Christmas Carol*, the nephew Fred doesn't complain about Scrooge's being tight-fisted at all: why should he? He is probably a Conservative himself— perhaps out of pocket, as Scrooge reminds him, but a Conservative. His morals are to do with family togetherness and a general affection for humankind. But how odd it is that Fred feels absolutely within his rights to insist that Scrooge be sociable—be talking and carrying on and eating in a large cheerful group. . . . Or the Duluth parents of my old elementary-school friends—"Come down! Come down!," these complacent extroverted parents had a way of shouting up the staircase. "Don't skulk about in your room! It's Christmas! We want to be all together!"

But in my father's household no one used the phrase "skulk about in your room," and it was all right to do it. It was all right to skulk about for hours and hours of the Christmas holidays home from school, or in my youngest brother's case, home from Notre Dame where the Navy had sent him. In fact, that house, big, ill-afforded, what with our now dead mother's doctors' bills, was perfect for skulking about in. Our father did it himself. He never promoted sociability—except for this: we had to meet the formal occasion. He had a way of mustering us—the two children he had left home to muster. Step up to meet someone, he would say. Square your shoulders. Don't give adults such a handshake that they feel as if they've got hold of a dead mouse. Don't do it!, he'd cry.

At five o'clock on Christmas Eve we would toast those who had left us and those now in danger, but we must stand up straight, please. Speak up clearly. Don't simper when we are toasting anyone, especially Mother. And don't grin. My widowed father liked form.

Covertly, he liked his office better than anywhere else, much as he loved the house. Even though his fourteen-year-old daughter had just got home from Massachusetts, he wanted to return to his office. He half-disguised the longing. I told him I was happy to have him leave. I told him, I will bring down the crèche, Dad. I have homework to do, Dad. . . .

My brothers and I came home from our schools in the 1940s on a Chicago and Northwestern Railroad train called The Duluth-Superior Ltd. It left Chicago in the afternoon, went all night through Wisconsin, paused in Superior, in the morning, and then came across the bay to Duluth at eight.

Our dad stood on the brick platform. He was always there, never late. He never wore his scarf high around his neck where it would do him any good: he kept his great-coat collar down. White shirt-collar and foulard showed. He was fifty-seven, a big, hale man with a face red with cold. He had met us at Christmas so many times—all three boys from their schools and their colleges, and now, in 1944, me, and the next day, my youngest brother—that he knew exactly where the Pullman cars stopped.

Dad drove me slowly home through the cold morning. "There's your city," he would point out happily, a little loudly. "There she blows! There's the old aerial bridge! They may have good things at Abbot (or The Hill School or Asheville, as the case might be—this year it was my school, Abbot) but they haven't got the aerial bridge!" He was advertising Duluth to me, since I would be home for two weeks. He was advertising his life to me, to welcome me back home.

No one would salt the streets of Duluth for another two decades, so we drove on fair whiteness, handily, snow tires creaking, my father brimming. We couldn't see them from where we were, but Dad reminded me that middle-aged men under his tutelage, the Temporary Coast Guard Reserve, were patrolling the docks and ways along the Harbor. . . .

Here we were, then, going home—not many friends left here, but a few good ones.

Mother was dead two years now, but Dad was here and Malcolm was coming to-morrow. My elder two brothers were away at war but they were alive. Our father had had only the good kind of telegram. On behalf of the President of the United States, the Secretary of War wished to assure my father that his John was making a satisfactory recovery from appendicitis surgery at Anzio, and would soon rejoin his unit.

Cheer up then. None of us had been killed. Now it was snowing on the tongue-in-groove yellow streetcar, and the streetcar—beloved, howling type of transport—joined us from Wallace Avenue and was grinding itself along with us. Being in Duluth for Christmas, I said to myself as we passed Lewis Street, is enough for now.

━━━━━•◦•━━━━━

### "We'll have a heavy load Christmas, too!"

Last year, when America was at peace, 12 times as many long-distance calls were made to many points on Christmas Eve and on Christmas as on an average business day—many calls were delayed and some did not get through at all.

This year with the nation at war, the situation will be much worse unless a great many people refrain from making long-distance calls at Christmas time.

To keep telephone lines open for military operations and other defense activities, it will help if everyone who possibly can will make their long distance calls at other times.

Message from Tri-State Telephone and Telegraph Co.,
*St. Paul Pioneer Press*, December 22, 1941

*Wartime soldiers gather at a St. Paul servicemen's canteen decorated with a small tree, about 1943*

• • •

# Driving My Parents Home at Christmas

### ROBERT BLY

As I drive my parents home through the snow,
their frailty hesitates on the edge of a mountainside.
I call over the cliff,
only snow answers.
They talk quietly
of hauling water, of eating an orange,
of a grandchild's photograph left behind last night.
When they open the door of their house, they disappear.
And the oak when it falls in the forest who hears it
through miles and miles of silence?
They sit so close to each other . . . as if pressed together
by the snow.

# "Everybody smile"

### MICHAEL FEDO

*For at least a hundred years or more, Christmas food rituals have been accompanied by the "say cheese" of that most ridiculed of figures—the self-appointed Family Photographer. In the family of Duluth-born Michael Fedo, that role was filled, not surprisingly, by Dad. It's perhaps exactly because the pictures are so "unremarkable," so unchanging year after year, that they hold such a precious place in the author's memory.*

My father has a collection of what he calls "The Christmas Slides." It includes 20 or so shots taken during the late 1940s through the mid-'60s. They are not, however, pictures of folks opening packages, or of decorative lighting, or of department store Santas hoisting my younger brothers and me atop the backs of stuffed reindeer.

*The Fedo-Norquist family waiting for the photographer*
· · ·

The slides are of the Fedo–Norquist clan sitting around Grandma Norquist's food-laden table partaking in the annual Christmas Eve feast. They are unremarkable pictures, the kind that would produce bored yawns from anyone outside the family, as there appears to be little difference from one year's slide to the next.

Seating never varied around Grandma's table: Dad at the east end; my mother's brother, Howard, at the west; and everyone else always assuming his or her position from the previous Christmas dinner.

No one except Dad seemed to enjoy either the taking or the viewing of the slides. Dad would wait until everyone, himself included, was seated, the food brought to the table and passed around. Then he'd jump up. "Wait—almost forgot the picture."

He'd squeeze around the table to get back to the living room for his Kodak, load it, and then ask us to pose. I think Dad took the slides for his own amusement, just to make everyone wait while plates heaped with holiday comestibles cooled before us.

The rest of us were not pleased. Our faces reflect impatience, indifference, or silliness, yet Dad remained dogged in his determination to capture our family tableau each year. Camera in hand, he would adjust his position, ask someone to move closer to the table, or request that someone else inch back just a bit.

"Good grief, Mike, just hurry up and take the picture," Uncle Howard would crab. "Stand still and take the picture so we can eat."

Ignoring Howard, whose appetite never seemed to be sated, Dad would say, "Smile at the birdy." Birdy was not one of Dad's words, and he used to wriggle his mustache and roll his eyes to try to arouse mirth.

"Damn the birdy," Uncle Howard muttered in 1950. That picture is distinguished from all the rest because my brother David and I are collapsed with giggles, while our sober, 65-year-old great-aunt Hilma, shocked by the epithet, is wide-eyed with mouth agape. Howard's head is in his hands, and his mass of russet hair dominates the lower right-hand corner of the slide.

In other slides, David and I would not smile but jam our mouths with carrot sticks and pose for Dad, cheeks bulging. Several early 1950s slides show both of us grinning stupidly at spoons mountained with boiled potatoes that we had positioned near our lips. In later shots we have left our clownish, awkward stages and grown into young men with crew cuts, wearing dark suits and exhibiting enigmatic smiles at Dad's ridiculous "birdy."

In every holiday slide at Grandma's the table groaned with traditional Swedish fare: lutefisk; rings of potato sausage; bowls of skinned potatoes, peas, and carrots; rye buns; silver platters with molded jello, cranberries, and various relishes.

I remember everything fondly, save the lutefisk, which David and I refused to eat. My Italian father tolerated the quivery mass of lye-soaked cod by inundating it with allspice and ladling on Grandma's white sauce.

Howard, on the other hand, heartily waded in, always slapping hefty portions on his plate. He would slurp the fish and slowly devour platters of food for nearly two hours, chewing slowly, taking a bit of bread to mop up sauces, and then wash everything down with strong coffee liberally laced with cream and sugar. Three desserts—pumpkin and mincemeat pies and rice pudding—were de rigueur for Howard, and he finished off with several of Grandma's paper-thin ginger Santas.

By the time Howard had gnawed his way to dessert, David and I were beside ourselves with the anticipation of opening our gifts, but we knew we still had to wait until all the dishes were washed and put away before presents could be opened.

Dad grew impatient as well. He preferred to listen to the Bing Crosby Christmas program on our large Philco console, but inevitably had to settle for scratchy snatches of "White Christmas" on Grandma's beige table-model Zenith because of Howard's marathon eating. Perhaps this was Howard's revenge on Dad for having to pose for the slides year after year.

In the early 1960s the pictures began to change. Aunt Hilma passed away in 1959, and viewing the slides now, I'm awash in memories of the stories she used to tell David and me—hair-raising tales of wolves howling and pawing at the barn door of the old family farm in Deerwood. The 1960 photo is somehow bleak without her stern countenance staring at the camera. Grandma's death followed in 1961, and Howard's wife, Gwen, died the next year. In 1963, I'm not there either, electing to spend the season singing with a folk group at an Omaha coffee house.

The slides were suspended in 1966, when Aunt Ada (my mother's older sister) and Howard came to our house instead of Grandma's, where Ada now lived alone. We no longer consumed lutefisk and potato sausage, but rather prime rib of beef with Yorkshire pudding, or sometimes crown pork roast. Once there was a Dickensian stuffed goose, but none of those viands are captured on film, for Dad seemed to lose his zeal for the Christmas photo after the tradition moved to our house.

Howard, frail and drawn, still mustered an appetite for the occasion, but was as apt to daub his tie in the gravy as his bread. Nobody seemed excited about opening gifts, and our conversations were more sedate without the presence of overstimulated children.

By 1975 I had married and spawned two daughters who seemed to heighten the mood for all of us. After dinner that year, Howard, now lean and crippled, appeared exhilarated. He called to Dad, "Get out your birdy, Mike. Take a birdy."

Dad had forgotten his old key word. "What do you mean, Howard?"

"A picture, Dad," I said. "A slide."

Dad protested weakly. It just wouldn't be the same. Besides, everyone was finished eating. Part of the fun, he said, was in having all the food on the table for the photo.

"Just take the picture," Howard groused.

Dad looked around at the rest of us and said it would take some time. He hadn't used the camera in ages and wasn't sure it would work properly. He spent several minutes loading the Kodak and adjusting his position, as in Christmases past. Howard, smoothing his hair, tightening his tie, demanded, ""Everybody smile."

Only Mom, Howard, Ada, and my young family are present. David and my youngest brother, Stephen, were living out of state and could not join us that year. It was the last Christmas Howard and Mother would celebrate. The following year they were ill, and our holiday festivities were somber. They died within three months of each other.

The images on those old slides are precious to me, as is the memory of Dad's Kodak routine. A few years back I took on the role of Christmas photographer, and my technique is reminiscent of Dad's. I putter with aperture, flash, and angles. Dad, in turn, resurrects Howard. "Stop fooling with that camera," he grumbles. "People are hungry and the food's getting cold."

———  ◆  ———

# "How am I doing, Dad?"

## Jon Hassler

*A family. Christmas dinner. A knotty pine bungalow. The north woods. But look again. This family is a divorced father and his son in recovery. Dinner is eaten out of fast-food bags in the front seat of Dad's car. The wintry setting is a fictional bucolic treatment center some-where north of Brainerd. A "typical" Christmas? Probably not. But with a ring of Minnesota truth? You betcha.*

Rookery lies four hours north of St. Andrew's, between Paul Bunyan State Forest and oblivion. Traffic is light, virtually all holiday visitors having already got where they're going. Stopping for coffee and gas in Brainerd, I notice that the few of us left on the road are mostly men like myself, traveling alone, with colorfully wrapped presents on the back seat and the gray look of fatigue and anxiety in our eyes. Divorced or estranged fathers, we're spending Christmas Day on the road in hopes that a beloved child some-where will love us in return.

I can't say for certain whether Bob loves me. He's always been hard to read. During his boyhood, I always thought of his reticence as part of his charm. He had an engag-ing little smile for polite occasions and a restrained little chuckle that told you he was greatly enjoying himself. During his teens this quality used to drive his mother nuts. "Bobby, will you please show some emotion!" she would call to him, during one of his track meets, say, or at the graduation party we threw for him. She'd long ago given up saying it to me.

Likewise, Bob had the stoic's way with pain and disappointment. I learned too late that his frown meant he was severely troubled, that his barely audible groan pointed to disaster. It was last spring that he came in from college near midnight and shook me awake, saying, "I'm expected to know all my lines by Friday, Dad. I can't possibly learn them all by Friday—there are over a hundred." He was a freshman, planning to major in Dramatic Arts. I turned over in bed and looked at him, and because I saw no real distress in his expression, only a slight scowl, I didn't realize he was out of his mind. He then said, "I need a break, Dad, let's go to Switzerland for the weekend. I'll take my script along. Or Norway. I could really concentrate in Norway."

Assuming he was kidding, I told him to get some sleep, and the instant he un-derstood I wasn't taking him seriously he gripped my arm so tightly he left bruise marks. "Please, Dad, come with me," he pleaded. "Get dressed and come with me to Norway . . . just for a coupla days . . ."

I don't know what he'd been indulging in that evening. I assumed it was some kind of upper given to him by a friend—a one-time mistake. What I didn't know, and what came out in treatment, was that he'd been secretly drinking vodka and using crack for the better part of a year. Already at nineteen our Bob was—without our catching on—a hopeless alcoholic and drug addict.

I say hopeless because he literally lost all hope. He hit bottom the day I packed up my belongings to move to St. Andrew's. I was carrying out my last box of books when I saw him standing in the street beside his little Honda CRX. He looked as if he was about to drive off somewhere. I went over to him and said good-bye. His response was a mumble—I expected no more—and then he surprised me with the tightest embrace of my life. He must have held me for fifteen or twenty seconds, and all the while he was making this strange sobbing or groaning noise in my ear. Then he hopped into his car and drove away. I noticed that he didn't buckle himself in—because, as he later told me, he stood a better chance of dying that way.

It was only about eight blocks and two stoplights from our house to the city limits, and yet by the time he hit the open road he was up to eighty-five miles an hour with a patrol car chasing him. He wasn't a mile from town when he turned off the highway and smashed into a power pole—not by accident, he later admitted. Because the pole was standing in a deep ditch, the car tipped sideways as it left the roadway and Bob was thrown flat across the front seat an instant before the pole tore the top off the car at windshield level. Bob came out of it with a concussion, a traffic citation, and a judge's order that he enter treatment. Had he worn his seat belt, he'd have been decapitated.

He went into treatment a zombie. Whether from trauma or drugs, he spent a week sitting deep in a couch with his eyes open and seeing nothing. I delayed my move to St. Andrew's and went to the hospital every day. I talked to him, trying to bring him back from wherever his mind had taken him. I talked until my voice wore out, mostly about some great games of pool we'd played together, but to no avail. After a while he'd turn and look at me as if to say, Who the hell are you?

We used to play a lot of pool, Bob and I. Some families, I'm told, relate to one another around the dinner table. Others go camping in the woods. Some fathers take their sons fishing. From the time Bob was in junior high, the pool table had been our meeting ground. At least once a week for years we went downtown to Oren's Beer Joint, where the green table felt is worn and torn, and there we'd play what we called Bob and Jay's World Series of Pool. The loser of four games out of seven not only paid, but was expected to blame his loss on the poor condition of the tables and the crooked cue sticks. Whenever I lost, which came to be well over half the time, Bob would give me a fatherly pat on the back and say, "Sorry, old man, better luck next time." Come spring it will be two years since we played a game of pool.

He was in treatment seven days before he came out of his trance—and just in time, since his counselors were about to kick him out (the goons!) for being uncooperative. His expression didn't change—he was still somber—but at least he was aware of his surroundings. I can't tell you how relieved I was. I remember saying, later, to Charlie, "Now I know how Lazarus's sisters felt when they saw him step out of the tomb."

But he's not the same son I used to have. He can't seem to warm up to me. He'll come around, his counselor tells me, recovery is slow. I've returned to Rookery twice a month to visit him, and each time, driving into town, I've prayed to God—as I'm praying now—that the two of us might recover something of our lives as father and son. To be met with a little embrace would be enough, not necessarily the bear hug he gave me the day he tried to take his own life. Or even a pat on the back would do it. Even a touch.

At the edge of town I stop along Fast-Food Avenue and come away with Christmas dinner. It's nearly two o'clock when I park in front of Bungalow Eight. I switch off the ignition and sit there a moment, rubbing my eyes, and suddenly my passenger door opens and Bob gets in and falls upon the sacks of food. So much for the embrace I'd hoped for.

While I eat a fish sandwich, he eats a Big Beef, a double cheeseburger, and a bag of fries. He's looking very healthy these days, heavier, more robust, happier than he's looked in years. Between bites he answers my questions about treatment. His only complaint is about the few men who don't cooperate with the counselors. "We vote on whether to keep 'em in or kick 'em out, and we always vote to keep 'em in. I think we ought to kick 'em out." A year ago, having said this, he would have shut communication down until tomorrow, having used up his daily limit of words. Now he goes on about his counselor, his daily schedule, his fellow residents. Can this articulate young man be my son?

He says he'll complete the twelve-step program in late January, but then—a great surprise—he wants to stay on and enroll in the counseling program. He admires his bungalow's counselor—Andy is his name—and he'd like to emulate him. . . .

"How about acting? You're giving up theatre?"

"Maybe I can do that on the side. You know, community theatre, that kind of thing?

I just figure, as a counselor . . ." He gives me a shy glance. "I could do more good for humanity." Then he adds, "Like you and Mom have been doing all your lives."

He holds me in his gaze while it dawns on me that this is the most—the only— heartwarming statement I've heard in months. I want to tell him so. "Bob," I begin, but he opens his door and gets out before I can finish.

He takes me for a sightseeing walk across the grounds, showing me what he's accomplished as a member of the hospital's grounds-keeping crew. "We hung all these big electric candles up on these lampposts." "See that fence over there—we just put that up last week." "Did you notice the road is smoother? We've been patching it with hot tar."

At the top of a windy hill I point out that I'm not dressed for the wintry outdoors. "Sorry," he says, and we hurry off toward Bungalow Eight. On the way he asks me, "How am I doing, Dad? How do you think I'm doing?"

"Wonderfully, Bob. You're doing wonderfully."

"All along here, come spring, we're going to have flower beds. We're going in with a roto-tiller and plow up this whole area and plant geraniums and a bunch of other stuff. It'll be the first thing you see when you drive in."

He is doing wonderfully. You'd never know he's living in a treatment center. His eyes are clear. So is his talk. He's shaven and neatly dressed. And yet he isn't my son. My son has never spoken at length on any subject. He might be some anonymous groundskeeper running on about his work, and I his anonymous visitor.

Bungalow Eight has been Bob's sprawling, pine-paneled home since August. He points out the circle of chairs in the front parlor, left over from this morning's group sessions.

"Even on Christmas?" I ask.

"'Specially on Christmas. There's certain guys get all screwed up thinking about Christmas." . . .

We buy two Cokes and sit at the window watching the people come and go in the parking lot. The majority of residents are accompanied by two generations of visitors (spouses and parents), and some by four (youngsters and grandparents as well). Here and there I spot a parent listening intently to something a son or daughter is saying. Oh, the fortitude required in pretending to be interested in such drivel. I spent the past several months listening patiently to Bob come up through the phases of recovery, the blaming phase, the guilty phase, the parroting-his-counselor phase.

A man goes by with his arm around a boy, and I wonder if it's this that sets Bob off. "Dad," he says, studying his Coke can, "I have to tell you, you don't look so hot."

"Aw, go on." I get halfway to my feet and smile into the mirror behind Bob. What's the problem? I might look a little tired, a little clenched, but I see nothing worse than weariness in my expression.

"No, really, Dad, you're not yourself. Probably nobody's told you, but you go around with this scowl on your face all the time, like you're mad at the world."

"I ain't mad at nobody," I tell him, quoting an old blues ballad. I'm about to explain that what he takes to be anger is fatigue, but he doesn't give me a chance.

"Well, whatever it is, it's very off-putting," he tells me. "It's a look I remember from when I was little and you were getting your doctor's degree. I wasn't allowed in your study till you were done, remember? Well, who'd want to go in there anyway, I used to think. I'd peek in and you'd have a book open and you'd be scowling at it.

"Bob, do you know what I was doing? I was writing the most boring dissertation ever conceived in the witless mind of any graduate committee anywhere on the face of this planet...."

"Okay, so it's not anger, it's depression, which is really suppressed anger. Did you know that, Dad? Andy says depression is really suppressed anger. I'm not blaming you in any way, Dad. You've been through hell. I mean, Mom moves out and then your only kid tries to kill himself. I'm only pointing out that for the last six, eight months you haven't been the same dad I used to know. It's like you're—I don't know—so distant all the time. I had to bring it up, Dad. One thing I've learned in this room is that straight talk is better than clamming up and never saying stuff."

Of course he's right. My doctoral work was very depressing. They were anxiety-filled years of make-work research with nothing at the end but the degree itself. Nothing learned except how to scowl. And now for the past several months I've been studying myself and not caring much for what I see. I see a man consumed by fear.

I stand at the window and ask, "You know what I'm feeling, Bob? I'm feeling..." It behooves me to explain myself, and yet "fear" is such an embarrassing little word to utter in connection with oneself. I need to tell him, since he brought it up, that ever since my life fell apart last summer I've been waiting for the next thing to go wrong. I've been walking tentatively, afraid that a misstep will cause the rest of the floor to give way. I need to tell him about my phobia concerning change. I can't stand to see people change the course of their lives. I need to tell him about Charlie, and how, in my obsession for the status quo, I blew my top and left the poor man in tears on Christmas morning. I need to tell him what happened to my old friendship with Jerry Randolph. I need to spill out my soul to my son.

And maybe I will, next trip. But for now I'm speechless, for Bob has his arms around me, and I'm fighting back tears and shuddering. When I gain control of myself, I turn away and try to say "Thanks," but it comes out like a quack. I blow my nose and am about to try it again when Bob pats me on the shoulder and says, "Sorry old man, how about a game of pool?"

"Pool?" My voice has a tremor in it. "I didn't know you had a pool table."

"Sure, down here." He opens a door off the parlor and flicks a light switch, revealing a flight of descending stairs. He starts down, saying, "Come on, the cues are straight and the table's fairly new, so you'll have to think up another excuse."

I follow my son the counselor into the basement.

---

# "I will never forget . . ."

*Getting someone to tell you a favorite Christmas story is usually not too hard: all you have to do is ask. That's just what the* St. Paul Pioneer Press-Dispatch *did in 1979 and 1980 in its "Christmas Memories" contests. Our families—being with them, being away from them— are almost always at the heart of our Christmas stories.*

I will never forget the Christmas of 1962. My first Christmas as a wife. I was 18, my husband 20. We had been married four months and had moved from St. Paul to Winona. We were looking forward to our first Christmas alone, together. How important it seemed to us to be grown up and away from home for the first time.

We are from large families so we knew how noisy Christmas can be. A quiet Christmas seemed so important. Christmas Eve came. All was quiet, the two of us sitting quietly in each other's arms, Christmas music on the stereo, staring at our first Christmas tree—aluminum—with a color wheel going around and around, how perfectly . . . boring! Boy, did we miss the noise of our families opening gifts, eating lots of goodies, singing carols, and we were doing just what we wanted to. We sure were homesick.

We opened our presents. One of the gifts from my husband was a stack of 50 brand new $1 bills. After all that excitement (must have taken 10 minutes) we went to bed early, me in tears, not looking forward to Christmas Day.

*A young couple stringing lights on their Christmas tree, 1940*

• • •

We woke early Christmas morning and decided to come home for Christmas. We didn't have a car, but we lived a block from the train station, so my husband got up and ran out in the dark, down to the station to see what time the train was leaving. He came running back and said, "The train is in and leaves in five minutes." I quickly got up, dressed, grabbed our coats, and ran out the door. It was freezing. The new snow crunched under us as we ran for the train. We just made it, the train started to move. We bought our tickets with crisp new $1 bills.

Very quickly we found our seats and looked out at the farmhouses. A few had lights on; they looked so cozy. The sky was clear; the stars were bright, and the snow sparkled.

We were so happy. We were going home for Christmas. —*Mrs. Roger Kutz, December 23, 1979*

◆ ◆ ◆

Christmas Eve 1976: I trimmed the tree alone that year as my husband of barely one year watched a basketball game on television. He wasn't being antisocial or unkind, just Jewish, and totally uninterested in what was to me the most special of all Christian feasts.

When we married we had decided never to interfere in each other's religious practices or to impose our respective religious beliefs on each other. But on that night, so rich in memories for me, I found it hard to live up to my side of that bargain. Compounding my loneliness was the fact that we were both transplanted Easterners, new to Minnesota, with all of our friends over a thousand miles away in Connecticut and New York.

I knew that I faced attending Christmas Mass alone for the first time in my life and I couldn't bear the thought. Yet when I suggested that my husband attend with me, one look at his face let me know that he would rather do anything else. Angry and hurt, I left for church in a huff, slamming the door behind me.

The service was long and crowded, and only served to reinforce my loneliness, as friends called out holiday greetings to each other. I realized sadly that for the first time in my life there was no one to wish me "Merry Christmas," not even my husband.

Yet, as I opened the door of my apartment, I got the loveliest surprise of my life. The apartment was lit entirely by candlelight and the tree was filled with red and silver paper hearts with "I Love You" written boldly across their fronts, which my husband had made while I was at church. "Merry Christmas!" greeted my husband, as I stood there gaping, too surprised and happy to speak.

Later that night, with the candlelight reflecting off the silver paper hearts, we would light our menorah and pray the ancient Jewish blessing to celebrate the last night of Hanukah: "Blessed are You, O Lord God of the Universe."

Since that night, we feel at home in Minnesota, with many new friends and two small sons. Our subsequent Christmases have been filled with much warmth and love. But I know that there will never be another Christmas for me so wonderful, so special and so happy as our first. —*Julia Harrison, December 23, 1979*

◆ ◆ ◆

The Christmas of 1970 really stands out more than any other for it was my second Christmas spent in the service, and this time in Vietnam away from family and friends. It was hard being in the service and even more difficult being in Vietnam, besides having to spend Christmas over there, of all places.

Two days before Christmas one of our company's aircraft with two pilots and a crew chief was seen exploding into a ball of fire and then going down into the ocean. This was my first personal encounter with death. I knew all the crew, as I was the flight records clerk and had personal contact with each one of them. Needless to say, my spirits were at rock bottom. . . .

After working late Christmas Eve, I was really tired, not to mention homesick, but decided to attend the church service next door at the medivac hospital. The service was held outside, and I was surprised to see so many servicemen there. People were everywhere: patients in casts, wheelchairs, stretchers, and even hanging out the windows and balconies—all in anticipation for the service to start.

As we all started singing those old but loved Christmas carols, the tears started running down my face. Soon I forgot where I was and in what seemed like minutes, I was caught up in the true spirit of Christ's birth and for the first time, I felt real peace in my heart and with my life. I truly believed that, despite the war and all the evidence of the war that were all around me, I knew that maybe the world would someday attain peace and good will for all people and myself. —G. *Burton, December 21, 1980*

*The joy of a snow angel, 1952*

✦  ✦  ✦

# Epilogue

·—◆—·

## Light, Darkness, Night

### NOAH ADAMS

*In this quiet essay, Noah Adams, former host of National Public Radio's "All Things Considered," reminds us that Christmas comes during the solstice, just at the moment that days begin to lengthen again. The unique emotional pull of Christmas may very well lie in this fact: it feels like a summing-up of our year, our yearnings and dreams, our anxieties and simple joys.*

24 December, 19 degrees, barometer 29.87 and rising.

There is full moonlight and the back steps are dangerously crunchy and icy, when I go out to read the other thermometer. We've had ice all week. But you still tend to forget and walk outside fast, then slip and catch yourself and gasp and almost pull a muscle. I think of my grandmother years ago, falling on the ice, walking to church one morning, breaking an arm, banging up her face. As you get older you begin to understand that it isn't so much the cold that makes you think about moving away, moving south, it's the ice, and the fear.

I did fall this week once, but not badly. I was out running with Will, holding his leash. I think he may have pulled me off balance, and I went down backward, an easy landing. I'm there on the sidewalk and the dog comes over, says with a look, "Well, this is a good place to stop."

This has been a difficult time for sleeping, this week, and the reasons involve the light and the darkness and the ice. I'm always restless, it seems, when the full moon approaches, and I spend a lot of time watching the sky.

Wednesday in the late afternoon the moon was rising, and it was luminous, as if you were looking through fogged-up glasses. Then Thursday night the sky was completely overcast, but the full moon was a strong white glow behind the clouds, a light you could sense, outside the house in the night.

It is the time of the solstice, the darkest night of our year. The sun has been rising later, more hesitantly.

That began to change Wednesday, as winter started. Now the days lengthen, and centuries ago this would have been a reason for celebration, the returning of the light. It would have been easy then, early in December long ago, to believe that the world was dying, and to feel each lengthening day as a reprieve.

At night—trying to sleep through all of this—in my dreams or maybe just the thoughts that come in the space between reality and fantasy, I am worried. Worried about tomorrow. Worried about something that happened today. Thinking of phone calls not returned and of a plane crash in Scotland. Does the Christmas tree have enough water? Does the cat have enough food? And just making up things to be worried about. Like what will I do tomorrow if I can't find a parking place in downtown Minneapolis? I won't find the right present, and then my marriage will be a failure.

If you realize at this point that you'll have trouble sleeping, you can go on down to the kitchen and heat up some milk. Have a cup of warm milk with some honey and just a touch of instant coffee for taste. Sit for a while and turn on the record player, listen to Samuel Barber's *Adagio for Strings*. And then, carefully, make your way upstairs in the dark to bed.

The house is quiet. The bed is still warm, and you know you're sleepy now. Why do I keep thinking about the moonlight and the way it looks on the snow and sparkles on the ice? Why do I think about the quiet cold of the countryside, and the darkness? . . .

An owl calls from high in a tree, there by the edge of the forest. And I move with the wind, along the ice of the river, fast and strong and gliding, one arm tucked behind me, the other one swinging. The long blades of the skates bite into the ice through the dusting of snow. The air rushes past the hood of my racing suit.

The moon is full and warm and empowering; the woods dark and friendly; the small towns peaceful, trusting, with Christmas lights; the church steeples lit in white.

The river runs through the town and under a bridge, and I sweep by fast, a whooshing sound, a child stirs in sleep, dreams of toys and adventure. And I race on, flying on the glistening surface of water, following the river in the dark. At daybreak I'll find a cave to sleep in, and travel again at night.

No one will know I'm there. But maybe I'll stop in the towns and solve problems and rescue people. They'll see me just as I'm disappearing around the bend of the river, a flash of skates, and someone will say, "Who was that?"

In the morning, sitting in the kitchen, strangely tired, I can have a cup of coffee and read the paper and listen to the radio and understand, in the light of day, that the things we worry most about are things that have already happened, or may not happen at all. I'm afraid sometimes that we teach children to do that, that we put the worry there on their faces as they grow older. But I guess we also teach them, especially at this time of year, about joy and being kind and smiling and singing, and about light and darkness.

We went up to the elementary school for a Christmas pageant presented by grade four. We parked out by the street and walked carefully over the ice into the school. There were last-minute giggles coming from the music room. We found the gym and a couple of seats. All the parents were there, and all the brothers and sisters. The lights went down, and spotlights came on.

The fourth grade classmates came out onstage, arranging themselves, grinning. They couldn't help it. Some of the parents waved, started taking pictures. Some of the kids waved, at just about everybody.

You can't look at fifty or so ten-year-olds waiting to sing without grinning yourself. The clothes and the haircuts are just the way they were when you were in school. And you know one child there, in the next to last row, wearing a white shirt and corduroy pants, is going to smile his way through the whole pageant and never sing a word.

The pageant has a fourth grade stage manager and sound effects people and a fourth grade light person. But the light is really coming from the stage to the audience, shining from the energy and pride of the young faces.

And you would like, in a way, to reassure each one: Yes, it becomes more serious, and at times tragic. But always through life, in late December, just about the time of the winter solstice, there will be a moment, every year, that will be almost more than you can stand. Just a thought, a carol on the radio, the face of an old friend, a stranger's smile, a baby's laugh, a moment that will bring a tear and a release of emotion, and you'll know it's Christmas.

*Santa welcomes chilly viewers from a decorated window at Minneapolis Dayton's department store, 1938*
*(Norton & Peel)*

• • •

# Sources

Some selections in the book are identified within the excerpts. Manuscript collections and newspapers are available at the Minnesota Historical Society, St. Paul.

## Chapter 1: Finding Christmas

Chronicles: Anna Ramsey letter in Alexander Ramsey and Family Papers; Catherine Goddard letter in Orrin F. Smith and Family Papers; "A Bachelor" report in *Minnesota Pioneer*, December 25, 1851; Mrs. C. A. Smith reminiscence (1858) and Mrs. W. I. Neimann reminiscence (1857) in Lucy Morris Wilder, *Old Rail Fence Corners* (1914; Minnesota Historical Society, 1976); Ann North letters in John Wesley North and Family Papers; Britania J. Livingston account in "Letters from a Pioneer Woman," *Fairmont Daily Sentinel*, June 6, 1925—all in the Minnesota Historical Society.

Excerpt from "A Swedish Visitor of the Early Seventies" (Roy W. Swanson, trans. and ed.), in *Minnesota History* 8 (December 1927) by Hugo Nisbeth (n. d.). Used by permission of the publisher.

Excerpt from *The Checkered Years: A Bonanza Farm Diary* (Caxton Press, 1937; Minnesota Historical Society, 1989) by Mary Dodge Woodward (1826–1890). Used by permission of the publisher.

Sidebar: Sister M. Grace McDonald, *With Lamps Burning* (Saint Benedict's Press, 1957). Used by permission of St. John's Abbey, Collegeville.

Excerpt from *The Bohemian Flats* (1941; Minnesota Historical Society Press, 1986) by Works Progress Administration writers.

Excerpt from "Sawmill City Boyhood," *Minnesota History* 47 (Winter 1980) by Melvin L. Frank (b. 1907). Used by permission of the publisher.

Excerpt from *Woman of the Boundary Waters: Canoeing, Guiding, Mushing, and Surviving* (1986; University of Minnesota Press, 1994) by Justine Kerfoot (1906–2001). Copyright © 1986, 1994 by Justine Kerfoot. Used by permission of the publisher.

## Chapter 2: Celebrating the Holidays

### Chapter 3: Coming Home

Excerpt from *The Great Gatsby* (Charles Scribner's Sons, 1925) by F. Scott Fitzgerald (1896–1940). Copyright © 1925 by Charles Scribner's Sons; renewed 1953 by Frances Scott Fitzgerald Lanahan. Used by permission of Scribner, an imprint of Simon & Schuster Adult Publishing Group.

Excerpt from *We Made It Through the Winter* (Minnesota Historical Society Press, 1974) by Walter O'Meara (1897–1989). Used by permission of the publisher.

Excerpt from *Christmas on West Seventh Street* (Afton Historical Society Press, 2000) by Jerry Fearing (b. 1930). Copyright © 2000 by Jerry Fearing. Used by permission of the publisher.

Excerpt from *Faces of Christmas Past* (Afton Historical Society Press, 1998) by Bill Holm (b. 1943). Copyright © 1998 by Bill Holm. Used by permission of the publisher.

Excerpt from *The F Word: How to Survive Your Family* (Warner Books, 2002) by Louie Anderson (b. 1953). Copyright © 2002 by Louie Anderson. Used by permission of Warner Books, Inc.

Excerpt from "Afterthoughts on Christmas Trees," in *Cold Comfort: Life at the Top of the Map* (University of Minnesota Press, 1998) by Barton Sutter (b. 1949). Copyright © 1998 by Barton Sutter. Used by permission of the publisher.

"Cold Feet: A Christmas Story," National Public Radio, December 25, 2001, by Emily Carter (b. 1960). Used by permission of National Public Radio.


### Chapter 4: The Giving Season

"A Gift of Oranges," *Christmas: The Annual of Christmas Literature and Art* 63 (Augsburg Publishing House, 1993) by Beatrice Fines (n. d.). Copyright © 1993 by Augsburg Publishing House.

Excerpt from *Down Town: A Betsy-Tacy Story* (Thomas Y. Crowell, 1943) by Maud Hart Lovelace (1892–1980), illustrations by Lois Lenski. Copyright © 2005 by the estate of Merian Kirchner. All rights reserved.

Excerpt from "What a Christmas Shopper Saw on Sixth Street," *St. Paul Pioneer Press*, December 12, 1915

Excerpt from "The Victorian City in the Midwest," by Harrison E. Salisbury (1908–1993), in *Growing Up in Minnesota: Ten Writers Remember Their Childhoods*, Chester G. Anderson, ed. (University of Minnesota Press, 1976). Copyright © 1976 by the University of Minnesota. Used by permission of the publisher.

Excerpts from Celia Tauer letters, James Jerome Hill and Family Papers, Minnesota Historical Society.

Excerpt from James Gray letter, January 2, 1930, James Gray and Family Papers, Minnesota Historical Society.

Excerpt from *The Days of Rondo* (Minnesota Historical Society Press, 1990) by Evelyn Fairbanks (1928–2001). Used by permission of the publisher.

Excerpt from *Packinghouse Daughter: A Memoir* (Minnesota Historical Society Press, 2000) by Cheri Register (b. 1945). Used by permission of the publisher.

Excerpt from *Up North* (1986; University of Minnesota Press, 2003) by Sam Cook (b. 1948). Copyright © 1986 by Sam Cook. Used by permission of the publisher.

Excerpt from "The Cut-Glass Christmas," *Redbook*, December 1980, by Susan Allen Toth (b. 1940). Used by permission of the author.

"Gifts" in *Glacier Wine* (Carnegie Mellon University Press, 2001) by Maura Stanton (b. 1946). Used by permission of the author.

Excerpt from Chapter 7, *The Growing Seasons: An American Boyhood Before the War* (Viking, 2003) by Samuel Hynes (b. 1924). Copyright © 2003 by Samuel Hynes. Used by permission of Viking Penguin, a division of Penguin Group (USA) Inc.

"The Gift," unpublished story by Kevin Kling (b. 1957). Used by permission of the author.

## Chapter 5: Eating and Making Merry

Excerpts from Book II, *Unto a Good Land* [1954] and Book III, *The Settlers* [1956] (both reprinted by Minnesota Historical Society Press, 1995; trans. Gustaf Lannestock), by Vilhelm Moberg (1898–1973). Used by permission.

Civil War accounts: Samuel Bloomer diary excerpt in Samuel Bloomer Papers; Knute Nelson reminiscence in "Three Christmas Days in the Civil War," *Yule Tide*, 1920; William Bircher excerpt in *A Drummer-Boy's Diary: Comprising Four Years of Service with the Second Regiment Minnesota Veteran Volunteers, 1861 to 1865* (St. Paul Book and Stationery, 1889); Thomas Christie letter in James C. Christie and Family Papers—all in the Minnesota Historical Society.

Excerpt from letter by Otis Terpening in Agnes J. Larson, *History of the White Pine Industry in Minnesota* (University of Minnesota Press, 1949). Copyright © 1949 by the University of Minnesota. Used by permission of the publisher.

Excerpt from *Mountain of Winter* (Coward McCann, 1965) by Shirley Schoonover (1936–2004). Copyright © 1965 by Shirley Schoonover.

"The Kookie Never Krumbles," *Minnesota Monthly*, December 2002, by Nick Fauchald (b. 1978). Used by permission of the publisher.

Excerpt from *The Gift of the Deer* (Alfred A. Knopf, 1966) by Helen Hoover (1910–1984) and Adrian Hoover (illus.). Copyright © 1965, 1966 by Helen Hoover and Adrian Hoover. Used by permission of Alfred A. Knopf, a division of Random House, Inc.

Excerpt from "Coins of the Realm" in *Meant to Be Read Out Loud* (Loonfeather Press, 1988) by Susan Carol Hauser (b. 1942). Used by permission of the author.

Sidebar: Gilbertson letter in *We Hold This Treasure: The Story of Gillette Children's Hospital* (Afton Historical Society Press, 1998) by Steven E. Koop (b. 1953). Copyright © 1998 by Steven E. Koop. Used by permission of the publisher.

"Mickey's Diner," original story by Colleen Kruse (b. 1968). Used by permission of the author.

## Chapter 6: Family Matters

Excerpt from "Black Ice," revised 2005 (Tunheim Santrizos, 1993, and in *Rescuing Little Roundhead: A Childhood in Stories* [Milkweed Editions, 1996]), by Syl Jones (b. 1951). Used by permission of the author.

Excerpt from *Main Street* (Harcourt, Brace and Howe, 1920) by Sinclair Lewis (1885–1951).

Excerpt from *An Adolescent's Christmas: 1944* (Afton Historical Society Press, 2000) by Carol Bly (b. 1930). Copyright © 2000 by Carol Bly. Used by permission of the publisher.

"Driving My Parents Home at Christmas," in *This Tree Will Be Here for a Thousand Years, Revised Edition* (HarperCollins Publishers, 1992) by Robert Bly (b. 1926). Copyright © 1979, 1992 by Robert Bly. Used by permission of the publisher.

"Christmas Slides: Smile for the Birdy," *Minnesota Monthly*, December 1985, by Michael Fedo (b. 1939). Used by permission of the author.

Excerpt from *Underground Christmas* (Afton Historical Society Press, 1999) by Jon Hassler (b. 1933). Copyright © 1999 by Jon Hassler. Used by permission of the publisher.

Letters: Kutz and Harrison, *St. Paul Pioneer Press*, December 23, 1979; Burton, *St. Paul Pioneer Press*, December 21, 1980, both Minnesota Historical Society.

## Epilogue

Excerpt from *Saint Croix Notes: River Mornings, Radio Nights* (W. W. Norton & Co., 1990) by Noah Adams (b. 1942). Copyright © 1990 by Noah Adams. Used by permission of the publisher.

## Illustration Credits

The photo p. 19 is from the Minneapolis Collection, Minneapolis Public Library; p. 22 and 157, by Francis Lee Jaques, are from *Snowshoe Country* (Minnesota Historical Society Press, 1989; copyright University of Minnesota Press); p. 28, TCF Holidazzle; p. 30 is a Flaten/Wage photo from the Clay County Historical Society; p. 53, Charles M. Schulz, PEANUTS © United Feature Syndicate, Inc.; p. 60–67, Lee Mero, "Christmas in the City," from *Christmas—The Annual of Christmas Literature and Art* 44 (Augsburg Publishing House, 1974); p. 74, Jerry Fearing, *Christmas on West Seventh Street* (Afton Historical Society Press, 2000); p. 81, Department 56, Eden Prairie; p. 104, Lois Lenski, illustrator, in Maude Hart Lovelace, *Down Town, A Betsy-Tacy Story* (Thomas Y. Crowell, 1943); p. 186, Michael Fedo.

Unless otherwise identified, the other images are in the Minnesota Historical Society, St. Paul, including: p. viii, Wanda Gág card (c. 1927); p. 37 and 84, Eric Mortenson/MHS; p. 40, Gold Medal flour ad, *The Bellman*, December 19, 1914; p. 101, Marilyn Ziebarth/MHS; and p. 112, Holtzermann's ad, *St. Paul Pioneer Press*, Dec. 23, 1900.

The Minnesota Historical Society photos on p. 33, 49, 56, 80, 113, 123, 129, 164, 177, and 181 (left; bottom right) are from the *St. Paul Dispatch Pioneer Press* photograph collection; on p. 18, 93, 160, 174, 181 (top), and 198, from the *Minneapolis Star Journal Tribune* photograph collection.